Presented to Purchase College
by
Gary Waller, PhD Cambridge

State University of New York
Distinguished Professor

Professor
of Literature & Cultural
Studies, and Theatre &
Performance, 1995-2019
Provost 1995-2004

Shakespeare
and the Sixteenth-Century Study
of Language

Shakespeare

AND THE

Sixteenth-Century Study

OF

Language

JANE DONAWERTH

University of Illinois Press

URBANA AND CHICAGO

Publication of this work was supported in part by a grant from the University of Maryland.

This book is printed on acid-free paper.

The following publishers have generously given their permission to quote from copyrighted materials: *Hamlet Studies* for "The Language of Voice, Expression, and Gesture in *Hamlet*" (3, no. 1 [Summer 1981]) and the University Press of America for "Shakespeare and Acting Theory in the English Renaissance," which appeared in *Shakespeare and the Arts*.

Library of Congress Cataloging in Publication Data

Donawerth, Jane, 1947–
    Shakespeare and the sixteenth-century study of
language.

    Based on the author's thesis (doctoral) — University
of Wisconsin, Madison, 1975.
    Includes index.
    1. Shakespeare, William, 1564–1616 — Knowledge — Language
and languages.   2. Shakespeare, William, 1564–1616 —
Language.   3. Rhetoric — 1500–1800.   I. Title.
PR3069.L3D6   1983   822.3'3   82–21740
ISBN 0-252-01038-8

To my Mother and Father,
who understood that love and education
are almost the same thing.

Contents

His plausive words
He scatter'd not in ears, but grafted them,
To grow there and to bear.
                    —*All's Well That Ends Well*

Preface

This book is an exploration of the relation between Shakespeare's plays and the sixteenth-century study of language. Although it is aimed primarily at students of Shakespeare and of Elizabethan drama in general, I hope that those interested in the history of linguistics or the history of rhetoric will also find it useful.

The organization is a familiar one: a study of background materials as they are relevant to Shakespeare's art followed by essays on plays, in this case on *Love's Labor's Lost, King John, The Merchant of Venice, All's Well That Ends Well,* and *Hamlet.* The first half of the book provides a survey of Elizabethan ideas about language, arranged by topics and focused on the implications for Shakespeare's drama. The second half offers close readings of five plays from that part of Shakespeare's career as a dramatist when he refers most frequently and explicitly to ideas taken from the sixteenth-century discussion of language, and when he is experimenting with ways of using the ideas to greatest dramatic effect. For convenience, I have divided the background materials into three chapters: the first concerned with basic ideas about the nature, history, and powers of language; the second, with ideas related to passion psychology and the body's language; and the third, with Elizabethan attitudes toward language. The remaining chapters, each a study of ideas about language in a particular play, also furnish a means of examining the important changes in Shakespeare's handling of the ideas as he masters the craft of making a play. In *Love's Labor's Lost* and *King John,* ideas about language contribute to shaping an atmosphere and a world for the play appropriate to the fables: play with the word as symbol reinforces the playful and artificial exploration of young love in the former, and the transience of voiced speech reinforces the fall of a weak king in the latter. In *The Merchant of*

Venice, All's Well That Ends Well, and *Hamlet,* ideas about language increasingly contribute to individuation of characters: in the first, attitudes toward the multiple meanings of words help to determine the characters' abilities to judge well; in the second, learning the differences between words and things marks the stages of growth toward wisdom in the young; and in the last, the language of voice, gesture, and passion separates truthful from hypocritical characters and enables Hamlet to assume a virtue that he does not have, acting the courageous role that events have thrust upon him.

The epigraph from *All's Well That Ends Well* appears in the King's speech praising his old friend and Bertram's father, now dead. A mature Shakespeare, somewhere in his thirties, wrote this celebration of the power of eloquence that increases as a man loses his youthful capacity for action. This passage, itself eloquent, commends a love of language characteristic of Renaissance English culture; it is a wonderful faith in the power of words to change minds, to effect action, and to remake human beings in the image of an ideal. While our society does not often encourage this faith, one benefit of the study of history and literature is learning to see with others' eyes and to hear with others' ears, thereby escaping the limitation of our time and minds. We may thus find renewal of our own humanism in the Elizabethan and Shakespearean ideas that words can replace ignorance with knowledge, that the transitory sounds of the human voice can produce ideas that last in the mind, and that, through listening to others, men and women can make something greater of themselves.

Now I may turn to thank those who enabled me to read and listen, and so to make this book something better than I could have made alone. I am grateful to the University of Maryland Research Board for summer grants, in 1976 and 1978, in order to complete the research on Elizabethan ideas about language; and to the Institute for Research in the Humanities at the University of Wisconsin, Madison, in 1979, and to the National Endowment for the Humanities, in 1980, for the time and support necessary to refine my thoughts and finish writing this book. I also wish to thank the staffs of those libraries where I pored over the lovely old pages of sixteenth-century texts: the Rare Book Room of the University of Wisconsin Memorial Library; the Huntington Library in San Marino, California; and the Folger Shakespeare Library in Washington, D.C. In addition, I greatly appreciate the hours put into typing two drafts of the book by the secretaries of the University of Maryland Department of English, especially Dorothy Zachmann and Julie Bicknell.

This book owes its existence—and some of its best phrases and clearest ideas—to the community of scholars and friends around me. Particular debts I acknowledge with gratitude: Professors Mark Eccles and Mary Jane Doherty commented on the dissertation that preceded this book; Professor Jan McKay reviewed the first section with an eye to modern linguistics; Professor Robert Coogan, with his knowledge of rhetoric, steered me through a portion of an early draft; Mrs. Virginia Clapper guided me in my Latin translations; Professors Theresa Coletti and Charles Mish aided me in overcoming a tedious beginning; Professor Richard Knowles, with magnificent patience, brought clarity to my muddled thoughts and prose both in the dissertation and also in the book; and Professors Charles Rutherford and Sandy Mack read and reread chapters in an attempt to teach me what a sentence and a book should be. That the book is not perfect after their generosity is my own fault. To Rosanne Sabatelli and the other friends who kept up my spirits when I sorrowed over my writing I extend heartfelt appreciation. And to my husband, Woody Scally, who lent me his strength, his ear, and his typing skills, I give much thanks. At the last, I appreciated the aid of reviews of the manuscript from Professors Howard Cole and Stephen Booth, whom I hope one day to meet and thank in person. My greatest debt, however, is to Professor Madeleine Doran, who directed my dissertation, commented on the book in several drafts, and eased me with her experience and friendship. In her teaching, in her conversation and advice, and in her own work, she is, like Bertram's father in *All's Well That Ends Well*,

> a copy to these younger times
> Which followed well, would demonstrate them now
> But goers backward.

Shakespeare
and the Sixteenth-Century Study
of Language

Introduction

This book is a study, historical in method, of ideas about language in Shakespeare's plays. There is something ungracious about a book on Shakespeare's ideas. It is hard to relinquish the romantic conception of Shakespeare as a natural artist: from the warmth of his imagination he gives us experience beyond the cold reaches of the intellect. What have the commonplaces of a grammatical textbook to do with the irreverence of Falstaff, or Elizabethan medical theory with the anguish of the woeful queens in *Richard III?* These characters seem derived from an understanding of human spirit and passions that transcends rational concerns. Yet Falstaff echoes the grammarians when he tells us what is in that word "honor": nothing but air.[1] And Queen Elizabeth claims, as do Renaissance physicians, that her words, though ineffectual, yet "ease the heart" of its burdensome humours (*R3* 4.4.130–31). It is Hamlet, the character best loved by the romantics, who argues that if man has reason to fust in him unused, to sleep and feed, he is no more than a beast. Shakespearean characters come alive not only by their desires and affections, but also by their ideas; and we are drawn into the worlds of their plays as much by their love of ideas as by the urgency of their passions.

In adopting the historical method, I have assumed that an artist shapes his works from the materials at hand, not that the culture shapes the artist. Others have made more eloquent defenses of this method than I could make,[2] and I shall only say that I do not intend to treat Shakespeare's plays as historical documents lacking in originality, nor do I expect us to be an Elizabethan audience, giving up our different tastes and our more removed critical perspective. Nevertheless, if we are to be a responsive audience, we must be an informed audience; if we are to participate in the creative act by

1

learning how and why Shakespeare made the play he did, we must seek to bridge the distance between Shakespeare's age and our own.

Thus the first three chapters posit information, but information of two sorts. I have included a great deal of information on the commonplaces and controversies concerning language current in sixteenth-century England—too much, perhaps, to make these easy and graceful chapters. The detail, however, seems necessary: no history of Elizabethan linguistics and philosophy of language has yet appeared; there are relevant studies of grammar, logic, and rhetoric, but there is no overview.[3] Still, these chapters are not meant to take the place of the history that remains to be written. Because my aim is to understand Shakespeare's plays, I have limited the historical sources to what Shakespeare might have known: textbooks used in sixteenth-century grammar schools, classics that were taught or widely read, continental works popular enough to be translated, and English books published from about 1500 to 1620. The English authors have been given more weight, even when there is less likelihood that Shakespeare knew them, because they reinterpret old ideas and record the controversies of Shakespeare's own lifetime and society. I have similarly limited the topics to those relevant to Shakespeare's art. The spelling controversy, for example, is excluded. The one reference to it in the canon, by Holofernes in *Love's Labor's Lost* (5.1.17-26), is not important enough to warrant its inclusion. Moreover, since my purpose is to gain insight into Shakespeare's plays, not to write a history of linguistics, I have emphasized the common ideas, however fallacious, that reveal the interests of the age, over the novel ideas that imply progress in the study of language. Finally, although I have drawn some illustrations from earlier plays, this is, by design, not a book on the adaptation of linguistic ideas to dramatic conventions throughout Elizabethan drama. The ideas we shall be working with, even when controversial, are common; one would expect them to appear in the earlier drama, just as one would expect Shakespeare's use of them to be modified accordingly. I have decided to concentrate on nondramatic sources because they are clearer: what the theorists spell out, the dramatists allude to or merely assume.

The first three chapters also include information, admittedly more speculative, on Shakespeare's handling of ideas about language throughout his plays. I have tried to point out what ideas

Shakespeare must have shared with other writers of his age, ideas that encouraged him to solve recurring dramatic problems in certain ways. In this attempt I am preceded by several Shakespeareans who have surveyed Elizabethan ideas and attitudes toward language.[4] Yet language was a subject more often for disagreement than consensus in sixteenth-century England, and these surveys, though valuable, underestimate this quarrelsome spirit. The fresh inquiry and controversy that Elizabethan writers bring to the question of language is matched by Shakespeare's eclecticism. Rather than taking a particular stand on linguistic issues, he draws on the whole Elizabethan vocabulary of ideas in stimulating the imagination. In his plays Shakespeare subordinates ideas about language to the dramatic purposes of individualizing characters and of shaping an imagined world where the story may credibly take place.

In the remaining chapters on plays I have concentrated even more on what Shakespeare made of the ideas. For each play I have suggested why Shakespeare chose particular ideas about language for emphasis, what they contribute to character, atmosphere, and story in the play, and how examining these ideas and their connection to style of language aids us by giving new insights, or by resolving the standing problems of critical interpretation. The chapters on plays taken all together also allow us to see something of Shakespeare's development as a dramatist over the course of the crucial first decade of plays. In the early plays Shakespeare uses ideas about language, as he does imagery or allusion, in establishing the norms and customs of a particular society, and in creating an appropriate and credible world for the play. In the middle plays ideas about language, like styles of language, are increasingly adapted to each character, allowing richer and more individualized characterization. In the mature plays ideas about language work to both ends: Shakespeare reveals the social world of the play emerging from the conflicting attitudes and ideas of the characters, and especially from their conceptions of language; speaking and listening, the characters create and transform their world — and themselves — for better or for worse.

The Elizabethan discussion of language is far richer than we have been led to believe by comparing only the commonplaces of the sixteenth- and seventeenth-century study of language. Despite the echoing of terms and ideas from writer in Elizabethan Eng-

land, language is more often a topic for debate than for agreement. "Herein it is," comments Henry Peacham, "that we do so far
passe and excell all other creatures, in that we haue the gifte of
speech and reason, and not they."[5] Even this general truth—that
language is the distinguishing mark of mankind—is open to question. In *Svmmers Last Will and Testament,* Thomas Nashe, whose
own style seems to proclaim the importance of language to men,
argues that dogs share this excellence:

> To come to speech, they haue it questionlesse,
>
> . . . .
>
> They barke as good old Saxon as may be,
> And that in more varietie than we.[6]

Nashe, to be sure, is mocking the importance man assigns himself in
God's scheme of things. But the disagreement is more serious if we
take into account two continental writers translated into English
about this time. Montaigne supposes that animals have a kind of
language—for "their jestures treate, and their motions discourse"
—and that this language is also "the proper and peculiar speech of
humane nature."[7] Du Bartas, on the other hand, distinguishes the
"dumbe discourse" of birds and beasts, only voiced sounds, from the
language of men, made up of words signifying "various sence."[8] Of
the many commonplaces in the Elizabethan discussion of language,
none stands uncontested.

There are several reasons that sixteenth-century writers disagree
on linguistic issues. Foremost is the encyclopedic spirit that pervades
all Renaissance learning. When Vives, the Spanish humanist who
tutored Mary, discusses the possibility of "true apellations" (words
that have a real and natural connection to things) he cites Plato and
the Bible in support, and Aristotle in opposition.[9] The question of
such words existing he leaves open. Classical authors who treat language—Plato, Aristotle, Varro, Lucretius, Cicero, Horace, and
Quintilian—differ on its history and nature, and their differences
carry over into the Renaissance. A sixteenth-century writer may
even refer to several classical sources in the same work, without
noting any inconsistency. Authority is authority, especially if it
serves the purpose of the moment.

And so follows the second reason for disagreement. Elizabethans
did not write treatises "On Language." They wrote on grammar,

logic, rhetoric, medicine — on all the arts and sciences, and on many
other topics. Where it is appropriate to their larger topic — speaking
correct Latin, persuasion, argument, or curing diseases — they discuss language.[10] But their ideas are colored by the context. The Bible may very well imply that language has existed since Adam
named the creatures and fell through Eve's invitation. Thomas Wilson, however, in the preface to his rhetoric prefers to reinterpret
Christian history in the light of Cicero: "Therefore euen nowe [after
the fall] when man was thus paste all hope of amendemente, God
. . . stirred vp his faythfull and elect, to perswade with reason, all
men to societye. And gaue his appoynted ministers knowledge bothe
to se the natures of men, and also graunted them the gift of vtteraunce . . . . And therefore, where as Menne lyued Brutyshlye in
open feldes, . . . these appoynted of God called theim together by
vtteraunce of speache."[11] When he introduces a student to eloquence, Wilson does not want to remind him that language is
dangerous. He wants to convince him that language raises men
above beasts, that it is civilizing and redemptive. For this purpose,
the opinion of the Greek rhetoricians popularized by Cicero, that
human civilization originated in the advent of language, is more
useful than a literal reading of the Bible.

The controversy over language as the distinguishing mark of man
illustrates a final source of disagreement: the nature of man. Nashe
and Montaigne, through their definition of language as voice and
gesture, view man as an animal, scarcely different from other animals. Peacham and Du Bartas find man's unique rational soul reflected in his language. Language may be the mark of man, but
what, after all, is man? If we add Ben Jonson's idea that language is
a social contract, based on custom,[12] we observe the full range of linguistic debate in the sixteenth century. Three terms recur: nature,
reason, and custom. They define not only conceptions of language,
but also conceptions of what man is. In the familiar Renaissance
definition, man is a rational and social animal. The definition
varies, however, according to which of the three terms receives most
emphasis.

This concentration on man is itself new with the Renaissance.
Medieval writers who discussed language perceived it as a reflection
of the divine, not the human. Although Augustine, a rhetorician as
well as a theologian, states that language is invented by reason and

based on custom, he finds in it the mystery of the Word made flesh, meaning incarnate in the body of sound.[13] For the Renaissance playwright Ben Jonson, on the other hand, the mystery of language is a human one: "In all speech, words and sense, are as the body, and the soule. The sense is as the life and soule of Language, without which all words are dead. Sense is wrought out of experience, the knowledge of humane life, and actions, or of the liberall Arts."[14] When Aquinas discusses language, it is to point out the reflection of God in the words that signify the perfections of his creatures.[15] In contrast, when the speakers of Castiglione's *The Courtier* discuss language, it is to define the perfect courtier, and ultimately the ideal man.[16] Nor is this difference observable only between medieval theologians and the later, secular men of letters. At the end of the Middle Ages, Dante writes, in *De Vulgari Eloquentia,* that God is the inventor of language, and that we would all be speaking the divine language were it not for the confusion of tongues at Babel and the later dispersion of the Jews.[17] In Sylvester's translation of the work of the Renaissance religious poet Du Bartas, Adam is the inventor of language, and the process of education (learning Latin, Greek, and Hebrew) repairs the curse of the tower.[18] I have chosen the most striking illustrations, but I think that the generalization still holds: the study of language in the sixteenth century shows a great increase in the role assigned to man. Language reflects man's history, and his rational and irrational powers; one studies language to know oneself. Man is the measure in the sixteenth century, and, judged by this subjective standard, language is not found wanting.

A different, more "objective" standard arises in the seventeenth century. Praising Bacon, Abraham Cowley sets forth the reason that many later writers distrust language:

> From Words, which are but Pictures of the Thought,
> (Though we our Thoughts from them perversely drew)
> To Things, the Minds right Object, he it brought.[19]

Seventeenth-century writers want language to reflect Nature not human nature, things not thoughts. This distrust of the subjectivity of language has descended to us, and our creative writers are caught in a cruel paradox: since they write in a medium that does not seem capable of expressing to others what they know, the impossibility of communication becomes a primary theme; their art denies what it makes. It is useful to remember that this modern theme is simply that — of an age, not for all time. Elizabethans had their own distrust of language, but they did not draw the conclusion that communication fails us. They saw that language has its limits, as do all things human; they also granted it something of the human creativity with which man transcends his limits.

In this respect, the Elizabethan dramatist might find encouragement for his endeavors in his society's view of language. Elizabethans found language to be a medium in its very nature expressive of the human condition. In the fleeting sounds of the human voice they noted the effect of the transience of all human life. In the rational and generative order of language they found an index of creative human intelligence. Through the double purposes of speech, purging the passions and expressing ideas, they believed man integrated his nature, at once physical and rational. Many wise men, they argued, had invented words as imitations, in sound or in etymological derivation, of the things they wished to name. To Elizabethans, language was itself mimetic, and in its invention society as a whole had taken the first step for the playwright who wished to hold the mirror up to nature. They further observed that a society is only as excellent as its language, and a man, only as good as his words. It is a playwright, Ben Jonson, who most clearly expresses the theme that runs throughout the Elizabethan discussion of language: "No glasse renders a mans forme, or likenesse, so true as his speech."[20]

In many other ways the sixteenth-century discussion of language must have defined the frame of reference in which the playwright worked, for the age was developing an aesthetic of poetry and of acting, and ideas drawn from other disciplines offered a starting point. Elizabethan ideas about language thus restricted Shakespeare in some ways and freed him in others. The notion of voice as the part of language given to emotional expression might have held Shakespeare in a melodramatic presentation of passion for his entire career, as it did during the early plays; certainly it at first hindered the players' development of a theory of acting as an independent art with purposes very different from rhetorical delivery. Furthermore, Shakespeare's age discouraged him from the self-consciousness about the nature of language as symbolic that we see everywhere in the poems and plays of our own age. In this connection we must beware of seeing language as a major theme of Elizabethan playwrights. Much more common than the modern idea that language has aesthetic value in itself was the idea that language is a medium for expressing the humane truths that have moral as well as aesthetic value. Yet other ideas, grand ideas about the social and moral importance of speech, partly account for the greatness of the drama at the time, and for its particular form — love of verbal display, grandeur of language. They freed Shakespeare, as well as other Elizabethans, to develop in a special way the ethical considerations of comedy and the moral dilemmas of tragedy. In our age of distrust in words we might look carefully at those freedoms Shakespeare saw in language. Such a look might well aid us in bringing our own age into perspective, just as it might well prevent us from an anachronistic reading of Shakespeare's plays.

One final comment seems appropriate. A student of mine reported that her roommate enjoyed Shakespeare's stories, but found his language given too much to cliché. What this person took for lack of creativity, of course, is the fullest creativity. Shakespeare's conception of language is of special interest to us because what he made of language has lasted, not only on our library shelves and in our theaters, but also on our tongues. Among Elizabethan writers the notion recurs that the poet shapes the world to come by shaping the language, by choosing the best words of his own and others' invention. Shakespeare achieved this ideal: his words have been grafted to our language, and when we look for a way to express ourselves we often reach back to imitate Shakespeare's words. In this respect, as in many others, all the world's a stage; choosing the best words to express our own lives, we find that they are often the words that Shakespeare chose to dramatize the many lives that he imagined.

Notes

Latin will be given only for those passages I have translated myself. The classical texts quoted from the Loeb Library editions and translations (Cambridge, Mass.: Harvard Univ. Press) will be noted in short form. Because we are interested in what Elizabethans read, not in Renaissance literature in general, the continental works by such authors as Castiglione, Montaigne, and Du Bartas will be cited in the English translations current in Shakespeare's lifetime, not in the original.

1. *1 Henry IV*, 5.1.134–35, in *The Riverside Shakespeare,* ed. G. Blakemore Evans (Boston: Houghton Mifflin Co., 1974). All references to Shakespeare's plays and poems will be to this edition.

2. See especially Madeleine Doran, *Endeavors of Art* (Madison: Univ. of Wisconsin Press, 1954), pp. 3–18; and D. C. Allen, *Image and Meaning* (Baltimore: Johns Hopkins Univ. Press, 1968 [enlrg. ed.]), p. vii.

3. There is no history of sixteenth-century linguistics, but both Francis P. Dinneen, in *An Introduction to General Linguistics* (New York: Holt, Rinehart, and Winston, 1967), and also R. H. Robins, in *A Short History of Linguistics* (Bloomington: Indiana Univ. Press, 1967), survey the subject briefly. Useful specialized studies will be noted in place, but the works most helpful for studying ideas about language in Elizabethan literature, because they treat those ideas in context, are Sr. Miriam Joseph's *Shakespeare's Use of the Arts of Language* (New York: Columbia Univ. Press, 1947); Richard F. Jones's *The Triumph of the English Language* (Stanford: Stanford Univ. Press, 1953); Madeleine Doran's *Endeavors of Art;* and Marion Trousdale's *Shakespeare and the Rhetoricians* (Chapel Hill: Univ. of North Carolina Press, 1982).

4. Surveys by Shakespeareans of Elizabethan views on language include Gladys Willcock, *Shakespeare as Critic of Language* (London: Oxford Univ. Press, 1934); "Language and Poetry in Shakespeare's Early Plays," *Proceedings of the British Academy* (London, 1954), XL, 103–17; and "Shakespeare and Elizabethan English," *ShS,* 7(1954), 12–24; M. M. Mahood, "A World of Words," in *Shakespeare's Wordplay* (London: Methuen & Co., 1957), pp. 164–88; Margreta de Grazia, "Shakespeare's View of Language," *SQ,* 29 (1978), 374–88; and James Calderwood, "Elizabethan Naming," in *Metadrama in Shakespeare's Henriad* (Berkeley: Univ. of California Press, 1979), pp. 183–220.

5. Henry Peacham, *The Garden of Eloquence* (London, 1577), sig. Aii^r. A revised edition appeared in 1593.

6. Thomas Nashe, *Svmmers Last Will and Testament* (1600), in *Works,* ed. Ronald B. McKerrow (London: A. H. Bullen, 1904–10), III, 254 (ll. 675–78).

7. Michel de Montaigne, "An Apologie of *Raymond Sebond,*" *The Essayes,* tr. John Florio (London, 1603), p. 261.

8. Guillaume de Saluste Du Bartas, *Bartas: His Deuine Weekes and Workes,* tr. Josuah Sylvester (London, 1605), p. 422.

9. Juan Luis Vives, *On Education* (1531), tr. Foster Watson (Cambridge: Cambridge Univ. Press, 1913), p. 92.

10. Perhaps the Elizabethan habit of studying language as a means to an end results from the pervasive influence of Aristotle on ancient and Re-

naissance thought; see Richard McKeon, "Aristotle's Conception of Language and the Arts of Language," *Classical Philology*, 41 (1946), 193-206, and 42 (1947), 21-50.

11. Thomas Wilson, *The Arte of Rhetorique* (London, 1553), sig. Aii^v. For the rhetoricians' idea that language preceded and caused the civilization of man, see Isocrates, "Nicocles," 5-9, and "Antidosis," 253-57; and also Cicero, *De Inventione*, I.ii.2-3, *De Re Publica*, III.ii.3, and especially *De Oratore*, I.viii.33: concerning language, Cicero asks, "what other power could have been strong enough either to gather scattered humanity into one place, or to lead it out of its brutish existence in the wilderness up to our present condition of civilization as men and as citizens?"

12. Ben Jonson, *Timber or Discoveries*, in *Ben Jonson*, ed. C. H. Herford, Percy Simpson, and Evelyn Simpson (Oxford: Clarendon Press, 1925-52), VIII, 621-22.

13. Augustine's comparisons of Christ the Word to the spoken word abound in *De Trinitate*, but the most succinct statement occurs in *De Doctrina Christiana*, tr. D. W. Robertson, Jr., as *On Christian Doctrine* (Indianapolis: Bobbs Merrill Co., 1958), p. 14 (I.xiii): "How did He come except that 'the Word was made flesh, and dwelt among us'? It is as when we speak. In order that what we are thinking may reach the mind of the listener through the fleshly ears, that which we have in mind is expressed in words and is called speech. But our thought is not transformed into sounds; it remains entire in itself and assumes the form of words by means of which it may reach the ears without suffering any deterioration in itself. In the same way the Word of God was made flesh without change that He might dwell among us."

14. *Timber*, in *Ben Jonson*, VIII, 621. While for Jonson significance in language comes from human experience, for Augustine significance comes from God: in *De Magistro (The Teacher)*, tr. Robert P. Russell, in The Fathers of the Church, 59 (Washington, D.C.: Catholic Univ. of America Press, 1968), pp. 53-54, Augustine argues that language does not teach anything, since words simply call to mind what knowledge, by the grace of God, is already there.

15. Thomas Aquinas, *Summa Theologiae*, tr. Thomas Gilby (New York: McGraw Hill Book Co., 1964), I, 53-55.

16. Baldassare Castiglione, *The Courtier*, tr. Thomas Hoby (1561; London, 1588), sigs. E1^v-F8^v.

17. Dante Alighieri, *De Vulgari Eloquentia*, tr. A. G. Ferrers Howell, in *A Translation of the Latin Works* (London: J. M. Dent and Co., 1904), pp. 16-20.

18. Du Bartas, *Deuine Weekes*, pp. 420-34.

19. Abraham Cowley, "To the Royal Society," preface to Thomas Sprat's *History of the Royal Society* (London, 1667).

20. *Timber,* in *Ben Jonson,* VIII, 625.

CHAPTER 1

"What Is in That Word?":
The Nature, History,
and Powers of Language

"*Language* most shewes a man: speake that I may see thee."[1] So observed Shakespeare's fellow playwright, Ben Jonson, voicing at once a principle of Elizabethan dramaturgy and a common theme in the sixteenth-century discussion of language. Just as the theorists argued that language is a reflection of human nature, the playwrights argued that their purpose was to mirror human character in their words. In his prologue to *Damon and Pithias* (1571), Richard Edwards assumed that "the greatest Skyll" necessary to a successful comedy is "rightly to touche / All thynges to the quicke: and eke to frame eche person so, / That by his common talke, you may his nature rightly know."[2] If an Elizabethan playwright were to come to terms with his medium, what he considered of first importance was the language.

Some visual elements—costume, dance, the dumb show, and pageantry—were, of course, important in the Elizabethan theater; but much of the burden that has since been assumed by scenery, lighting, and the director's orchestration of actors into stage images was then carried by the language. The Elizabethan idiom for attending a play further illustrates this difference between their theater and ours. "There is a lord will hear you play to-night" (l. 93), the actors are told in the induction to *The Taming of the Shrew;* and they are warned not to wonder at their patron's odd behavior, "For yet his honor never heard a play" (l. 96). Elizabethans went to "hear" a play, not as we do to "see" one.[3] Even when the playwrights invoked the traditional metaphor of the mirror for their plays, they were offering not so much a realistic representation on the stage, as lan-

13

guage that would enable the audience to see the play imaginatively through the mind's eye. Thus, when Marlowe invites his audience to "view" Tamburlaine's "picture in this tragicke glasse," the visual image stands for what we hear:

> Weele leade you to the stately tent of War,
> Where you shall heare the Scythian *Tamburlaine,*
> Threatning the world with high astounding tearms
> And scourging kingdoms with his conquering sword.[4]

And we do "hear" Tamburlaine "scourging kingdoms": his first victory is to overcome Theridamas with words, and many of his ensuing conquests are presented to our ears, through "astounding tearms," rather than to our eyes. When Elizabethan playwrights held the mirror up to nature, their mirror, like that in old fairy tales, was a speaking one.

In this chapter we shall begin exploring this connection between ideas about language and dramaturgy in Shakespeare's plays. From the point of view of the playwright, we shall imagine what questions Shakespeare might have asked about the nature of language as his dramatic medium. If a play is a mirror of nature, how much help does language give the playwright? What of human nature or society is reflected in language? What connection is there between language and reality? How much license does the poet have to create his own language, and what is his responsibility to his society when he chooses his words? And what power is there in language to engage and move an audience? These are questions that Shakespeare and other Elizabethan playwrights answered mainly by their practice, and only rarely in theory; we may, however, avoid misunderstanding their practice by considering what answers their culture would have encouraged them to make.

Also in this chapter, from the point of view of the critic, we shall explore what end ideas about language serve in Shakespeare's plays. Given the verbal exuberance of Renaissance drama, and especially Shakespeare's, the importance of words and styles of language to character, story, and setting is a critical commonplace. But what do *ideas* about language do in the plays? If our observation of the connection between the Elizabethan discussion of language and the dramatic medium holds, then we may be able to say that they possess a similar importance. Both ideas about language and also styles of language help to create the characters, to keep the plot moving in debate, and to shape the imagined world of the play on a stage without scenery. Both aid in showing "the very age and body of the time his form and pressure" (*Ham.* 3.2.23–24).

Let us begin, then, with the most basic questions. What is in that word? What definitions of language do Shakespeare's characters offer, and why? What is a playwright working with, according to Elizabethans, when he makes his play out of words?

Definitions of Language

Shakespeare's characters pause to wonder what is in a word, and to explain what speech is. When Falstaff, for example, considers "that word honor," he defines it as "air." To Falstaff words have no lasting effect: the word "honor" cannot "set to a leg," or "take away the grief of a wound"; it is "insensible" to the hearing of the dead who possess it, and contradicted among the living, who hear the words of "detraction" as well as praise (*1H4* 5.1.131–39). In contrast, the King in *All's Well That Ends Well* finds the "plausive words" of Bertram's father almost tangible, "grafted" to the ears of the listener, valuable precisely because they "grow" and "bear," becoming something that lasts (1.2.53–55). In yet another context, Ulysses tells us that Nestor's speech, only a "bond of air," is by a fortunate irony "strong as the axle-tree / On which heaven rides" (*Tro.* 1.3.66–67); with his tongue, Nestor binds all the Greeks together in a community attentive to his words. Transitory and lasting, powerful and ineffective—very different conceptions of speech claim attention from Shakespeare's characters.

In this instance, the plays reflect their age. Elizabethans had several choices in conception of language. They might hold with the medieval definitions taught in school. They might adopt the notion of language advanced by the later humanists in their English textbooks. Or they might, along with Ramus, entertain the new ideas that eventually led to a revolution in linguistic studies in the seventeenth century.[5] Because of the wealth of ideas, Shakespeare need not take a particular stand on linguistic issues in his plays; his characters may speak for themselves, revealing their personalities in their ideas.

The advanced grammars of Donatus and Priscian, philosophical texts from the early Middle Ages, furnished the definitions that an Elizabethan learned in school: in a general way language is *vox*, voiced sound; specifically it is *dictio* and *oratio*, sound shaped into symbols of thoughts and things. These texts had been part of Latin education for so many centuries that their ideas were echoed everywhere: in the most recent grammars and logics, even in popular literature.[6] The advanced grammars began with a definition of *vox* that had been first stated by the fourth-century teacher of St. Jerome, Aelius Donatus: *"Vox est aer ictus sensibilis auditu, quantum in ipso est"*[7] — voice is air that has been struck and that can be perceived by the hearing, as long as it lasts. Thus, when Falstaff reduces the word "honor" to "air" (*1H4* 5.1.134-35), he is doing so on the authority of a thousand years of Latin grammarians. Two hundred years before Falstaff, the pedantic eagle in Chaucer's *House of Fame* had come to similar ironic conclusions on the nature of speech:

> "Soun ys noght but eyr ybroken,
> And every speche that ys spoken,
> Lowd or pryvee, foul or fair,
> In his substaunce ys but air."[8]

If Chaucer and Shakespeare did not borrow their definitions from Donatus, then they probably did from Priscian, who had elaborated Donatus's idea in the sixth century: voice is not only *"aerem tenuissimum ictum,"* a very small quantity of air that has been struck; it is also *"suum sensibile aurium, id est, quod pro prie auribus accidit,"* the perception of it by the ears, that is, that characteristically falls on the ears. The second definition, advises Priscian, is taken from nonessential qualities, for *"Accidit enim uoci auditus quantum in ipsa est"* — hearing simply happens to the sound as long as it lasts.[9] Thus, voiced sound is essentially air, and hearing it is only accidental, as Falstaff implies when he reminds us that the word "honor" is not Priscian's *"sensibile"* to a fallen soldier: "Doth he hear it? No. 'Tis insensible then? Yea, to the dead" (*1H4* 5.1.137-38).

The grammarians developed two main implications of the definition of *vox*. First, speech is a physical process with material results. Hence, wrote one commentator, the etymology of *verbum* ("word" or "verb"): this part of speech gets its name because it is brought about by air that has been *"verberato"* — moved by the motion of the tongue.[10] Because it is air, argues Priscian, voice has height, width, and length (which are properties of matter) and so can be heard from all directions.[11]

Perhaps from the grammars Shakespeare derives his conception of speech as actually substantial and energetic. In his plays, as in the grammars, speech is a material fact — "the converse of breath," the Princess calls it in *Love's Labor's Lost* (5.2.735) — and a physical event: thoughts sounded on the tongue *(MM* 2.2.140-41); words coined by the lungs (*Cor.* 3.1.77-78); murmured on the lips (*Jn.* 4.2.53); buzzed in the ear (*R2* 2.1.24-26); "Splitting the air with noise" (*Cor.* 5.6.51). Speech is so much a part of the physical world that it may be pictured, not only in these figurative expressions, but also literally. Echoing Priscian's definition, *"aerem tenuissimum,"* the narrator in *Lucrece* explains that the painting of Troy includes even Nestor's speech: "Thin winding breath, which purl'd up to the sky" (l. 1407).

The second implication of the definition of *vox* makes itself felt when the grammarians attempt to define the elements of speech: the smallest unit of linguistic sound, the letter, is a "simple voice";[12] and the basic unit of voiced language, the syllable, is "the pronouncing of one letter or mo, with one breath."[13] Yet the syllable, as Priscian analyzes it, has no significance in itself: *"syllaba . . . non omnimodo aliquid significat per se"* — a syllable does not signify something entirely by itself. Thus, continues Priscian, words of one syllable are only syllables in a certain sense, *"quia nunquam syllaba per se potest aliquid significare"* — because a syllable can never mean anything alone. As an example, Priscian cites the syllable *"-am,"* which may be recognized as a syllable, but has no tense, mood, voice, or meaning until it is comprehended as part of a word.[14] The definition of the syllable as a meaningless unit of sound enables the grammarians to explain why animals and infants may imitate speech sounds, and yet not truly speak, since they intend no meaning.[15] But the definition also creates a logical paradox: speech both is, and is not, significant. If, as Macbeth imagines in his famous soliloquy, the days ahead creep "To the last syllable of recorded time" (*Mac.* 5.5.21), then life indeed "is a tale / . . . full of sound and fury, / Signifying nothing" (ll. 26-28).

Insofar as it is air, speech seems a reflection of the physical, perishable aspect of human existence to many Renaissance writers. Contemplating the words that die out of a language, even the entire tongues that are lost, the Count in Castiglione's *The Courtier* presses home to the inevitable conclusion: "time [doth] make those first wordes to fall, and vse maketh other to spring a fresh . . . vntil they in like sorte consumed litle and litle with the enuyous byting of time, come to their end, because at the last both wee and whatsoeuer is ours, are mortall."[16] At the end of this period, in 1617, Robert Robinson eloquently assesses the mutability of speech: "And though the voice be a more liuely kind of speech, yet in respect it is but onely a sleight accident made of so light a substance as the ayre, it is no sooner vttered but it is dissolued, euery simple sound doth expell and extinguish the sound going before it, so that the eare can haue but one touch of the ayre beating vpon it to declare the speech vnto the mind."[17] As man is a living being but mortal, so his speech is lively but transient. When they considered speech as voice, Renaissance men saw reflected in it human limitations: speech is accidental, of slight substance, not inherently significant, filled with life only for the briefest moment.

It is the mutability of speech that Falstaff calls upon to protect himself from "that word honor" (*1H4* 5.1.134). The fat knight need not obey the command of a word, for words are intangible, ineffectual, and of transitory significance. Falstaff, of course, is equivocating, confusing the word "honor" with what it symbolizes. Just as a child who wants to win changes the rules of a game, Falstaff changes the meaning of the word; he is a mirror of human mutability in his use of words, as well as in his definition of them. This wordsmith who pays his tavern bill with words, however, is thus denying himself, as well as the value of language. As a result, our response to Falstaff's witty subversion of language is mixed. Seen through his view of language, Falstaff seems sadly mortal: if words are insignificant, dying the moment they are uttered, so much the more is the lonely man who speaks them. Poetic justice triumphs over this side of Falstaff when we realize, from Hal's epitaphs on the spirit of Hotspur and the body of Falstaff, that the former will remain honorable to the living, and the latter merely, for a brief time, sensible (*1H4* 5.4.87–110). Yet Falstaff and his words, in this comic context, show a more positive side, as well. Master of changeable meanings, Falstaff creates and recreates language each time he opens his mouth to talk someone out of a glass of sack or into a robbery. This side of Falstaff is Dionysian: neither Falstaff nor his words last, but both fall and die, only to rise again with the next breath.

Unlike Falstaff, the Latin grammarians balance the idea of speech as *vox* with another: speech as *oratio*. As stated by Priscian, the definition of *oratio*—"*ordinatio dictionum congruam sententiam perfectamque,*"[18] the arrangement of words into an agreeing (i.e., grammatical) and complete thought or meaning—implies that significance in language depends on the whole structure of the sentence or larger unit of discourse. Still an authority for the Renaissance, Isidore of Seville explains that *"oratio,"* derived from *"oris ratio"*—reason from the mouth, is rational because it is not the mere uniting of words, but the weaving together of words with overall significance.[19] It is this order providing significance that Quince's prologue lacks in *A Midsummer Night's Dream* when he fails to use appropriate intonational cues: Hippolyta judges his speech "a sound, but not in government"[20] (5.1.123–24); and Theseus adds, "His speech was like a tangled chain; nothing impair'd, but all disorder'd" (ll. 125–26).

The grammarians extend the idea of significance resulting from grammatical structure to the point of denying the significance of many parts of speech: only the noun and the verb are truly significant; all other parts of speech are "consignificant," signifying only in conjunction with significant words.[21] It follows that speech is naturally creative since the sentence is a whole greater than its parts: order creates significance out of insignificant parts. Applying these ideas to Quince's prologue, we may say that we take delight not simply in his failure to order, but rather in the unintentional significance in his speech. Language, a creative system, makes a meaning for him, and one on the whole more appropriate than what he intended: "That you should here repent you, / The actors are at hand" (5.3.115–16).

Priscian furthermore argues that words are words, rather than merely sounds, only by virtue of their structured context. A word is *"pars minima orationis constructae"*—the smallest part of structured speech, a part necessary not only to the order, but also to understanding the whole thought. A word thus differs from a syllable both because a syllable is part of a word, and also because *"dictio dicendum (hoc est intelligendum) aliquid habet"*—because a

word has something to be communicated (that is, to be understood).[22] These definitions suggest that the speaker imposes meaning
on sound when he orders the sentence, and that words acquire
meaning as they are given a place in discourse, and interpreted by
the hearer. Of this supposition Theseus reminds Hippolyta when he
agrees to hear the mechanicals' play: when the "great clerks" made
"periods in the midst of sentences" (as Quince is about to do) Theseus yet "pick'd a welcome" by understanding their intention of
dutiful love (*MND* 5.1.93–105). Communication depends upon the
overall structure of speech, as it is created and understood by speaker and hearer in a specific context.

While Renaissance writers saw man's mortal limits reflected in
speech considered as voice, they saw his ability to transcend limits
reflected in the rational significance of language. Mourning the al-
terations of time in spoken words, Richard Mulcaster exults in the
permanence of written words: "So that books giue life where bodies
bring but death."[23] Henry Peacham, alternatively, celebrates man's
raising himself above the beasts by means of language: speech is the
"key of conceptions, whereby we open the secreates of our hartes, &
declare our thoughts to other, and herein it is that we do so far . . .
excell all other creatures, in that we haue the gifte of speech and
reason, and not they."[24] In language man reveals himself as the
creative orderer, the maker of significance set over the rest of nature
according to his exceptional abilities. Whereas the medieval grammarians emphasize that speech is not truly speech unless it is ordered
and rational, these sixteenth-century writers emphasize that reason
is not fulfilled until it is made known in speech—not merely to
others, but even to the speaker himself.

In *Titus Andronicus,* we feel as much horror from Lavinia's loss
of language as from her rape and mutilation: without tongue and
hands, she lacks the means to convey her thoughts in intelligible
form. Titus's zeal to "wrest an alphabet" from her signs, to "learn
[her] thought" and "know [her] meaning" (3.2.39–45), is to restore
to her her human significance, and the frantic attempts to communicate by gestures indicate the degree to which men and women
define themselves by their ability to signify. That Ovid's book opens
the way to this restoration is no accident: his words on Philomela,
alive in their significance for Lavinia, serve as an emblem of the aid
language gives men in overcoming their limitations. When the An-

dronici do succeed, and Lavinia communicates her thoughts despite the debility of her body, signifying becomes a human triumph.[25] This whole scene seems to me very overdone. Yet the effect that Shakespeare is striving for is the same admiration for the greatness of the human intellect that we saw in the passages from Mulcaster and Peacham. Signifying his thoughts through symbols allows man to transcend the restraints imposed on his spirit by his physical and mortal nature.

A few books in sixteenth-century England anticipated the ideas of the next century. In definitions like that in the English translation of Ramus's grammar—"A *word* is a note whereby a thing is called"— the importance of the oral quality of language is giving way to the visual, and words are becoming expressions of things, not human thoughts.[26] These ideas, however, did not yet find wide acceptance. More influential was the English humanists' conception of language, differing from that of the medieval grammarians mainly in emphasis. In *The Petie Schole,* the closest thing to an English grammar written in the sixteenth century, Francis Clement explains that "A Word is an absolute & perfect voice, whereby something is ment and signified."[27] This writer and other humanists are following in the tradition of the Latin grammars, but, in popularizing ideas, they simplify them and do away with the logical categories. Shakespeare offers a similar definition in Sonnet 69: "tongues" are "the voice of souls" (l. 3), where "souls," I think, carries the sense of "rational soul" (as in the Latin *anima*). Rhetoric has taken hold over the other disciplines, and the humanists celebrate the expressive powers of speech, even at the level of the word. A most eloquent definition is that of the English logician, Ralph Lever: "Words are voyces framed with hart and toung, vttering the thoughtes of the mynde."[28] Lever's conception of language is oral and subjective: speech is a physical process, and it expresses human thoughts, not things.

Simply by combining the older definitions of *vox* and *oratio,* moreover, the humanists change the conception of language. Speech is not two things existing in a hierarchy, mutable voice and transcendent significance. Speech is rather an integration of human nature, physical and rational: heart, tongue, and mind. When Ben Jonson explains that "words and sense" are the "body" and "soule" of language, he does not mean that significance is transcendent, but that it makes language what it is, giving it "life." Through language man is thus a creator of himself, for Jonson continues, "Sense is wrought out of experience, the knowledge of humane life, and actions, or of the liberall Arts."[29] Speaking, man not only unites his own nature, but also places himself in a significant relation to his world. So it is that speech may be as Ulysses describes it, "a bond of air," but yet one "strong as the axle-tree / On which heaven rides" (*Tro.* 1.3.66–67). When the slight substance of air takes on the weight of human thought, it acquires the strength—comparable to that holding up the heavens—to support human society.

As we have seen in the examples of Falstaff and the Andronici, Shakespeare's characters define themselves by their conceptions of language; in this way, as in linguistic styles, language is a mirror for the Elizabethan dramatist. In *Measure for Measure,* Mariana and Angelo similarly reveal themselves and their relation to society in their understanding of language as a union or a divorce of voice and significance. In the final scene Mariana asserts that Angelo is her husband by natural, moral, and linguistic certitudes. Indeed, her assertion has force because the interrelation of these physical and metaphysical truths supports her claim of union. If there is a connection between body and spirit, then she and Angelo are one:

> As there comes light from heaven, and words from breath,
> As there is sense in truth, and truth in virtue,
> I am affianc'd this man's wife as strongly
> As words could make up vows; and, my good lord,
> But Tuesday night last gone, in 's garden-house,
> He knew me as a wife.
>
> (5.1.225–30)

Words come from breath and vows from words: by these linguistic facts, as well as by the natural light of heaven and the truth implicit in virtue, Mariana vows that Angelo is her husband *because* of their physical union. Even the syntax of the statement, one thing issuing from another, reinforces her affirmation of unity. To Mariana the breath of voice, the meaning of words, the strength of vows—all these are integrated in herself, and also into a vast scheme of things that has moral significance, as well as physical existence. She sees herself whole, and connected to her society as part of this scheme; so, too, she sees Angelo, whether he wishes to be so or not.

Earlier in *Measure for Measure,* in contrast, Angelo had depicted the battle within himself by a description of sound divorced from sense:

> Heaven hath my empty words,
> Whilst my invention, hearing not my tongue,
> Anchors on Isabel; heaven in my mouth,
> As if I did but only chew his name,
> And in my heart the strong and swelling evil
> Of my conception.
>
> (2.4.2–7)

Tongue and mouth form words, but they remain lifeless; Angelo's thoughts of Isabella empty the symbols of meaning.[30] As the natural and intellectual oppose each other, the separation of voice from significance in Angelo's words mirrors his moral disintegration. He is a man who literally does not know what he is saying. His failure to unify himself also isolates him from his society: "The state, whereon I studied, / Is like a good thing, being often read, / Grown sere and tedious" (2.4.7–9). In their response to the double nature of language, Shakespeare's characters disclose their personal vision: at odds with their words and themselves, or unified and reflecting a larger concord.

The definitions taught in school and adapted by the English humanists emphasize language as human communication over language as an abstract system of symbols: significance does not inhere in words, but arises from the interaction of speaker and listener as they order and understand the words. We may infer the view of the dramatic medium resulting from this view of language: one would regard a play not as an artistic artifact made from words, with aesthetic value depending only on the verbal construct, but as a communication through words, with aesthetic value depending on the experience that words engender in the audience.[31] This, in fact, is the conception of his medium that Shakespeare presents in the choruses and epilogues where he speaks either on his own behalf as a dramatist, or on behalf of the actors. In *Pericles*, for example, Gower, who serves as chorus and represents, if not Shakespeare, then the generic poet as Shakespeare saw him, espouses a view of dramatic language very close to the view of language of the English humanists. That a play is as transitory as the voices of its speakers Gower indicates near the end: "Now our sands are almost run, /

More a little, and then dumb" (5.2.1-2). The words of the play are not meant to form an artistic artifact valuable in itself, according to Gower, for they cannot create a realistic representation of the events and setting: the dramatist must use one language to stand for many, and mere rhymes to imply the passage of time and the movement from place to place (4.cho.45-50 and 4.4.1-7). It is only with the aid of the audience's response that the play comes to have aesthetic value: in his speeches Gower invokes the audience to imagine the realistic world that the language and the theater cannot fully represent (3.cho.58-60 and 4.cho.45-50). At the end of the play, Gower, the characters, and the words are gone, but the sense wrought out of human experience remains: in his last speech, Gower focuses on the moral implications of the story that we should carry with us; and in his first speech, he had called the play an old song, the immediate end of which is "To glad [the] ear and please [the] eyes" (Pro., l. 4), but the final end of which is "to make men glorious" (l. 9). To Gower a play is a union of the voices and actions of the speakers, the human experience that they communicate, and the imagination of the audience, who help to make sense of it. What glads the ear — the words and their beauty — is transitory. What makes men glorious — the imaginative experience arising from the words — is not.

Shakespeare's epilogues further acknowledge the bond of communication between author or performers and audience. Apologizing for the "all-unable pen" of "Our bending author" (ll. 1-2), the epilogue of *Henry V* urges that, for the sake of the story about English heroes, the play will find "acceptance" in the "fair minds" (l. 14) of the audience. Similarly, in *The Two Noble Kinsmen*, the actor speaking the epilogue hopes that "the tale we have told" will "content" the listeners (ll. 12-13). At the end of *The Tempest*, the actor playing Prospero speaks directly to the audience and requests a reply: "Gentle breath of yours my sails / Must fill, or else my project fails, / Which was to please" (ll. 11-13). The "breath" he asks is not only the voice of the audience acclaiming the performance, but also the imagination to sustain the ending, Prospero's voyage home — the same imagination that has helped to create Prospero's world and its meaning throughout the play. As language is presented in the English humanists' writings, an integration of human faculties and experience, so is a play presented in Shakespeare's epilogues: a union of the pen of the playwright, the voices of the actors, the ears of the audience, and the minds of all. And, if everyone performs well, the humane exchange occurs of experience and hearts:

> Ours be your patience then, and yours our parts;
> Your gentle hands lend us, and take our hearts.
>
> (*AWW*, epi., ll. 5–6)

The Connection between Words and Things

The excitement of studying language in the Renaissance lay in discovering the supreme importance of humankind. Language reflects man's physical limits and his rational powers to order and create. Accordingly, the playwright might find in language an ideal medium for creating the semblance of human nature. But what, then, is the connection between language and reality? More particularly, if words express thoughts, what is the connection between words and things? Shakespeare's characters reveal opinions on this matter as divergent as their opinions on what language is. Juliet maintains that the relation between her lover and his name is only arbitrary: "What's Montague? It is nor hand nor foot, / . . . nor any other part / Belonging to a man" (*Rom.* 2.2.40–42); like the word "rose," symbolizing the flower but having no real connection to it, the name "Montague" applies to Romeo without binding him to his family. In *Measure for Measure,* in contrast, Escalus unravels Elbow's case against Pompey Bum, and shrewdly perceives that a more than superficial logic lies behind the imposition of names: "Troth, and your bum is the greatest thing about you, so that in the beastliest sense you are Pompey the Great" (2.1.217–19). Similarly, the soothsayer in *Cymbeline* interprets the oracle — and unravels the confusions of the fable — by explaining the connection between words and reality, between the "lion's whelp" and Leonatus, between the metaphorical "cedar" and Cymbeline, and between the Latin word *"mulier"* and Imogen's tender loyalty (5.5.443–58). Words that to others appeared nonsense are, to the soothsayer, connected to the workings of the world by a certain and profound link.

Just as a difference of opinion exists among Shakespeare's characters, so on a more sophisticated level existed a lively disagreement among Elizabethan writers. Historians of linguistics have identified the discussion of the relation between a word and what it represents as the "nature-convention controversy": they see two sides to the debate.[32] Shakespeareans have generally assumed that what D. P. Walker and Frances Yates found in continental Neoplatonists must hold for educated Elizabethans as well: both believed in a real and natural connection between words and things — and so presumably did Shakespeare.[33] Yet in Elizabethan writings three possible positions in the controversy may be discerned, that of a real connection being least common.

Those Renaissance men who postulated a real and natural connection between words and things were strictly following Pythagorean and Neoplatonist doctrine. If all things in the cosmos are shadowy manifestations of the Ideas in the mind of God, then words as well as things are such manifestations, and are connected to things, as all things are connected, by astral influences and divine harmony: this is Agrippa's explanation in *De Occulta Philosophia* (1533). He qualifies it to an extent; some names men have imposed arbitrarily, and so only certain names signify "by the influence of the Celestiall harmony."[34] Continental writers of this school who were especially influenced by Cabalistic studies argued that Hebrew, because of its origin in the language that God gave to Adam, contains more "true names" than other languages.[35] John Dee is the rare Englishman who espouses this view of language, and he attributes these qualities not to Hebrew, but to a language taught him, he claims, by angels through his medium Edward Kelly. In this divine language each letter signifies "the quiddity of the substance," and the letters "are by numbers gathered together" so that the angels "teach proper words . . . signifying substantially the thing that is spoken of in the center of his Creator."[36] As Walker points out in *Spiritual and Demonic Magic*, Protestants were less likely than Catholics to hold a Neoplatonic view of language.[37] Perhaps it is Protestantism that led the English generally to other explanations.

Most Elizabethans, unlike Dee, found words to be the imprints of human, not supernatural, significance. As a result, the controversy on the relation of words to things takes place in England between those who take the positions of the two speakers in Erasmus's humanist treatise, *De Pronunciatione*. Concerning *"voces"* (words) Leo says, *"Arbitrabar fortuito natas, aut certe pro arbitratu instituentium repertas"* — I judged them born by chance, or at least invented according to the whim of teachers.[38] Leo sees only an arbitrary relation between words and things; in doing so, he has many classical and medieval precursors,[39] as well as sixteenth-century followers. In his English logic, for example, Abraham Fraunce observes that some things were named "by the imposition and fancie of man."[40] When, in *The Advancement of Learning*, Bacon declares that words signify *"Ad Placitum* [at pleasure], hauing force onely by *Contract* or *Acceptation,"*[41] he is not taking a new stand, but rather continuing a very old debate.

What marks those Renaissance thinkers sharing Leo's view is skepticism about man's superior powers as they are manifested in his institutions, which are merely conventional, and which include language: words are imposed by speakers' whims and retained only by habit. On this matter Shakespeare's Juliet anticipates Florio's English translation of Montaigne: "the name, is a voyce which noteth, and signifieth the thing: the name, is neither part of thing nor of substance: it is a stranger-piece ioyned to the thing, and from it."[42] When Juliet denies that a real connection exists between Romeo and his family name, she sounds very much like the French skeptic:

> What's Montague? It is nor hand nor foot,
> Nor arm nor face, nor any other part
> Belonging to a man. O, be some other name!
> What's in a name? That which we call a rose
> By any other word would smell as sweet;
> So Romeo would, were he not Romeo call'd,
> Retain that dear perfection which he owes
> Without that title.
>
> (*Rom.* 2.2.40–47)

Juliet consorts with the skeptics out of desperation. As if telling beads, she works her way around the problem of Romeo's paternity, seizing upon the argument from his name: if there is no real bond between the man and his name, then there is no real bond between her lover and the family who are her enemies. Might not these two deny fathers and quarrels and all, as easily as they would give up their separate names to be joined together? Juliet's hope is not realized: even though Romeo denies his name, his bond to his family remains tragically real and natural. Not the name of Montague, but the social ties and discords signified by it destroy the lovers.

In his debate with Leo in Erasmus's *De Pronunciatione*, Ursus

takes the remaining position on the connection between words and
things. Arguing that certain letters are associated with particular
qualities (an "r" in a word often points to a rough quality in the
thing named, "l" to a gentle or slow quality) Ursus concludes that
the imposition of words has a logical basis. Words do not necessarily
reproduce by their letters and sound the things that they signify, admits Ursus; nor is the whole thing represented by the word. Still,
"satis est aliquam similitudinem apparere"—it is enough that some
likeness is clear. Even if the likeness between word and thing is not
clear, he cautions, *"tamen aliquid causae subest, cur huic rei
uocabulum hoc sit impositum"*—nevertheless, something is there
which has caused this name to be imposed upon this thing.[43] According to Ursus, words are neither naturally nor arbitrarily connected to things; rather, words are representative of things in a
rational manner. If we look to the classical and medieval precursors
of Ursus, we find that language imitates reality in two ways: in an
obvious way, when sound mirrors sense, as in onomatopoeic words;
in a less obvious way, when words characterize things or their
qualities, as in compounds, metaphors, and derivatives.[44] Richard
Carew finds these characteristics in the English language, where
words have proper "Significancie": "for example, in *Moldwarpe* we
express the Nature of the Animal; in *Handkercher* the thing and the
use; in the word *upright,* that Virtue by a Metaphore; in *Wisdome*
and *Doomesday,* so many Sentences as Words; and so of the rest."
English, he avers, passes even the classical languages in one respect,
"that all the proper Names of our People do in a manner import
somewhat."[45]

In Shakespeare's plays, as well, a man is often "like" his name. At
work may be merely dramatic convention when Shakespeare provides charactonyms for the audience alone; no one in Hamlet's
world comments on the name of "Fortinbras," despite its significance for us. In other cases, however, Shakespeare makes the dramatic convention part of the world of the characters; a broader
principle operates when a character recognizes the surprising connection between a man and his name. "I would not have you ac-
quainted with tapsters," Escalus advises Pompey's companion when
he judges him in *Measure for Measure;* "they will draw you, Master
Froth, and you will hang them" (2.1.204–6). In Escalus's world,
names may "import somewhat," characterizing what they name;

and so Master Froth's name represents by a metaphor his frivolity
and his willingness to be "drawn in" by tapsters (l. 210). Escalus's
discovery of what the name in each case imports dramatizes his ability to see to the heart of a matter, and to make the connections between words and reality that bring order into the confusions of the
testimony. After his insight into the beastly sense in which Pompey
Bum deserves his name, he further couches his reprimand as an analogy between Pompey and his name: "I advise you let me not find
you before me again upon any complaint whatsoever. . . . If I do,
Pompey, I shall beat you to your tent, and prove a shrewd Caesar
to you; in plain-dealing, Pompey, I shall have you whipt"
(2.1.245–50).

It is the likeness between words and things that justifies the medieval and Renaissance science of etymology. Bacon, who is skeptical
of the claims of etymologists, yet thinks that "examining the power
and Nature of Wordes, as they are the foot-steppes and prints of
Reason: which kinde of Analogie betweene *Woordes,* and *Reason* is
handled *Sparsim,* brokenly . . . [is] worthy to be reduced into a
Science by it selfe."[46] Many earlier English humanists were less cautious. A name may be imposed on a thing "according to his naturall
proprietie," declares Abraham Fraunce; and he consequently
defines etymology as the study of the connection between words and
things: "Notation or Etymologie, is the interpretation of the woord.
For woords bee notes of thinges, and of all woords eyther deriuatiue
or compound, you may yeelde some reason fet from the first arguments, if the notation bee well made."[47] Thus Othello fetches his
reasons from the first arguments, those of the name-makers, when
he explains to Iago his right to marry Desdemona: unless he loved
"the gentle Desdemona," he "would not [his] unhoused free condition / Put into circumscription and confine" (*Oth.* 1.2.25–27);
unless he loved Desdemona, he would not wish to become a husband, "house-bound."

One need not go to Plato or Aristotle, asserts the English educator Richard Mulcaster, to prove that words are "voluntarie, and
appointed vpon cause": "For euen God himself, who brought the
creatures . . . vnto that first man . . . that he might name them, according to their properties, doth planelie declare . . . what a cunning thing it is to giue right names, and how necessarie it is, to know
their forces, which be allredie giuen, bycause the word being

knowen, which implyeth the propertie the thing is half known, whose propertie is emplyed."[48] God himself acknowledges that men are also creators: by bestowing names that characterize things, men make an imitation of the order and significance of God's creation. Language reflects reality because wise men imprinted their knowledge of the properties of things even in the elements of words. By learning why a certain name was imposed on a thing, one may actually learn something of the nature of the thing itself.

The soothsayer in *Cymbeline* follows these recognized principles of Renaissance etymology when he interprets the oracle. His interpretation, in fact, depends on demonstrating that the words are notations well made: Leonatus corresponds to "the lion's whelp" because "The fit and apt construction of [his] name / . . . doth import so much" (5.5.443–45); that is, his name means "lion-born." Similarly, Imogen corresponds to the "piece of tender air" because the Latin *"mulier,"* compounded of *"mollis"* and *"aer,"* expresses a characteristic quality of women[49]—and particularly of the gentle wife who is hanging about the neck of the husband who wanted her murdered (ll. 446–52). Finding the oracle, Posthumus had judged it "senseless speaking, or a speaking such / As sense cannot untie" (5.4.147–48); yet he kept it because, "The action of my life is like it" (l. 149). At the end of the play, the soothsayer reveals Posthumus's life to be like the oracle, not because both are senseless, but because there is an analogical relation between its words and the events of Posthumus's life: his constant wife is like the tender air; Cymbeline is like the cedar; and the King's two sons returned to him are like the branches revived. In teaching the "fit and apt construction" of words, the soothsayer actually teaches that the universe, reflected in language, has an order and a significance not immediately apparent, but nonetheless profound. Cymbeline instantly makes peace with the Romans, fulfilling the last statement of the oracle, and thereby making his life simulate divine order. The good man, the play seems to tell us, creates his life in the same way that wise men invent words, as an imitation of the significance of a divinely created world.

This last view of the connection between words and things was favored in Renaissance England, and its popularity may explain some of the reverence in which the ancient words of Latin, Greek,

Hebrew, and even Anglo-Saxon were held. In their etymological elements, words were thought to communicate knowledge not immediately obvious, a legacy of the wisdom of the past. One was delving into deep mysteries by studying words, learning what former wise men thought of the things they named. In a sense, the maker of a name was considered an artist, creating an imitation in little of a portion of the world around him. When the soothsayer who perceives the likeness of words to things in the oracle speaks his final speech in *Cymbeline,* we may see that Shakespeare carries the principle of imitative names into his own art: it is Philharmonus, the lover of harmony, who tells us that "The fingers of the pow'rs above do tune / The harmony of this peace" (5.5.466–67). The playwright, like the soothsayer, may take advantage of the fact that language is mimetic to reveal the order and meaning in the apparent insignificance of human life.

The Cause and History of Language

As part of his history of poetry, the Elizabethan George Puttenham considers it necessary to explain the causes of language: "Vtterance also and language is giuen by nature to man for perswasion of others, and aide of them selues, I meane the first abilite to speake. For speech it selfe is artificiall and made by man."[50] Elizabethans wrote no books entirely devoted to the history of language, but many writers, like Puttenham, treated some of the issues. We shall review three major ones: whether the cause of language is nature or custom; whether the history of language shows progressive decline or cyclical rebirth; and whether a man's responsibility to his language is to retard or to accept change in diction. Many Shakespeareans have assumed that the model of language history for sixteenth-century writers was the Bible: the cause of language is God, and its origin the naming of the creatures; after the Tower of Babel, language became hopelessly corrupted. For many hundreds of years, from Isidore of Seville to Dante, these ideas had indeed controlled European study of the history of language.[51] But in the Renaissance, with classical theories revitalized and a new pride in native tongues appearing, the biblical model was reinterpreted to give men a greater role in the history of language. Puttenham, for example,

may also have believed that speech is a gift from God, but the two
causes he emphasizes are human ones: speech is a natural capability
and a human invention.

Not all men agreed with Puttenham that language has two
causes. Sixteenth-century anatomists, demonstrating variously that
the human larynx differs from that of animals, or that the entire
oral apparatus of man is adapted to speaking, as well as to eating
and breathing, saw nature as the main cause of speech.[52] After considering the commonplace that communication is natural to animals, but that speech is artificially learned by man, Montaigne
denies it, here in Florio's English: "As for speech, sure it is, that if it
be not naturall, it is not necessarie. . . . It is not to be imagined,
that nature hath refused vs that meane, and barred vs that helpe,
which she hath bestowed vpon many and divers other creatures."[53]
Montaigne is so convinced that language is innate that he thinks a
child raised without human contact would yet speak and invent a
language. These men rely on classical authority, the anatomists on
Galen and Montaigne on Lucretius;[54] yet they also show a new spirit
of inquiry, since they base their ideas on direct observation of human and animal physiology and behavior.

Those who hold that language is natural, however, are a minority
in this century. Shakespeare, for example, imagines that Caliban,
raised alone, has no language until he is taught one by Miranda and
Prospero. Most Elizabethans with an opinion on it saw language as
an invention, and one dependent on an entire society, not just on an
individual. In his logic, Ralph Lever maintains that "no man is of
power to change or to make a language when he will: but when fit
names are deuised and spoken, they force the hearers to like of them
and to vse them: and so do they by consent of manye, growe to a
speache."[55] More closely following Quintilian, who was probably
also Lever's source, Ben Jonson takes a less democratic stand: "*Custome* is the most certaine Misstresse of Language. . . . Yet when I
name Custome, I understand not the vulgar Custome: For that were
a precept no lesse dangerous to Language, then life, if wee should
speake or live after the manners of the vulgar: But that I call Custome of speech, which is the consent of the Learned; as Custome of
life, which is the consent of the good."[56] Not all sixteenth-century
writers, though, found in custom the rational order that Lever and
Jonson did. In *Of the Vanitie of Artes and Sciences*, Agrippa dis-

misses the grammarians' rules with the argument that language is mutable and based only on common custom; and, in his logic, Abraham Fraunce mournfully echoes Horace: "Woordes are lyke leaues, as Horace reporteth: leaues spring before Summer, and fall before Winter; and the same inconstancy is in words."[57]

In *Hamlet,* in a brief choric speech by a minor character, Shakespeare employs the idea of custom as the foundation of language to emphasize the uncertainty that eventually results from Claudius's rule and Hamlet's fatal opposition to it:

> The rabble call him lord,
> And as the world were now but to begin,
> Antiquity forgot, custom not known,
> The ratifiers and props of every word,
> They cry, "Choose we, Laertes shall be king!"
>
> (4.5.103-7)

Even more disapproving than Jonson at a language based only on vulgar usage is the gentleman who brings the news of Laertes' rebellion: as if the mob inherited no language or social structure, the gentleman reports with horror, they think that they can bestow names where they will. Behind his speech lies the idea that kingship and language are similar and related social institutions: no man has the right to choose his own king, any more than he has the right to make his own language; both kingship and language depend on ancient practice, and on the consent of the whole society as it is manifested in custom. We understand, of course, that Claudius faces only the disorder begun by him: he has already knocked the prop from under the title "king" by depriving it of its true significance— Hamlet. In doing so, Claudius has unloosed the forces of mutability and corruption that custom controls. When any man can appoint a king, there can be no true king; when any man can invent his own meaning for words, words also lose their validity.

Like the gentleman who sees the corruption of the word "king" as a sign of social disruption, Elizabethan writers generally see language, based on custom and varying with changes in society, as an index of social history. The educator John Brinsley, writing at the beginning of the seventeenth century, assumes that change in language indicates the increasing corruption of men: in the "confusion [at Babel], som words were changed altogether, in others the significations were altered, & many haue bin depraued and corrupted by continuance & succession of time."[58] Earlier, Agrippa had seen linguistic change as evidence of the uncertainty of all human knowledge: no one now knows the original letters, or understands the forms of any of the ancient languages.[59] To Brinsley and Agrippa, the history of language reflects the general decline of human morality and wisdom.

The early humanists also saw change as degeneration in language, but their model was Latin, pure in Cicero's age, afterwards corrupted by voluptuous poets, and even more by barbarous scholastics. In their attempts to restore Latin to its former purity, and in their discussion of the birth of the vernaculars from Latin, they nevertheless provide later writers with a model of decay and renewal in language.[60] Castiglione, writing in Italian, points out that the history of language is a series of cycles: Italian reached a peak of excellence in the Tuscan dialect of Petrarch and Boccaccio, and it may again be renewed through the sense of educated men and the revolutions of time.[61] Many Elizabethan writers judged the language of Chaucer, Lydgate, and Gower to be such a peak; and Camden likewise praised the mixed English of his own age, refined by *"Pregnant wits"* and the Tudors' encouragement of learning, and so raised to an excellence equal to the height of English-Saxon before the Norman conquest.[62] In the decade before Shakespeare's plays appear, Mulcaster supposes that languages have "ascent" and "discent," depending on whether the state grows "to better countenance," or falls off "to the more corrupt." His theory does not depend on condemning change: although change may be "decaie," it soon brings in a new language, "different from the old, tho excellent in the altered kinde." Such a language he finds the English he writes in, "the best for substance . . . so capable of ornament," which will yet "make roum for another, when the circular turn shall haue ripened alteration."[63] To these vernacular writers, the history of language reflects the rise and fall of human history: a society and its language may decline, but a society rebuilding itself also renews its language.

The historians of language thus reinforced for the poets and playwrights the necessity of decorum in language. Language "springs out of the most retired, and inmost parts of us," writes Ben Jonson, "and is the Image of the Parent of it, the mind."[64] Just as the individual's style reflects his character, so the language of a society mirrors its collective character. Defining Spenser's archaic terms as appropriate to the world of shepherds, E. K. cites the "auncient solemne wordes" of Livy, " labouring to set forth in hys worke an eternall image of antiquitie."[65] For Shakespeare, on a stage with little scenery and with costumes mainly contemporary, the character of an ancient or imagined society must be seen in the language, if seen at all. Thus the plain speech of Brutus's oratory and the florid of Antony's not only characterize the two men in *Julius Caesar,* but also provide a taste of the ancient world, whose orators consciously developed Attic or Asiatic styles. The principle operates most obviously in plays where there are competing worlds: in *1 Henry IV,* for example, where the witty prose of the tavern denotes the license of its frequenters, where the periodic sentences and formal verse of Henry's court represents its stern and self-imposed order, and where the hyperboles and run-on sentences of the rebels, in a mixture of prose and verse, embody the unrestrained ambitions of the northern and western lords. In addition, Shakespeare occasionally introduces characters, such as the Bastard in *King John* and Lavache in *All's Well That Ends Well,* who comment on the corruption of language as an indication of the times.

The theory of cyclical renewal in language generated a further debate among the vernacular writers: how does one bring a language to a peak of excellence, by restoring it to a former purity of diction, or by borrowing from other languages and inventing new words? In *The Courtier* Castiglione represents both sides: Sir Frederick argues that the courtier's vocabulary should be based on antiquity and authority, those ancient Tuscan words used in Petrarch and Boccaccio; the Count argues that the courtier must participate with other learned men in remaking his language, by choosing the best words in current use and by inventing new words and deriving them from other tongues. Both speakers borrow their terms from Quintilian, but reinterpret them according to their own opinions on the purpose of society: whether society functions to preserve old wisdom and values or to reorder itself continually in the light of contemporary taste and new knowledge.[66]

As R. F. Jones records in *The Triumph of the English Language,* the English of the latter half of the sixteenth century were intent on bringing their language to a peak of expressiveness, and were also debating how to do so.[67] Sir John Cheke, in his preface to Hoby's translation of *The Courtier,* took the conservative Sir Frederick's side; he urged his countrymen to preserve their own words, borrowing or inventing only if absolutely necessary.[68] Camden, in opposition, thinks that English has reached its present excellence by "enfranchising" words from "other good tongues," and by "implanting new wordes with artificiall composition."[69] Closer in spirit to Quintilian, Ben Jonson strikes a mean between these extremes:

> But wee must not be too frequent with the mint, every day coyning. Nor fetch words from the extreme and utmost ages; since the chiefe vertue of a style is perspicuitie, and nothing so vitious in it, as to need an Interpreter. Words borrow'd of Antiquity, doe lend a kind of Majesty to style, and are not without their delight sometimes. For they have the Authority of yeares, and out of their intermission doe win to themselves a kind of grace like newnesse. But the eldest of the present, and newest of the past Language is the best.[70]

Jonson thinks that excellence in language derives from a combination of the familiar words that make a style clear and the new or archaic words that lend majesty, grace, and freshness. Earlier in this same passage in *Timber,* he advises that "Words are the Peoples; yet there is a choise of them to be made" (p. 621): to choose well is a major responsibility of the poet.

Asking why "with the time" he does not choose "new-found methods and . . . compounds strange," Shakespeare touches on the issue of diction in Sonnet 76, in order to explain why his words are appropriate to his topic. The position in this sonnet is slightly more conservative than Jonson's:

> O know, sweet love, I always write of you,
> And you and love are still my argument;
> So all my best is dressing old words new,
> Spending again what is already spent:
>   For as the sun is daily new and old,
>   So is my love still telling what is told.
>
>   (ll. 9–14)

Preserving old values—"you and love"—the poet must respect the custom that is the foundation of language. He cannot create his own language any more than he can coin his own money; he must use the tokens provided him by society. What the poet can do is to renew old words. Shakespeare's metaphor—"dressing old words new"—seems a modest presentation of the poet's ability until we recall that dress in Elizabethan society signified by law one's social status, and livery granted by a patron signified special loyalty.[71] The poet thus raises old words to a higher status by making us see their significance afresh. In this poem the poet's modesty becomes a defense of his loyalty: just as the best language is old and new, so the best love is old in loyalty and new in its realization, and the best poem repeats the old story of fidelity, but in words revitalized by a fresh understanding of it. The poet fulfills his responsibility to language when he observes the ancient custom and yet renews it by giving it something significant to say.[72]

Old words renewed with fresh significance might serve as well to describe the sixteenth-century discussion of the history of language. Sylvester, in his 1605 translation and augmentation of Du Bartas's poem, is "still telling what is told," the old story of the biblical history of language, but a story renewed with a significance appropriate to his own age. In *Deuine Weekes,* speech is viewed as a gift of God in the sense that he made man able to voice sounds and to signify the ideas of his inner soul. Adam, however, invented the original names for things; he and later name-makers created in Hebrew an ideal language, wherein sound mirrored sense to reveal God's creation fully, and each word recorded the tale of a thing's nature in brief. After Babel, all nations except the Hebrew spoke varied and corrupt languages based on usage. Since then, Time has changed all tongues and created new ones; words are like leaves that spring and fall. The diversity of languages is a curse, but only because it makes human intercourse more difficult: men must labor half a lifetime learning languages in order to acquire the knowledge once available in their native tongue. Yet each language still performs the functions of the original: civilizing and educating men, persuading them to good, and allowing them conversation with God. Furthermore, a good education in the tongues repairs the curse of the tower: witness "the Great Eliza," Elizabeth I of England.[73]

During the sixteenth century, men learn to see language in their own image: human beings and their society are the cause of language; the history of language is one of continual renewal, as men restore with their wit what habit, time, and moral decadence take away. Many Elizabethan writers, wishing their language to serve as a model for their society, feel a responsibility to participate in this renewal. Whether by preserving the authority of ancient words, by inventing new words, or by bringing old words alive with fresh meaning, the poets hope to increase the quality of their society by choosing the best words.

The Power of Language

The whole of Elizabethan culture testifies to the power imagined in words: the religious disputes over translations of the Bible and over the necessity of vows; the ritual of cursing, and the duels resulting from insults to someone's good name; the achievements of the literature, and its most characteristic failure, sheer verbal excess; even the strict censorship of books and drama. Yet there existed no agreement on the possible nature of such power; opinions ranged from superstitious belief in the innate power of words to fear of devilish influence, from faith in the arts of benign magic to trust in the arts of rhetoric and poetry. Shakespeare frequently takes advantage of these differing attitudes to heighten dramatic tension by assigning opposing ideas to characters in emotional conflict. As is often the case in drama, in Shakespeare's plays it is not the dogma of the playwright that lends life to the worlds he creates, but, instead, his sensitivity to the resonance of conflicting possibilities.

Shakespeare's critical portrait of Jack Cade and his followers in *2 Henry VI* includes a superstitious belief in the innate power of words. Assuming books and eloquence to be a kind of magic directed against common people, the rebels decide to kill all learned men. Accused of having "a book . . . with red letters in't," the clerk of Chatham is condemned by Cade: "Nay, then he is a conjuror. . . . Hang him with his pen and inkhorn about his neck" (4.2.90–110). Fearing the pity aroused in him by reasoned speech, Cade furthermore sends the Lord Say—the name is apt—to his death: "He shall die, and it be but for pleading so well for his life. —Away with him, he has a familiar under his tongue" (4.7.106–8). In *Religion and the Decline of Magic*, Keith Thomas has documented the widespread belief in word-magic among the common people of Renaissance England, and the attempts of church and state to discredit it. Among many illustrations, he cites the woman in Stowmarket in the mid-sixteenth century who alleged that she could cure diseases by "words of conjuration," and the practice in

Nottingham in the early seventeenth century of selling copies of St. John's Gospel as protection against witchcraft.[74] Thomas concludes that the illiterate made little distinction between word-magic and prayers, or between magic and medicine: all were mysteries to be believed, but not understood. Some of Shakespeare's contemporaries came to the same conclusion. Henry Chettle, dramatist and pamphleteer, mocks the charlatan who professes to work wonders with the power of words: "First, he must know your name, then your age, which in a little paper he sets downe. On the top are these words: *In verbis, et in herbis, et in lapidibus sunt virtutes:* vnderneath he writes in capitall letters, AAB ILLA, HYRS GIBELLA, which he sweares is pure Chalde, and the names of three spirites that enter into the bloud and cause rewmes, and so consequently the toothach." But, Chettle declares, "all is foppery, for this I find to be the only remedy for the tooth paine, either to haue patience, or to pull them out."[75] Similarly, in his *Daemonologie,* King James inveighs against incantations, surmising that "vnlearned men" find "these practises to prooue true . . . by the power of the Devill for deceauing men, and not by anie inherent vertue in these vaine wordes and freites."[76]

If in *2 Henry VI* sympathy lies with the rational Lord Say, not the credulous rebels, in *1 Henry VI* opinions conflict on the power of the words of Joan, *La Pucelle.* The bastard of Orleance believes that she has come because of "a vision sent to her from heaven" (1.2.52). "Astonish'd" by her "high terms" (1.2.93), Charles sees her as the "glorious prophetess" of France: "Thy promises are like Adonis' garden, / That one day bloom'd and fruitful were the next" (1.6.6–8). To English Talbot, on the other hand, Joan seems a "damned sorceress" (3.2.38), who can "practice and converse with spirits" (2.1.25); and York calls her a "Fell banning hag" and "enchantress" (5.3.42), whose own words condemn her for a "strumpet" (5.4.84). Won back from the side of England by Joan's "fair persuasions, mix'd with sug'red words" (3.3.18), but doubting any innate power in her speeches, Burgundy stands undecided between theories just as he stands undecided between countries: "Either she hath bewitch'd me with her words, / Or nature makes me suddenly relent" (3.3.58–59). And even though we see the devils that Joan calls up by her "ancient incantations" (5.3.27), the play encourages us to admire those men like Burgundy who do not succumb entirely to credulity. Blaming men not spirits, Talbot also doubts the efficacy of Joan's powers: "A witch by fear, not force, . . . / Drives back our troops and conquers as she lists" (1.6.21–22). Perhaps Joan's words have no more power than those of the English soldier who collects spoils from the French, "Using no other weapon but [Talbot's] name" (2.1.81).

From *The Second Shepherds' Play* to *The Tempest,* English drama sustains a fascination with exploring the magical powers of words. Yet the widespread continental interest in philosophical word-magic finds no parallel in England. During the late sixteenth century, John Dee does assert that some words have magical force. His angels, he records, explained to him that the words of their special language — not Hebrew, but God's creative language — have a sympathetic power over things: "the creatures of God [are] stirred up in themselves, when they hear the words wherewithal they were nursed and brought forth."[77] As we have seen, however, Dee is the rare Englishman who believed in a real and natural connection between words and things, which is the basis for Renaissance speculation on word-magic. Having spent many years in the academies and courts of Europe, Dee is closer to continental than to other English thinkers.

The English literary men, who are intrigued by the idea of an innate power in language in their fiction, are hostile to it in their pamphlets and histories. We have already listened to Chettle and King James holding forth against popular superstition. Sir Walter Raleigh similarly criticizes the erudite but still superstitious "doctrine of *Characters,* numbers, and incantations"; it is the devil, he warns, who "taught men to beleeue in the strength of wordes and letters: (which without faith in God are but inke or common breath)."[78] Raleigh does not rule out the force of prayer, where men use words to request divine intervention, but he does rule out any power in words themselves. Less indignant than Raleigh, William Camden, friend of Sidney and teacher of Jonson, admits that "Of the effectuall power of words, great disputes have beene of great wits in all ages." He first considers the Pythagoreans and "the impious Iewes," concluding, "and strange it is what *Samonicus Serenus* ascribed to the word ABRADACABRA [*sic*], against agues." Camden then turns to a story from English history that, at first, seems to support these pagan beliefs: with the force of the word "Niding" (which means "coward") King William Rufus "levied Armies, and subdued rebellious enemies"; having sent a message that any subject not coming to his aid would be known as a "Niding," Rufus discovered that his subjects "swarmed to him . . . in such numbers, that he had in few daies an infinite Armie, and the rebells therewith weere so terrified, that they forthwith yeelded."[79] Camden's irony is ultimately clear: Rufus put his faith not in the innate power of words, but in the honor of his subjects and the force of numbers; the word "Niding" had power not through magic, but because of its significance. "Suche force hath the tongue," wrote Thomas Wilson a generation before Camden, "and such is the power of eloquence and reason, that most men are forced euen to yelde in that, which most standeth againste their will."[80] Against the pagan belief in a magical force in words, Camden sets English common sense and the humanists' belief in the power of language to change men's minds.

Of Shakespeare's opinion there is no record. Even if he was not as open as Camden to disparate beliefs, the playwright did see the value of increasing dramatic tension through equally plausible but dissenting views. In the first act of *Othello,* such is the tension between Brabantio and Othello, increased by their different conceptions of the power of words. Frightened by the midnight cries, Brabantio grasps for an explanation of his daughter's "treason": "Is there not charms / By which the property of youth and maidhood / May be abus'd? Have you not read, Roderigo, / Of some such thing?" (1.1.169–74). At first tentative — "That thou hast practic'd on her with foul charms, / . . . . I'll have it disputed on, / 'Tis probable, and palpable to thinking" (1.2.73–76) — Brabantio gradually convinces himself that Desdemona's unnatural act required an unnatural cause: "She is abus'd, stol'n from me, and corrupted / By spells and medicines bought of mountebanks; / For nature so prepost'rously to err / . . . Sans witchcraft could not" (1.3.60–64). When Othello initially hears of Brabantio's anger, he remains calm: "My services which I have done the signiory / Shall out-tongue his complaints" (1.1.18–19). And calmly he promises to the council, "a round unvarnish'd tale" recounting "what drugs, what charms, / What conjuration, and what mighty magic" (1.3.90–92) he used to win his wife. In fulfillment, Othello summarizes the story of his adventures that moved Desdemona to pity and love him. Othello answers Brabantio's rage with self-possession, and sets his reasoned eloquence against Brabantio's accusations of magic. "This only is the witchcraft I have us'd" (1.3.169), Othello ends, and we may catch his irony: the power of Othello's speech lies in his catalogue of wondrous adventures, not in the magical properties of incantatory words. The scene is not about language and its powers; nor does it force a belief on the audience. Like the Duke, who vows Brabantio "the bloody book of law" against the man who has "thus beguil'd your daughter" (1.3.66–67), and then reassures Othello, "I think this tale would win my daughter, too" (l. 171), the audience may respond to the conflicting emotions and ideas with sympathy for both sides.

Our century has seen a Zulu production of *Macbeth* in which the spells of the witches necessarily had magical influence over reality, and a Japanese film where the prophecies demonstrated foresight but not efficacy. Both productions were insightful studies of their own cultures refracted through Shakespeare's story. But neither version captured the ambiguous world of Shakespeare's play, where Macbeth must try without the help of certainties to reconcile ambition and humanity. Hecate claims complete power for the "riddles," "spells," and "charms," of the weird sisters (*Mac.* 3.5.3–29).[81] On the other hand, Macbeth concludes that the witches' powers to tempt are greater than their powers to do:

> And be these juggling fiends no more believ'd,
> That palter with us in a double sense,
> That keep the word of promise to our ear,
> And break it to our hope.
>
> (5.8.19–22)

The play requires neither belief nor skepticism for the witches' claims, but rather the ability to entertain both possibilities.

In the more realistic worlds of the tragedies and histories, the skeptics may eventually prove themselves justified; in the golden worlds of the romantic comedies, however, the characters who believe in incantations generally appear the wiser sort. In *A Midsummer Night's Dream* we are asked to believe in love charms and the fairies' incantatory blessings of the household, and we may feel superior to Theseus, who unwisely denies the magical forces at play in his own world and language. Similarly, in the worlds of *As You Like It* and *The Tempest*, words have special powers: the chanted

vows of the lovers in Arden are answered by the appearance of
Hymen; and Prospero opens graves and commands the elements
with his magical words. Nevertheless, even in these plays, Shakespeare gives the skeptics some voice: in his epilogue, Puck tells us
that we may take his world for a "dream"; Ganymede brings back
Rosalind not by charms, but by a change of clothes; and Caliban
appears foolish because he thinks that Prospero's power resides in his
books, rather than in his knowledge and virtue.

Thus Shakespeare discovered early that the credibility of an imagined world results more often from conflicting perspectives among
the characters than from consistent ones. In addition, however,
Shakespeare reveals a typically Renaissance habit of mind when he
puts ideas about the power of language to dramatic use. In a certain
respect, the great works of the English Renaissance— *The Arcadia,
The Faerie Queene, Hamlet*—as well as the lesser works— *The
Gouenour, The Anatomie of Melancholy*—are encyclopedias. The
very souls of the men were encyclopedic. To play with ideas, to try
them on for size, to see if men measured up to them or were overwhelmed by them: these were essential purposes of most Elizabethan
writers. The potential powers and sources of power of words called
forth this exploratory response from Shakespeare, as well as from
many other Elizabethan writers. Was there a power in language that
made men smaller by tempting them to reach beyond themselves, or
was there a power that aided them to grow into the greatness naturally waiting for them? Or were men required to choose between
these powers?

Elizabethan fiction and treatises taken together thus suggest that
the poets might imagine a world of men who speak a language in-
nately powerful, but that they did not believe themselves to live in
one. Surprisingly, the English writers found the powers of eloquence
to be more exciting than those of magic, even when, like Camden,
they entertained the possibility of arcane powers in words. These
powers result not from words alone, but rather from the force of
knowledge and virtue expressed in language. Eloquence depends on
"weight of matter," Mulcaster determines, not "folie in words."[82]
The choice of a good metaphor, Richard Sherry advises his readers,
must not "be referred onely to the name of the thing, but much
more to the strength and power of the signification."[83] "The quaint-
nesse or liuelinesse of the conceit" Montaigne judges to be the source

of the "filling and ravishing" power of Lucretius's eloquence: faced
with such eloquence, Montaigne concludes, "I say not this is to
speake well, but to thinke well."[84] Ben Jonson concurs with Montaigne on the source of eloquence: "The sense is as the life and soule
of Language, without which all words are dead."[85] What all these
writers are talking about is obvious: the Renaissance ideal of wise
eloquence. Through language men move others to conviction by
the force of knowledge. Shakespeare's contemporaries rightly believed that this power of language over men's minds is to be wondered at.

On occasion, Shakespeare uses even the humanists' pervasive notion of the power of language as the basis for dramatic conflict.
"Conceit, more rich in matter than in words," Juliet advises Romeo,
"Brags of his substance, not of ornament" (*Rom.* 2.6.30–31).
Romeo has just requested that she "sweeten with [her] breath / This
neighbor air, and let rich music's tongue / Unfold the imagin'd happiness" of their love (2.6.26–28). In his romantic metaphor Romeo
suggests that love comes as easily as singing a tune, as naturally as
voice. In her reply, Juliet is correcting his assumptions about eloquence, as well as love. She more realistically believes that love, like
a gold mine, must be worked to produce riches: just as the power of
language lies in its significance, not its sound, so love must be
judged by its hidden depths, not by its outward expression. In *King
Lear* we may see that Lear has turned these values around when he
misjudges his daughters, and Kent cannot stop himself from rebuk-
ing his master's folly: "Nor are those empty-hearted whose low
sounds / Reverb no hollowness" (*Lr.* 1.1.153–54).

In artful language, especially in poetry, Renaissance humanists
found another power to equal that of significance in language: harmony. In rhetoric, Henry Peacham explains, wisdom "exerciseth
her power, working in the minde of the hearer, partly by a pleasant
proportion, & as it were by a sweet & musicall harmonie, and partly
by the secret and mightie power of perswasion."[86] Because of its harmony, Puttenham argues in his *Arte of English Poesie,* poetry better
persuades men than prose: more "voluble and slipper vpon the
tong," sounded with more "gallant and harmonical accents," more
"sweet and ciuill," poetry has more "efficacie" than prose.[87] Furthermore, in the Renaissance interpretation of the myths of Am-
phion and Orpheus, as Madeleine Doran and others have shown,

the comparison of music with poetic and rhetorical speech is based on the power to civilize men that these arts share.[88] Although Elizabethans denied that the power of speech lay in sound alone, they praised the harmonies of voice and music, reflections of divine proportion and order, which might move men on a higher plane, one on a level with the force of significance in speech.

Shakespeare's metaphors for the power of speech to enchant, in fact, are based not on the magical properties of words, but on the likeness of speech to music. Adonis must stop his ears against Venus's "deceiving harmony," (*Ven.*, 1. 781), "Bewitching like the wanton mermaids' songs" (1. 777). More often Shakespeare's mermaid is an anticlassical one, who leads men to civility rather than shipwreck. Oberon begins his tale of the love-flower by describing a mermaid, "Uttering such dulcet and harmonious breath / That the rude sea grew civil at her song" (*MND* 2.1.151-52). That a higher order of speech manifests itself in harmony is suggested by Nestor's eloquence; in the painting in *Lucrece,* the crowd around Nestor "swallow up his sound advice, / . . . As if some mermaid did their ears entice" (ll. 1409-11).

Shakespeare counts on the harmonious power of metrical speech to move men to comprehend the extraordinary. In *A Midsummer Night's Dream,* the young lovers' chiming couplets and the fairies' lilting ballad meters help us to comprehend two forms of "unnatural" experience: love and magic. Indeed, a promising trend among actors is not to resist Shakespeare's verse, but instead to emphasize it and let it do its work. Enobarbus, whose verse is generally as loose as his sense is caustic, describes Cleopatra in meters more strictly patterned than his usual; when he has concluded his praise of Cleopatra — fanned by dimpled Cupids, her barge and its purple sails tended by seeming mermaids, the queen herself an earthly Venus — the prosy soldiers, who ordinarily define greatness as discipline and valor, have heard in the subtle harmonies that greatness may be something else: beauty, grace, and extravagance. Enobarbus, moving from loose to more formal verse, and Hamlet, moving from the prose of his antic disposition to the verse of his philosophic soliloquies, allow us, too, to be moved, not emotionally but intellectually, from one perspective to another. The distinctions between verse and prose and between kinds of verse gave Shakespeare a variety in form to equal and emphasize the variety of ideas. Signaling far more than decorum of social class or genre, changes in the rhythms of prose and verse mark changes in the minds of the characters and in our responses to the events of the play.

In his introduction to Ulysses' speech in *Troilus and Cressida,* Agamemnon defines what he expects to hear from the ideally eloquent speaker: "music, wit, and oracle" (1.3.74). These are also the powers of speech that the Elizabethan poet and playwright hoped for: harmony and significance. It is with these powers, Sidney writes in his *Defense of Poesy,* not an innate power in language, that poets move men: "Although it were a very vain and godless superstition . . . (to think spirits were commanded by such verses, whereupon this word "charms," derived of *carmina,* comes) so yet serves it to show the great reverence those wits were held in. And altogether not without ground, since both the oracles of Delphos and Sibylla's prophecies were wholly delivered in verses, for that same exquisite observing of number and measure in the words and that high-flying liberty of conceit proper to the poet did seem to have some divine force in it."[89] If the poet longs at times for an innate power in language, its absence is yet a fortunate one, because it requires him to be a maker: his language grows powerful as he invests it with harmony, knowledge, and imagination. It is through these means that the poet moves his audience with a force that seems divine.

Notes

1. *Timber,* in *Ben Jonson,* VIII, 625.

2. Richard Edwards, *The excellent Comedie of . . . Damon and Pithias* (London, 1571), sig. Aii[r].

3. The courtiers "hear" the mechanicals' play in *MND* (5.1.76, 77, and 81); and the prologue begs us "Gently to hear" the play of *H5* (l. 34). Stephen Orgel finds Inigo Jones's idea of the theater as a visual illusion to be a revolutionary one for the Jacobeans, in *The Jonsonian Masque* (Cambridge, Mass.: Harvard Univ. Press, 1965), pp. 1 and 201–2.

4. Christopher Marlowe, *Tamburlaine, Part I,* in *Complete Works,* ed. Fredson Bowers (Cambridge: Cambridge Univ. Press, 1973), I, 79.

5. On seventeenth-century linguistics see Murray Cohen, *Sensible Words* (Baltimore: Johns Hopkins Univ. Press, 1977), esp. pp. 8–21.

6. For the influence of Donatus's definitions on medieval and Renaissance Europe, see Wayland J. Chase's introduction to *The Ars Minor of Donatus,* Univ. of Wisconsin Studies in Language and Literature, No. 11

(Madison, 1926), pp. 16–23. On the influence of Donatus's and Priscian's advanced grammars on the fifteenth- and sixteenth-century grammarians, see G. A. Padley, *Grammatical Theory in Western Europe 1500–1700* (Cambridge: Cambridge Univ. Press, 1976), pp. 15–29.

7. Donatus, *Ars Grammatica [Ars maior]*, in *Grammatici Latini*, ed. Heinrich Keil (Leipzig: B. G. Teubner, 1864), IV, 367.

8. *The House of Fame*, ll. 765–68, in *The Works of Geoffrey Chaucer*, ed. F. N. Robinson (Boston: Houghton Mifflin Co., 1957), p. 289.

9. Priscian, *Institutio Grammaticarum*, in *Libri Omnes* (Basel, 1568), p. 1.

10. Marius Servius, *Commentarius*, in *Grammatici Latini*, ed. Keil, IV, 405. Cf. John Seton's definition of voice as the sound of a living being, produced by the throat and other parts of the mouth, in *Dialectica*, ed. Peter Carter (London, 1584), sig. Ai[r]. Seton's text was the standard logic in sixteenth-century English universities.

11. Priscian, *Institutio*, p. 2.

12. See, for example, Francis Clement, *The Petie Schole* (London, 1587), p. 11: "A letter is an element, or simple voice apt to expresse a word, either one by it selfe vttered or moe ioined together."

13. William Lilly and John Colet, *A Shorte Introduction of Grammar* (London, 1584), sig. A6[r].

14. Priscian, *Institutio*, p. 35.

15. See Donatus, *Ars Grammatica*, in *Grammatici Latini*, ed. Keil, IV, 367–68; Sergius, *Explanationum in Artem Donati*, in *Grammatici Latini*, ed. Keil, IV, 487; Dante, *De Vulgari Eloquentia*, in *Latin Works*, p. 8; and Juan Luis Vives, *Tudor School-Boy Life, The Dialogues of . . . Vives*, tr. Foster Watson (London: J. M. Dent & Co., 1908), p. 19.

16. Castiglione, *The Courtier*, sig. F3[v]. Cf. Sir Francis Bacon, *The Twoo Bookes . . . of the proficiencie and aduancement of Learning* (London, 1605), sig. Pp3[v]: gestures are to hieroglyphics "as *Words spoken* are to *Wordes written*, in that they abide not."

17. Robert Robinson, *The Art of Pronuntiation* (London, 1617), sig. A3[v].

18. Priscian, *Institutio*, p. 44. For a different text and, consequently, a slightly different interpretation, see Ian Michael, *English Grammatical Categories* (Cambridge: Cambridge Univ. Press, 1970), p. 40: "a proper arrangement of words, expressing fully what the speaker wants to say *(ordinatio dictionum congrua, sententiam perfectam demonstrans)*." My conclusion—that significance depends on the whole structure of the *"oratio"*—remains consonant with Michael's reading, even though his text is quite different from the 1568 Priscian that I used.

19. Isidore of Seville, *Etymologiae*, *PL*, LXXXII, 81.

20. Hippolyta's objection to Quince's lack of "government" may be a technical grammatical criticism. "Government" in grammar is the influence of one word on the form and function of another one, as in Latin the preposition or verb determines the case of its object. Quince lacks proper government because his reading changes which phrases determine the function of other ones. In 5.1.113-15, for example—"We do not come, as minding to content you, / Our true intent is. All for your delight / We are not here."—"All for your delight" is an adverbial phrase modifying "here" according to Quince's reading, but it should be a predicate nominative following "intent is."

21. See Priscian, *Institutio*, pp. 44-45; and Seton, *Dialectica*, sigs. A1ʳ⁻ᵛ. On the theory of consignificants in the Renaissance, see Padley, *Grammatical Theory*, p. 36, and Michael, *English Grammatical Categories*, p. 50.

22. Priscian, *Institutio*, pp. 43-44. For a fuller explanation of Priscian's idea, see Padley, *Grammatical Theory*, p. 33; and Michael, *English Grammatical Categories*, pp. 44-46. Priscian's definition may have descended from Aristotle, *On Interpretation*, 16a: "No sound is by nature a noun: it becomes one, becoming a symbol."

23. Richard Mulcaster, *The First Part of the Elementarie* (London, 1582), p. 157.

24. Peacham, *Garden* (1577), sig. Aiiʳ.

25. Lawrence Danson's interpretation of Lavinia's speechlessness, although partly in accord with Renaissance ideas about language, does not take into account her overcoming her handicap; in *Tragic Alphabet* (New Haven: Yale Univ. Press, 1974), p. 11: "The mutilated Lavinia is . . . a conceit for the nearness of man to monster when deprived of the humanizing gift of expression, and (more narrowly) an emblem for the plight of the voiceless Andronici in a now alien Rome."

26. Peter Ramus, *The Latine Grammar*, tr. anon. (London, 1585), p. 1. This definition is repeated in Ramus, *The Logike*, tr. Roland MacIlmaine (London, 1581), p. 51. Ramus's definition probably originates in the traditional definition of "noun" and the fanciful etymology of *"nomen"* from *"nota"*; see Isidore of Seville, *Etymologiae, PL*, LXXXII, 82; and Servius, *Commentarius*, in *Grammatici Latini*, ed. Keil, IV, 405. In *Grammatical Theory*, p. 63, Padley observes that Scaliger defines *"orationes"* as *"notae rei"* in *De causis linguae Latinae* (1540); Padley links Ramus to seventeenth-century developments, p. 111.

27. Francis Clement, *Petie Schole*, p. 11.

28. Ralph Lever, *The Arte of Reason* (London, 1573), p. 1.

29. *Timber*, in *Ben Jonson*, VIII, 621.

30. John L. Harrison, in "The Convention of 'Heart and Tongue' and

the Meaning of Measure for Measure," SQ, 5 (1954), 1-10, sees the unity of heart and tongue as an indication of moral goodness in *MM*, the division between the two (primarily in Angelo and Lucio) as an indication of evil character.

31. Cf. Trousdale, *Shakespeare and the Rhetoricians*, p. 145: "Although the play is the occasion for instruction, the spectator, by active participation, must discover his own truth, not in it but by means of it."

32. See, for example, R. H. Robins, *Ancient and Medieval Grammatical Theory* (London: G. Bell & Sons, 1951), p. 7; and *Short History*, pp. 17-19; Dinneen, *Introduction*, pp. 74-76, and 93-95; and Padley, *Grammatical Theory*, pp. 12 and 98.

33. See D. P. Walker, *Spiritual and Demonic Magic*, Studies of the Warburg Institute, vol. 22 (London, 1958), esp. pp. 80-81; and Frances A. Yates, *Giordano Bruno and the Hermetic Tradition* (Chicago: Univ. of Chicago Press, 1964), esp. pp. 263-64. On the ostensible Elizabethan belief in this Neoplatonic idea, see Mahood, *Shakespeare's Wordplay*, pp. 170-71; and Calderwood, *Metadrama in Shakespeare's Henriad*, pp. 184-89.

34. Henry Cornelius Agrippa, *Three Books of Occult Philosophy*, tr. J. F. (London, 1651), sig. L5^r. On the reasons in Renaissance Pythagorean philosophy for a real connection between words and things, see S. K. Heninger, Jr., *Touches of Sweet Harmony* (San Marino: Huntington Library, 1974), pp. 247-48.

35. See Joseph Blau, *The Christian Interpretation of the Cabala in the Renaissance* (New York: Columbia Univ. Press, 1944), pp. 22, 43-44, and 80-81.

36. John Dee, *A True and Faithful Relation*, ed. M. Causabon (London, 1659), p. 92. Dee's angelic language, in keeping with his mathematical mysticism, includes the divine Numbers—the forms and proportions of the universe—as well as the words for the divine Ideas or substances. On Dee's "Pythagorean Platonism" see Peter French, *John Dee* (London: Routledge & Kegan Paul, 1972), pp. 103-11.

37. Walker, *Spiritual and Demonic Magic*, pp. 153-55. See also Keith Thomas, *Religion and the Decline of Magic* (New York: Charles Scribner's Sons, 1971), esp. pp. 51-68, 178-82, 224-30, 267-68, and 646. Thomas finds many uneducated Englishmen to be believers in magic, a few educated ones to be attracted to the continental Neoplatonic study of magic, and by far the greatest number of educated Elizabethans to be skeptical of magic; he attributes part of the decline of magic to the influence of Protestantism.

38. Desiderius Erasmus, *De Recta . . . pronunciatione* (Basel, 1558), p. 123.

39. For the position that there is an arbitrary relation between words and things, see Hippocrates, "The Art," ii.14–18 (the earliest statement on the relation of words to things if the editor's assignation of this treatise to a sophist is correct; he suggests Hippias); Hermogenes' speeches in Plato, *Cratylus*, 384c-d; Aristotle, *On Interpretation*, 16a, 17a; Sextus Empiricus, *Against the Professors*, I.iv.37–38; Augustine, *On Christian Doctrine*, pp. 34–36; and Dante, *De Vulgari Eloquentia*, in *Latin Works*, pp. 11 and 28–29.

40. Abraham Fraunce, *The Lawier's Logike* (London, 1588), sig. Ciiii^v.

41. Bacon, *Advancement*, sig. Pp3^v.

42. Montaigne, "Of Glory," *Essayes*, p. 359.

43. Erasmus, *De . . . pronunciatione*, p. 123.

44. For the position that words characterize or imitate things, see Socrates' speeches in the first half of Plato's *Cratylus*, 389a–426a; Varro, *On the Latin Language*, VI.ii.3 and X.iii.51–53; Isidore, *Etymologiae*, *PL*, LXXXII, 105–6; John of Salisbury, *The Metalogicon*, tr. Daniel D. McGarry (Berkeley: Univ. of California Press, 1955), p. 39; and Aquinas, *Summa Theologiae*, I, 49. In *Grammatical Theory*, pp. 63–65, Padley discusses Scaliger's theory (from *De causis linguae Latinae*, 1540), that words imitate things.

45. Richard Carew, "An Epistle Concerning the Excellencies of the English Tongue," (1595–6?), published with *The Survey of Cornwall* (London, 1723), pp. 5–6. Cf. William Camden, *Remaines Concerning Britaine* (London, 1605), p. 26: "Heereby may be seene the originall of some english words, and the *Etymology* or reason whence many other are derived, beside them alreadie specified may as well be found in our tongue, as in the learned tongues, although hardly; for that heerein as in other tongues, the truth lieth hidden and is not easilie found, as both *Varro* and *Isidor* do acknowledge."

46. Bacon, *Advancement*, sigs. Pp4^{r-v}.

47. Fraunce, *Lawier's Logike*, sigs. Ciiii^v and Oiiii^r.

48. Mulcaster, *Elementarie*, pp. 168–69. Cf. Isidore, *Etymologiae*, *PL*, LXXXII, 105: *"Nam cum videris unde ortum est nomen, citius vim ejus intelligis. Omnis enim rei inspectio, etymologia cognita, planior est."* [For when you have seen from what source a name comes, you understand its meaning more quickly. For the investigation of all things is more intelligible once the etymology is well known.]

49. See Isidore, *Etymologiae*, *PL*, LXXXII, 417: " '*Mulier*' vero, a '*mollitie*,' tanquam '*mollier*,' detracta littera, vel mutata, appellata est '*mulier*.' " [*Mulier* (woman) indeed was derived from *mollitie* (tenderness); so that *mollier*, with the deletion or change of letters, has become *mulier*.]

50. George Puttenham, *The Arte of English Poesie* (London, 1589), p. 5; Puttenham further explains the origin of speech in the physical nature and customs of men, pp. 119-20.

51. Among Shakespeareans who emphasize the biblical history of language are Mahood, *Shakespeare's Wordplay*, pp. 169-71; de Grazia, "Shakespeare's View of Language," pp. 376-79; Calderwood, *Metadrama in Shakespeare's Henriad*, pp. 186-92; and Joseph A. Porter, *The Drama of Speech Acts* (Berkeley: Univ. of California Press, 1979), pp. 42-47, 123-25, and 152-53. For the biblical history of language, see Gen. 2:19-20, Adam naming the creatures; Gen. 11:1-9, the Tower of Babel; and Acts 2:1-18, the gift of tongues at Pentecost. For medieval interpretations, see Isidore, *Etymologiae, PL,* LXXXII, 325, on Babel; and Dante, *De Vulgari Eloquentia,* in *Latin Works,* pp. 16-20, on God's gift of speech and the corruption at Babel.

52. On the human larynx, see John Banister, *The Historie of Man* (London, 1578), fols. 17^r and 49^v-50^v; on the adaptation of the breathing organs in man to speech, see Stephen Batman's English version of Bartholomaeus Anglicus's *De Proprietatibus Rerum, Batman vppon Bartholome* (London, 1582), fol. 47^r.

53. Montaigne, "Apologie," *Essayes,* p. 264.

54. See Galen, *"De Voce et Anhelitu," C. L. Galeni Pergameni [Opera] Omnia* (Basel, 1562), V, pt. 2, fols. 60^v-62^r; and Lucretius, *De Rerum Natura,* V.1028-90.

55. Lever, *Arte of Reason,* pp. vi^v-vii^r; see also p. 116, Lever's example of a syllogism: "Nothing lerned by imitation is natural; euery language is lerned by imitation; therefore, no language is naturall."

56. *Timber,* in *Ben Jonson,* VIII, 622. Cf. George H. McKnight, *The Evolution of the English Language* (1928; rpt., New York: Dover Publications, 1968), p. 22, who translates from the 1572 edition of Ramus's Latin grammar: " 'According to the judgment of Plato, Aristotle, Varro, Cicero . . . the people is sovereign lord in language—one owes recognition to no other master.' " Quintilian, the probable source for both Lever and Jonson, states that language depends on four bases—*reason* in the orderly pattern of the paradigms, *antiquity* or past language, *authority* in recorded models, and current *usage*—all finally manifestations of custom *(consuetudo),* which is "the agreed practice of educated men," not simply the consent of the majority, in *Institutio Oratoria,* I.vi.1-45. Other classical sources are Varro, in *On the Latin Language,* IX.i.3, who holds that all language depends upon custom, or the acceptance of a word by the majority of speakers; and Horace, in *Ars Poetica,* ll. 70-72, who explains that usage is the authority, the law, and the rule of speaking.

57. Henry Cornelius Agrippa, *Of the Vanitie . . . of Artes and Sciences,*

tr. James Sanford (London, 1569), fols. 7^r-11^r; and Fraunce, *Lawier's Logike*, sig. ¶¶ 2^r. The passage that Fraunce quotes from Horace, *Ars Poetica*, ll. 58-62, is also quoted by Castiglione, *The Courtier*, sig. F3^v; and Puttenham, *Arte of English Poesie*, p. 123.

58. John Brinsley, *Ludus Literarius* (London, 1612), p. 247.

59. Agrippa, *Vanitie*, fols. 6^r-7^r.

60. On the corruption of Hebrew and the birth of the vernaculars, see Dante, *De Vulgari Eloquentia*, in *Latin Works*, pp. 19-29; on the corruption of Latin and the rise of the vernaculars, see Vives, *On Education*, pp. 93-95; on the rise and fall of Greek and Latin, see Roger Ascham, *The Scholemaster* (London, 1570), sigs. Oii^{r-v} and Rii^v. C. S. Lewis, in *English Literature in the Sixteenth Century* (Oxford: Oxford Univ. Press, 1954), p. 21, castigates the humanists, to whom "we owe the curious conception of the 'classical' period in a language, the correct or normative period before which all was immature or archaic and after which all was decadent"; because of this idea, Lewis maintains, the humanists, trying to return Latin to its former purity, killed it. Lewis's historic analysis may be justified, but later humanists also used the idea of the rise and fall of language to accept linguistic change and to support the vernaculars as worthy media for science and literature.

61. Castiglione, *The Courtier*, sigs. El^v-F7^v.

62. Camden, *Remaines*, p. 20; see p. 15, on the two kinds of English speech, and p. 18, on the peak of English-Saxon. On the language of Chaucer, Lydgate, and Gower as a peak of excellence to Elizabethans, see R. F. Jones, *Triumph*, pp. 116-19. Sir Philip Sidney, in *The Defense of Poesy*, ed. Lewis Soens (Lincoln: Univ. of Nebraska Press, 1970), p. 5, is typical: "so in the Italian language, the first that made it aspire to be a treasure-house of science were the poets Dante, Boccaccio, and Petrarch; so in our English were Gower and Chaucer, after whom, encouraged and delighted with their excellent fore-going, others have followed to beautify our mother tongue, as well in the same kind as in other arts."

63. Mulcaster, *Elementarie*, p. 74 and pp. 157-59. Cf. Seneca, *Epistulae Morales*, CXIV.

64. *Timber*, in *Ben Jonson*, VIII, 625. See Doran's discussion of speech as *"mentis character,"* in *Endeavors*, p. 44.

65. "Epistle," to *The Shepheardes Calendar* (1579), in *Spenser: Poetical Works*, ed. J. C. Smith and E. de Selincourt (London: Oxford Univ. Press, 1912), p. 417.

66. Castiglione, *The Courtier*, sigs. El^v-F7^v. Sir Frederick borrows from Quintilian, *Institutio Oratoria*, I.vi.1-2 and 39-42, the ideas that language must be based on *antiquity* or past language, and *authority* in re-

corded models; the Count borrows from Quintilian, I.vi.45, the idea that language is based on current *usage*, the agreed practice of educated men.

67. R. F. Jones, *Triumph*, pp. 68–141 and 168–213.

68. E. K. also sides with the antiquarians in his praise of Spenser's diction in *The Shepheardes Calendar*, in *Spenser: Poetical Works*, p. 417.

69. Camden, *Remaines*, p. 20. Mulcaster also favors borrowing and inventing words, in *Elementarie*, p. 154.

70. *Timber*, in *Ben Jonson*, VIII, 622; this passage is a paraphrase of Quintilian, *Institutio Oratoria*, I.vi.39–41 and 44–45.

71. For the law on dress according to social hierarchy, see Elizabeth I, *A declaration . . . against the excesse of Apparell* (London, 13 Feb. 1588), STC 8168. See also S. Schoenbaum's discussion of Shakespeare's being granted livery in the King's color for the coronation procession in 1604, in *William Shakespeare: A Compact Documentary Life* (New York: Oxford Univ. Press, 1977), pp. 251–52.

72. Cf. Florio's Montaigne, "Vpon some verses of Virgil," in *Essayes*, p. 524: the "employment of good wittes, endeareth and giveth grace vnto a tongue: Notsomuch innovating as filling the same with more forcible and diuers services. . . . They bring no wordes vnto it, but enritch their owne, waigh-downe and cram-in their signification and custome; teaching it vnwonted motions; but wisely and ingeniouslie."

73. Du Bartas, *Deuine Weekes*, pp. 419–33. For further elaboration, see Simon Goulart, *A Learned Summarie*, tr. Thomas Lodge (London, 1621), esp. sigs. Sss2^v-Ttt2^v. Cf. Alexander Top, in *The Olive Leaf* (London, 1603), sigs. C2^r-C3^r, who sees Adam as the inventor of words and the confusion at Babel only what would have happened naturally with more time; and Bacon, *Advancement*, sig. Pp4^r, who says that the science of grammar aims to relieve the effects of the curse at Babel.

74. Thomas, *Religion and the Decline of Magic*, pp. 249–50. See also p. 232: "Jack Cade was accused of raising the Devil and using magical books to promote his rebellion in 1450." Thomas's conclusions are the opposite of Mahood's in *Shakespeare's Wordplay*, pp. 169–71; she suggests that educated Elizabethans were inclined to belief in the magical power of words, while the uneducated were skeptical of it.

75. Henry Chettle, *Kind-Heart's Dream*, ed. E. F. Rimbault, Percy Society Early English Poetry, Ballads, and Popular Literature, V (London, 1841), 29–30.

76. James I, *Daemonologie* (Edinburgh, 1597), sig. C2^v.

77. Dee, *True Relation*, p. 92. Many critics have inferred that Shakespeare must have trusted in the same innate force in words postulated by Renaissance magicians. See, for example, Arnold Stein, "*Macbeth* and

Word-Magic," *SR*, 59 (1951), 271–84; Mahood, *Shakespeare's Wordplay*, pp. 170–71; D. J. Gordon, "Name and Fame: Shakespeare's Coriolanus," in *Papers, Mainly Shakespearian*, ed. George Duthie (Edinburgh: Oliver & Boyd, 1964), pp. 52–53; Yates, *Giordano Bruno*, pp. 356–57; Calderwood, *Metadrama in Shakespeare's Henriad*, pp. 201–4.

78. Sir Walter Raleigh, *The History of the World* (London, 1614), p. 206. Cf. Florio's Montaigne, "Of Praiers and Orisons," in *Essayes*, p. 177: "Verely, it seemeth, that we make no other vse of our praiers, then of a companie of gibrish phrases: And as those who employ holy and sacred words about witchcraft and magicall effects; and that we imagine their effect dependeth of the contexture, or sound, or succession of words."

79. Camden, *Remaines*, pp. 27–28. Camden begins and ends this chapter on "The Languages" by mocking the scholars and pedants and by praising simple explanations and plain English (pp. 12–28).

80. Wilson, *Arte of Rhetorique*, sig. Aii[v].

81. The question of magic in *Macbeth* is complicated by the probable hand of someone other than Shakespeare in Hecate's speeches (3.5; 4.1.39–43, 125–32); see Evans's note in *The Riverside Shakespeare*, p. 1340. The three sisters, however, perform a charm in an uncontested scene, 1.3.32–34; thus Hecate's claims are of a piece with the powers imagined for the witches, even if Shakespeare did not author them.

82. Mulcaster, *Elementarie*, p. 257. Cf. Quintilian, *Institutio Oratoria*, VIII. Pr. 26: "But nowadays our rhetoricians regard Cicero as lacking both polish and learning; we are far superior, for we . . . seek not for the true ornaments of speech, but for meretricious finery, as though there were any real virtue in words save in their power to represent facts." For further background on the power of eloquent speech, its influence on poetic, and its results in the Elizabethan drama, see Doran, *Endeavors*, pp. 25–52.

83. Richard Sherry, *A Treatise of Schemes and Tropes* (London, 1550), sig. Bii[v].

84. Florio's Montaigne, "Vpon some verses of Virgil," *Essayes*, p. 524. The passage continues, "*Plutarch* sayeth, that he discerned the Latine tongue by things. Here likewise the sence enlightneth and produceth the words. . . . They signifie more then they vtter."

85. *Timber*, in *Ben Jonson*, VIII, 621. Jonson's passage must have a classical source with which I am unfamiliar, for both John of Salisbury, in *The Metalogicon*, p. 81, and Castiglione, in *The Courtier*, sig. E7[v], use the same analogy of body and soul to word and sense.

86. Peacham, *Garden* (1593), sig. ABiii[r].

87. Puttenham, *Arte of English Poesie*, pp. 5–6. Cf. Seneca, *Epistulae Morales*, CVIII.

88. See Madeleine Doran, " 'Yet Am I Inland Bred,' " *SQ*, 15 (1964), 107–11.

89. Sidney, *Defense*, pp. 7–8.

CHAPTER 2

"The Modesty of Nature":
Passion Psychology
and the Body's Language

In the preceding chapter we concentrated on the basic issues of the sixteenth-century study of language: the nature and history of language, its causes and powers, and the connection between words and things. These topics not only allowed us to gain a sense of the variety and controversy of the Renaissance discussion of language, but also to explore Shakespeare's eclectic use of the ideas: rather than taking a stand in the controversies, and so developing ideas about language thematically, Shakespeare employs them in shaping the worlds of his plays, in giving characters particularity, and in enhancing the debate form of his plots. In this chapter we shall concentrate on some of the less controversial Elizabethan assumptions about language: its double purpose of purging passion and communicating reason, the relation between speech and death, the physical language of voice, expression, and gesture, and the actors' additions to the playwright's words. While these topics all touch on passion psychology and the physiology of speech, they have been gathered together primarily because they illustrate the effects of the ideas on Shakespeare's art. Although the assumptions about language do not change throughout Shakespeare's career, the dramatic effects he achieves with them do.

"The modesty of nature" is Hamlet's description of the boundary the good actor does not cross if he wants to adhere to "the purpose of playing" (*Ham.* 3.2.19-20). The successful actor remains within the province of natural, appropriate voice and movement. It is helpful to approach Shakespeare's growth as an artist as if it were his gradual redefinition of this kind of boundary. His province is always what is natural and appropriate: he employs the ideas we shall discuss in this chapter to motivate speeches, to justify their form and content, to individualize characters, and to direct his actors' contributions to characterization. Nevertheless, his concept of what is natural and appropriate changes. As his mastery of styles of languages develops, as his actors' skills expand, Shakespeare finds in his culture's assumptions about speech increasingly fruitful means to dramatize the richness of human experience.

Let us begin, then, with a fundamental question: why do men speak? While Shakespeare's characters give similar answers throughout the plays—to relieve passions and to express reason—Shakespeare's dramatic practice changes as he discovers more convincing and more complex ways to embody these purposes in their speech.

The Purposes of Speech

In *Romeo and Juliet* Shakespeare casts the scene where Romeo learns of his banishment as an argument between Romeo, speaking out of passion, and the Friar, speaking out of reason. While Romeo reacts with "the breath of heart-sick groans" (3.3.72) and exclamations against his fate, the Friar proposes "Adversity's sweet milk, philosophy" (l. 55) and control over passion. The Friar seems to be a didactic chorus asking us to discount Romeo's emotional display as self-indulgence; but the style of the scene works against the Friar's ideas because Romeo's language interests us more than the Friar's. The young lover's hyperboles on his loss, his extravagant imagery (the "carrion flies," for example, that may kiss Juliet when he may not), his hysterical wordplay on "banish" and "fly"—all make us more attentive to his emotions than to the Friar's philosophy. The older man's regular verse, his sententious and balanced clauses, his severe list of arguments that Romeo has betrayed his shape, his love, and his wit by his passion—these reflect his philosophical temperament, but do not engage our sympathies and do not move us to any mature evaluation of Romeo's passion. The characters acquire some individuality—Romeo by his emotions and the Friar by his ideas—but they do not seem whole; and their dialogue is not truly communication since neither recognizes the validity of the other's response.

The weakness of this scene from *Romeo and Juliet* results partly, I think, from Shakespeare's understanding of why men speak. In the

1593 edition of his *Garden of Eloquence,* Henry Peacham explained
that speech was given to man for a double purpose: "to powre forth
the inward passions of his heart," and "to shew foorth . . . the priuie
thoughts . . . of his mind."[1] A decade earlier, Richard Mulcaster
had designed his program of education to take advantage of these
two purposes: since speech is "an instrument . . . to utter that,
which the minde conceiueth," one studies the classical tongues for
knowledge, and the arts of language for reasoned, eloquent expression; since speech is also an exercise that "practiseth and stirreth the
inward partes," purging the body of excess humours, one also de-
claims and reads aloud to better his health.[2] These contemporaries
of Shakespeare are bringing together ideas from very different
earlier sources: medical theory and humanist rhetoric and education.
In a similar way, Shakespeare brings together the two traditions, their
conceptions of the purpose of speech and their vocabularies for explaining it, in those scenes throughout his plays where passionate and
reasonable speakers confront each other. In the early plays, the characters generally speak for one or the other purpose, and so seem either
melodramatic or didactic. Only gradually does Shakespeare achieve
livelier characters, who show both sides of themselves and speak for
all their purposes at once.

Generally not mentioned by rhetoricians, Peacham's first purpose, relieving the passions, is an idea borrowed from the passion
psychology of Renaissance medicine. "Vociferation, whiche is
syngynge, redynge, or crienge," writes Sir Thomas Elyot in *The
Castel of Helth,* has "the propertie, that it purgeth naturall heate,
and maketh it also subtyll and stable"; furthermore, "By high crieng
& loude redinge, are expelled superfluous humors."[3] Not the
modern idea that speech is an emotional release, that talking about
a problem helps to solve it, this is a more ancient conception of
speech as a necessary part of a physiological process. According to
many Tudor physicians (and their classical precursors, from
Hippocrates to Celsus), voice relieves the heart of the excess heat
and wasted humours that result from disease and overwrought
emotions.[4]

This purgative effect of speech became an important element of
popular psychology during the sixteenth century. Mulcaster incor-
porates *"vociferatio"* in his educational program because, he main-

tains, such exercise "maketh the blood suttle and fine, purgeth all the veines, openeth all the arteries, [and] suffereth not superfluous humours to thicken"; the mad, the melancholy, and the phlegmatic especially "receiue comfort from speeche, which makes roome for health, where reume kept residence."[5] Tudor poets, moreover, adopted this medical notion as a justification for writing lyrics. "Where grefe tormentes the man that suffreth secret smart," writes the Earl of Surrey, "To breke it forth vnto som frend it easeth well the hart."[6] Surrey's phrasing is not very technical, but that of other poets is more so. Spenser, one of Mulcaster's students who presumably used speech exercises, argues in a sonnet that he must speak his love: for "if I silent be, my hart will breake, / or choked be with ouerflowing gall."[7] Repeatedly in English lyrics from Wyatt on, the poets maintain that their hearts are literally too full to hold in their passions; especially in the love complaints, speech is seen as a means of easing the heart of a lover whose lady refuses him any other sort of "ease."[8]

From popular psychology and lyric poetry, a motivation for passionate speeches came ready-made to Elizabethan dramatists.[9] A man speaks his passions because he cannot do otherwise: his full heart must overflow in words if his heart is not to swell and break. When Titus rages at his sorrows, having sent the Emperor his hand as ransom for his sons, his brother Marcus speaks against such excess: "do not break into these deep extremes. / . . . let reason govern thy lament" (*Tit.* 3.1.215–18). Further pouring out his misery in descriptions of sighs like winds and tears like seas, the earth deluged by the tempest of his passion, Titus ends with a physiological justification. If floods are necessary to the earth, as part of the natural order, then passionate speeches are necessary to men:

> For why my bowels cannot hide her woes,
> But like a drunkard I must vomit them.
> Then give me leave, for losers will have leave
> To ease their stomachs with their bitter tongues.
>
> (3.1.230–33)

The metaphor is repugnant; his speech is retching, a throwing up of his passions from within — but natural. In Shakespeare's early histories and tragedies, a motive for the earth-shaking, heaven-reaching hyperboles is thus found in the relation of speech to pertur-bation: the purgative quality of speech is a way of making "natural" the ranting speeches of grief and revenge. Most of Shakespeare's ear-ly choleric characters—Richard, Duke of York; Richard, Duke of Gloucester (in the *Henry VI* plays as choleric as his father); Suffolk; and even the later Hotspur—support their right to long speeches and cosmic comparisons by the fact that hot hearts require the relief of passionate words.[10] In these early plays, moreover, the objections of the reasonable speaker serve mainly as an opportunity to justify the passionate response, and so to display the inner, emotional life of the character. Indeed, in the scene from *Titus Andronicus,* Mar-cus gives up his defense of reason when the heads of his nephews are brought in: "Ah, now no more will I control thy griefs. / . . . Now is a time to storm" (ll. 259–63).

This way of motivating speeches in turn influences characteriza-tion. In *Richard III,* when the women of both factions—the Lan-castrian Queen Margaret and the Yorkist Queen Elizabeth and Duchess of York—join to lament their losses, the Duchess of York asks a question we might ask of these wordy women: "Why should calamity be full of words?" (4.4.126). Queen Elizabeth answers:

> Windy attorneys to their client's woes,
> Aery succeeders to intestate joys,
> Poor breathing orators of miseries,
> Let them have scope! though what they will impart
> Help nothing else, yet do they ease the heart.
>
> (4.4.127–31)

Words only nominally represent woes, they follow after joy without a clear title to it, and they lack the full power to voice misery. Although words do not fully express passion or remedy its cause, they still ease the heart of its burdensome humours. This psychology of language thus encourages melodramatic characterization: the passion that cannot be signified may yet be represented by many words and extravagant images, as the character floods the stage with the outpouring of her heart; these characters, as aware as we are that they are speaking purely out of passion, appear grand but self-indulgent. We may suppose that Shakespeare realized the weakness of this way of justifying emotional expression because he makes fun of it in *The Taming of the Shrew.* Claiming, "I am no child, no babe," Kate asserts,

> My tongue will tell the anger of my heart,
> Or else my heart concealing it will break,
> And rather than it shall, I will be free,
> Even to the uttermost, as I please, in words.
>
> (4.3.74–80)

Despite the demur, this is clearly childish; hot-hearted Kate, who justifies her wordy complaints in the manner of a tragic victim, is facing not rape, murder, and the fall of kingdoms, but Petruchio's rejection of her new clothes. The characters of the histories and tragedies, of course, have better warrant for their claims, but it is nevertheless the extravagance of the motive that allows Shakespeare a comic use of it here: characters who tell us they cannot control their passions lose a large portion of their dignity.

"As houses without doores are vnprofitable; so are men that haue no rule of their speech"[11] — so Francis Meres in his commonplace book. Most humanist rhetoricians and educators found a purpose in speech very different from the relief of passions; they saw speech almost entirely as an instrument of reason. Thomas Wilson, for instance, explains that "The tongue is ordeined to expresse the mynde, that one mighte vnderstande anothers meanyng."[12] In his first edition of *The Garden of Eloquence,* Peacham does not even mention the passions; man is given speech "to the end that this soueraign rule of reason, might spread abroade her bewtifull branches, & that wisdome might bring forth most plentifully her sweete and pleasaunt fruites."[13] Language is what we see of reason, Peacham observes, the tangible green leaf at the end of the hidden process of growth. Thus the purpose of speech in men, as described in Sylvester's Du Bartas, is higher than that in animals: men speak words that make sense, while the sounds of animals "are not words, but bare expressions / Of violent fits of certaine passions."[14]

Since its purpose is expressing reason, these humanists argue, language naturally civilizes men and binds them together in society. "For the exercise of the social instinct," Vives proclaims, "speech has been given to men, how otherwise could society exist, since our minds are hidden away in so dense a body? How completely dead and torpid would the mind be if it only found expression in the look of the eyes?"[15] Language is the only means men have to come out of the dark corners of their own minds and into the colorful bustle of intercourse with others. "Our intelligence being onely conducted by the way of the Worde," Montaigne warns, "Who so falsifieth the same, betraieth publike society. It is the onely instrument, by meanes wherof our wils and thoughts are communicated: it is the interpretour of our souls: If that faile vs we hold our selves no more, we enterknow one another no longer."[16] If we do not honestly speak our thoughts and freely share our knowledge, we destroy society. Equally important, we betray ourselves, because it is only through social intercourse that our minds come alive and discover for us our own humanity. Sir Thomas Elyot advises even in his medical treatise that this self-knowledge is as important as medical aid: cures of affections "not only require the helpe of phisyke corporall, but also the counsell of a man wyse and well lerned in morall philosophye."[17] Words may purge the unhealthy effects of passion, but wise counsel and reason in control are more truly medicinal.

Shakespeare's characters also claim to speak for these rational and social motives. For these purposes, Miranda reminds Caliban, she taught him language:

> When thou didst not, savage,
> Know thine own meaning, but wouldst gabble like
> A thing most brutish, I endow'd thy purposes
> With words that made them known.
>
> (*Tmp.* 1.2.355-58)

Many of the long speeches that develop character, but do not advance the story, are motivated by a simple "methinks" or "I think": the "molehill" speech of King Henry VI, Launce's on his dog Crab, the dialogue of Jessica and Lorenzo on all the lovers who precede them, even Cleopatra's dying speech.[18] The Elizabethan conviction that men speak because they think renders the contemplative soliloquy and the set speech less artificial conventions than would otherwise be the case: we hear the characters shaping their identities in words, by the oddities of knowledge and rumination that make human beings unique. The Elizabethan emphasis on the priority of reason over passion in speech may even have affected the general pattern of character development. Modern playwrights often moti-

vate their characters' speeches in a pattern we are taught by our culture and psychology to expect: characters at first speak mechanically,
from social reflex, and only gradually from personal reasons —
and so comes the obligatory, often alcoholic, stripping away of social
niceties to reveal the "true" self. Elizabethan conceptions of the purpose of speech encouraged a different pattern: from emotional to
more revealing rational language. Hieronimo's private speeches progress from laments for his son to a rational contemplation of the
morality of revenge; Hamlet's soliloquies begin with the outpouring
of his grief and anger and become increasingly objective assessments
of his situation, until his final soliloquy is a contemplation of honor
and a celebration of reason. In Shakespeare's early plays, the change
from passionate to thoughtful speeches seems anticlimactic to modern audiences. How can Kate give up her emotional liveliness to
speak that sober sermon on wifely duties? How can we appreciate
Richmond's commonplace truths, however "right," after listening to
the families of York and Lancaster open the dark recesses of their
ambitious and grieving hearts to us? In the early plays Shakespeare
develops melodramatic characters who are salvaged at the last by
didacticism.

Shakespeare, however, gradually modified this pattern of motivating speeches and individualizing characters. In the scenes from
Titus Andronicus and *Romeo and Juliet* that we have already examined, we may see what Shakespeare must have discovered: the speaker motivated only by passion forfeits our admiration but upstages
the speaker motivated by reason; the rational speaker loses much of
our interest and sympathy, even though he retains his dignity. A
scene in *Much Ado about Nothing*, where Leonato grieves for his
slandered daughter and Antonio argues for the "wisdom" of restraint (5.1.2-3), reveals an advance in Shakespeare's dramatic
strategy for pitting a passionate against a reasonable speaker. Unlike
Titus or Romeo, Leonato justifies his passionate speeches by a general comment on human weakness: men "Can counsel and speak
comfort to that grief / Which they themselves not feel" (ll. 21-22);
but no man has "virtue nor sufficiency / To be so moral when he
shall endure / The like himself" (ll. 29-31). Leonato makes a strong
argument for seeing men as what they are, rather than what they
should be, and by this means retains our admiration, despite his loss
of control: "My griefs cry louder than advertisement" (l. 32). Anto-

nio, less self-righteous than the Friar or Marcus, sadly acknowledges this truth of human nature: "Therein do men from children nothing differ" (l. 33). Because he modifies his position, accepting that human weakness must be reckoned with in any expectation of virtue, Antonio does not lose our interest and sympathy. Leonato vows he "will be flesh and blood" (l. 34), and we feel his grief with him. But Antonio shows the advantage of a reasonable response: "Yet bend not all the harm upon yourself; / Make those that do offend you suffer too" (ll. 39-40). "There thou speak'st reason" (l. 41), agrees Leonato, and the final compromise of the two brothers is reasonable in a different way from the Friar's philosophy: rational control is here taken to be not the denial of passion in speech, but rather turning it to an appropriate purpose. Thus when Claudio and Don Pedro enter, Leonato eases his full heart and forces them to face the effect of their slander at the same time. Shakespeare has recognized the complexities of the moral problem of controlling speech, and his characterization has benefited from it.

In the later plays, Shakespeare handles passionate and reasonable motivation in speech to even greater advantage. When Lear confronts Regan, he complains bitterly about Goneril:

> O Regan, she hath tied
> Sharp-tooth'd unkindness, like a vulture, here.
> I can scarce speak to thee; thou 'lt not believe
> With how deprav'd a quality — O Regan!
>
> (*Lr.* 2.4.134-37)

Lear, of course, is not restrained in speech, but Shakespeare handles the expression of emotion in Lear's speeches with more artistic restraint. Pointing to his swelling heart (at "here"), Lear implies the effect of his passion. His emotion realistically resists articulation, and the broken sentence suggests that his rising passion almost chokes off words. His grief finally erupts in a simple exclamation — "O Regan!"[19] Rather than depicting passion in a character's hyperbolic description of it, Shakespeare has found a way to embody it in style. Shakespeare gains further interest, moreover, by having the rational speaker clearly in the wrong: "I pray you, sir," counsels Regan, "take patience" (l. 138). When Lear finally pours out his heart in this scene, his grief and anger are warranted. Even then, he retains his dignity by finally controlling his terrible rage, and at utmost cost:

> You think I'll weep:
> No, I'll not weep.
> I have full cause of weeping, but this heart
> Shall break into a hundred thousand flaws
> Or ere I'll weep.
>
> (ll. 282-86)

Characters in the later plays more often control their passions, and must be coaxed into purging their hearts in speech. Malcolm thus stirs Macduff: "Give sorrow words. The grief that does not speak / Whispers the o'er-fraught heart, and bids it break" (*Mac.* 4.3.209-10). Similarly, Camillo urges Perdita's adopted father to release his fear of Polixenes: "Speak ere thou diest" (*WT* 4.4.451). Since they are responding to another's request, these later passionate speakers no longer forfeit our admiration by self-indulgence. Shakespeare has found ways for them to open their hearts to us without appearing ignobly to surrender themselves to their passions.

Even in *Coriolanus,* Shakespeare forces us to acknowledge the dignity as well as the weakness of the soldier who believes that any control of speech is insincerity.[20] The tribunes give us the bleakest picture of the hot-hearted patrician. "Put him to choler straight" (*Cor.* 3.3.25), Brutus says:

> Being once chaf'd, he cannot
> Be rein'd again to temperance; then he speaks
> What's in his heart, and that is there which looks
> With us to break his neck.
>
> (3.3.27-30)

From the tribunes' analysis, we may see that Coriolanus's speech is natural, but uncivil. Thinking himself in control by his refusal to flatter, Coriolanus has actually given up control to his choleric heart, and so to those who would use his hot words against him. Volumnia, in contrast, offers him a compromise similar to that of Leonato and Antonio: "I have a heart as little apt as yours, / But yet a brain that leads my use of anger / To better vantage" (3.2.29-31). Understanding his nature, even admiring his courage in speaking straight out, she yet admonishes him that political circumstances require him to conceal his anger:

> Go, and be rul'd; although I know thou hadst rather
> Follow thine enemy in a fiery gulf
> Than flatter him in a bower.
>
> (3.2.90–92)

Menenius goes even further in admiration for Coriolanus's passionate spontaneity. Although he counsels the soldier to restraint, he yet defends him from others:

> His nature is too noble for the world;
> He would not flatter Neptune for his trident,
> Or Jove for 's power to thunder. His heart's his mouth;
> What his breast forges, that his tongue must vent,
> And, being angry, does forget that ever
> He heard the name of death.
>
> (3.1.254–59)

Menenius's judgment evokes in us the suspicion that we, too, often control our speech from fear, rather than from reason. When the old Roman does urge temperance, he argues political expedience, and his heart is not in it:

> Before he should thus stoop to th' herd, but that
> The violent fit a' th' time craves it as physic
> For the whole state, I would put mine armor on,
> Which I can scarcely bear.
>
> (3.2.32–35)

We share both responses to Coriolanus, admiring and condemning him at once. Coriolanus is tragic in the Aristotelian sense: he has faults that a weaker, lesser man might avoid. He does not fear death, and we do; his passions are too large to be held in, and ours are not that grand. When Aufidius calls him "boy," fears do not crowd in upon him, as they would on us. The great heart simply impels him to speech: "Measureless liar, thou has made my heart / Too great for what contains it. 'Boy'? O slave!" (5.6.102–3). To Coriolanus's passionate words we can have no simple moral response: they are wrong and noble. The more complex the moral problem of controlled speech has become, the more interesting the characters have become: as if in overcoming the dramatic problems of the conflict between reasonable and passionate speakers, Shakespeare has become increasingly aware of the difficulty of the moral problem.

In *The Winter's Tale,* reason and controlled speech are no longer synonymous. Bringing the newborn child to Leontes, Paulina bristles at the lords who fear Leontes' distemper and block her way:

> Not so hot, good sir,
> I come to bring him sleep. 'Tis such as you,
> That creep like shadows by him, and do sigh
> At each his needless heaving, such as you
> Nourish the cause of his awaking. I
> Do come with words as medicinal as true,
> Honest as either, to purge him of that humor
> That presses him from sleep.
>
> (2.3.32–39)

Purgative words are not those that ease Paulina's heart of her grief for Hermione, although her passionate eloquence might be analyzed that way. Nor is the control of the lords beneficial. Instead, purgative words are a metaphor for the wise counsel that Leontes needs to conquer his jealousy. Paulina's speech is medicinal in a higher sense, one recognized by Sir Thomas Elyot when he recommends that cure of affections requires the help of a person "wyse and well lerned in morall philosophye." Leontes, of course, has passionate words erupting from his full heart as well, but passion is no longer set opposite reason as motivation, and so the reasonable speaker is as energetic and interesting as the irrational one. When she reprimands Leontes, Paulina speaks with all her selves, fully integrated, in her words: "I beseech you hear me, who professes / Myself your loyal servant, your physician, / Your most obedient counsellor" (2.3.53–55). The humane speaker here is not one who represses passion, but one who unites the forces of her personality and, as Peacham would say, pours forth her inward passions and her secret thoughts in an honest cause.

Speech and Death

According to Renaissance medical theory, speech is generally beneficial, expelling wasted humours and excess heat and thereby restoring man's body to the balance requisite for health and sanity.

Not so, however, when the speaker is already weakened by wounds or disease. Then speech may drain away the heat and spirits essential to life. The Elizabethan concept of the harmful effect of speech on the dying influences Shakespeare's handling of death scenes throughout the plays. But the way Shakespeare dramatizes this concept changes. In the plays before 1600, the person near death generally gives long speeches of advice marked by the idea that speech wastes vital breath and brings death closer. In the later plays, speech usually brings death with a different style and effect: elliptical and exclamatory, the dying speeches figure forth the breath rushing from the body, rather than state it.

First, we must consider that death was not always defined as we now perceive it. An ancient Greek, whose ideas early editors attributed to Hippocrates, described death in this way: "The boundary of death is passed when the heat of the soul has risen above the navel . . . and all the moisture has been burnt up. . . . [Then] there passes away all at once the breath of the heat (wherefrom the whole was contructed) . . . partly through the flesh and partly through the breathing organs in the head, whence we call it the 'breath of life.' And the soul, leaving the tabernacle of the body, gives up the cold, mortal image to bile, blood, phlegm and flesh."[21] The soul in this passage is the vital center of heat and spirits of the body, and death is the rush of heat and breath from a weakened body. Many centuries later, Elizabethans could still describe death in the same way. In *The Historie of Life and Death,* Bacon warns against the dangers of "sweatings and outward breathings": "the good spirits and moysture being not easily repayred, are exhaled and consumed with the excrementious humours and vapours."[22] And in his sixteenth-century version of Bartholomaeus's encyclopedia, Stephen Batman writes that death often comes by "too great exhalation and wasting of the kinde heate."[23]

To Elizabethans, then, speech may seem to hasten death, for words waste vital heat and spirits. This idea is the basis of Gertrude's vow of silence:

> Be thou assur'd, if words be made of breath,
> And breath of life, I have no life to breathe
> What thou hast said to me.
>
> (*Ham.* 3.4.197-99)

Gertrude's hyperbole describes an actual state for many of Shakespeare's dying characters—for Henry IV, whose breath does not stir
the feather, and for Cordelia, whose breath does not cloud the looking glass. Violent as Elizabethan tragedy is, death is not always
bursting hearts or bleeding wounds. Just as often, death is breath
rushing the heart's fires into nothingness.

Or, since words are breath, death may come by speech, leaching
away vital heat and spirits. In *1 Henry VI*, for example, Mortimer
loses his life not in violence, but in words. Embracing his nephew
Richard, Mortimer desires to "spend [his] latter gasp" (2.5.38) with
him. We may take his expression literally: he is spending his last
breath in his family's interest, warning Richard of Henry's fear of
their family—"if," he adds, "my fading breath permit / And death
approach not ere my tale be done" (2.5.61-62). Mortimer's reference to his fading breath lends urgency to the scene: it is important
that the whole history of family grief be told before his breath is
gone. As he finishes the long tale of Henry IV's usurpation, first dis-
placing Richard II, and then fearing Mortimer, he also declares the
consequence of his speech: "my fainting words do warrant death"
(l. 95). His words have additional power because they are a
sacrifice; he is wasting breath and bringing death closer to ensure
his family's royal inheritance, to tell Richard that he is what his dying uncle was: true heir to the throne.

In this same play, Old Talbot addresses his dying son, again with
reference to life passing in the breath of words:

> O thou whose wounds become hard-favored Death,
> Speak to thy father ere thou yield thy breath!
> Brave Death by speaking, whether he will or no;
> Imagine him a Frenchman, and thy foe.
>
> (4.7.23-26)

"Brave" means "challenge," and so the father is asking his son to put
himself in danger by speaking, by this means showing his fear-
lessness of Death. But the boy has too little life for words, and Talbot must read his bravery in his smile, "as who should say, / Had
Death been French, then Death had died to-day" (ll. 27-28). Lacking even the movement of breath, man is only the cold, mortal image of what he was, and death seems a fact sufficiently tragic in
itself. The passing of life in speech, however, indicates the larger

tragic irony of man's own nature working against his purpose: faced with death, man struggles to hand on love and truth in his dying words, only to have those very words open the gates to his enemy.

Often in Shakespeare's plays what the dying man passes on is wise counsel. In these cases, another commonplace influences Shakespeare: a dying man always speaks the truth for fear of his soul. This idea remains part of the Anglo-American legal code: the dying declaration is the only form of hearsay admissible as evidence.[24] In *King John*, Melune uses this commonplace to urge Salisbury's belief in his dying confession: "Why should I then be false, since it is true / That I must die here and live hence by truth?" (5.4.28-29). A man tells the truth in his dying words because he no longer can gain anything by lies; only by honesty will his soul continue to live.

In a scene in *Richard II*, Shakespeare sets Gaunt's desire to speak the truth to Richard against York's concern for his futile sacrifice of life and breath. "Will the King come," asks Gaunt, "that I may breathe my last / In wholesome counsel to his unstayed youth?" (2.1.1-2). "Vex not yourself," replies York, "nor strive not with your breath, / For all in vain comes counsel to his ear" (ll. 3-4). Idealistic Gaunt hopes that his last words will be listened to as his former advice was not, that even foolish Richard will value the truth of a man's dying speech:

> O but they say the tongues of dying men
> Enforce attention like deep harmony.
> Where words are scarce, they are seldom spent in vain,
> For they breathe truth that breathe their words in pain.
> He that no more must say is listened more
> Than they whom youth and ease have taught to glose.
>
> . . . .
>
> Though Richard my live's counsel would not hear,
> My death's sad tale may yet undeaf his ear.
>
> (ll. 5-16)

Pragmatic York believes that Gaunt will only waste precious breath and hasten his death through words that will be disregarded: "Direct not him whose way himself will choose, / 'Tis breath thou lack'st, and that breath wilt thou lose" (ll. 29-30). York, who has already decided that this king is not worth such sacrifice, brings into relief the unassuming heroism of Gaunt, who values his duty as a counselor above his life.

Gaunt's language, here and elsewhere a pastiche of common-places, reflects his venerability.[25] We can see how the feckless king might be bored by these old maxims, worn thin by handling; but we can also see the values they speak, though not always freshly. North-umberland's sarcastic epitaph—"Words, life, and all, old Lancaster has spent" (2.1.150)—is thus more appropriate than he knows. Flat-tering Richard, Northumberland means that Gaunt had only words to give, and he is glad that the tedious speeches are over. We, how-ever, thinking back to the sacrifice in Gaunt's last speeches, under-stand that he has indeed offered his life in the service of his king. Such a scene evokes a pity that is not balanced by the excitement that we feel when a soldier-hero takes up his sword to die in battle. Gaunt, and others who meet death in speech, move us with a quieter feeling of admiration. Theirs is the humble courage sometimes nec-essary for speaking the simple truth.

Men who acknowledge their approaching death acquire dignity, especially when speaking their knowledge brings death closer still. Our greatest sympathy for Henry IV comes from his dying speeches, in which Shakespeare follows a formula he had used before in the early histories: to Hal, Henry gives long speeches of advice marked by the idea that speech wastes breath and brings his death closer. "O foolish youth," Henry admonishes Hal,

> Thou seek'st the greatness that will overwhelm thee.
> Stay but a little, for my cloud of dignity
> Is held from falling with so weak a wind
> That it will quickly drop; my day is dim.
>
> (2H4 4.5.96–100)

First comes direct anger, then the return of dignity, as Henry dresses even his death in majestic words: the "wind" yet holding his office high is his fading breath, his weakened speech. And how typical of Henry, who by his majestic speech—the regular verse, the periodic sentences, the formal schemes and similes—has held up his reign merely with the force of his will. Now comes this Harry, whose style seems unbearably common to him, to topple the authority he has strained to build: "Pluck down my officers, break my decrees, / For now a time is come to mock at form. / Harry the Fift is crown'd! Up vanity!" (4.5.117–119). Harry's defense, nothing exciting to us who have seen him wear his wild wit, is an expostulation with the crown, regular in verse, long in clause, filled with the figures of sound and syntax that mark his father's style. Henry forgives, as if he is reassured by Hal's majestic language, as well as by his sentiments of care for his father and the office. "Come hither, Harry," the dying King commands, "And hear (I think) the very latest counsel / That ever I shall breathe" (ll. 181–83). The speech that follows is Henry's death, and his making it despite this knowledge reflects his courage:

> God knows, my son,
> By what by-paths and indirect crook'd ways
> I met this crown, and I myself know well
> How troublesome it sate upon my head.
> To thee it shall descend with better quiet.
>
> (ll. 183–87)

Still, Henry's urgency is sad, because his counsel is self-centered: do what I have done, and fulfill my dreams, he tells Hal; trust no one, curb the power of ambitious men, lead them away from rebellion to foreign wars. What is most significant to our understanding of Henry, that he came by the crown through "crook'd ways," is but a digression to him. The advice ends with spent breath:

> More would I, but my lungs are wasted so
> That strength of speech is utterly denied me.
> How I came by the crown, O God forgive,
> And grant it may with thee in true peace live!
>
> (ll. 216–19)

Henry's last words reveal the truth of his ambition, set right his soul with God, and pray for his son's peaceful rule. These are noble words, and worth the sacrifice; but they are less selfless than Gaunt's. Gaunt's race against death is to hand on wisdom. Henry's, like Mortimer's, is to father in his heir the dynasty that his life's work could not accomplish singly.

Gaining power at the expense of realism was a bargain struck as a matter of course by Elizabethan playwrights. Despite their claims, Mortimer, Gaunt, and Henry never seem to reach their last breaths, and leave to die offstage. As late as *Hamlet,* whose hero gives up his last moments of life to offer his "dying voice" to Fortinbras (5.2.356), Shakespeare employs the technique of long, sacrificial speeches. Nevertheless, Shakespeare gradually gave over the dying speeches that challenge their own credibility by their length, at first admitting a new technique side by side with the old. In *1 Henry IV* Hotspur meets death in speech, but with a novel style and effect. Hotspur dies with these words:

> O, I could prophesy,
> But that the earthy and cold hand of death
> Lies on my tongue. No, Percy, thou art dust,
> And food for—
>
> (5.4.83-86)

Having briefly lamented the loss of youth and proud titles, Hotspur steps beyond himself with characteristic flash and quickness to see the larger irony of fortune's change. He who was always full of hot words now can summon too little heat to finish his proverb. What is left, the cold and dry, belongs to dust. Hotspur faces his death with a dignity equal to those who died after long speeches, but his style is new: elliptical, exclamatory, ending with a broken sentence, portraying the sudden rush of breath and spirits from the body, rather than stating it.

This new, more dramatic handling of the idea Shakespeare carries over into the later plays. The realism of Mardian's description of Cleopatra's supposed death makes credible Antony's belief. She spends her last breath, Mardian tells him, as a sacrifice to Antony:

> Then in the midst a tearing groan did break
> The name of Antony; it was divided
> Between her heart and lips. She rend'red life,
> Thy name so buried in her.
>
> (*Ant.* 4.14.31-34)

This is like Cleopatra, to leave in a whirlwind, her passionate words taking the last heat from her heart. Antony's anger drops from him, not to return even when he learns that Cleopatra lives. The awkward staging, when Antony, dying, is lugged into the monument, may tell our eyes that he is too old a soldier for this passionate carrying-on. He himself advises Cleopatra not to lament "The miserable change now at my end" (4.15.51). But his words are not awkward, as he seeks his queen's safety in the midst of his dying "O's," and asserts that he is not a man to be conquered by the boy Caesar:

> but please your thoughts
> In feeding them with those my former fortunes
> Wherein I liv'd, the greatest prince o' th' world,
> The noblest; and do now not basely die,
> Not cowardly put off my helmet to
> My countryman—a Roman by a Roman
> Valiantly vanquish'd. Now my spirit is going,
> I can no more.
>
> (4.15.52-59)

Conjunctions, then even a main clause, drop from his speech as he struggles for breath to put straight his honor and to speak, himself, the story of his valiant death. The "spirit" that departs is both his soul and also the vital heat and breath from his heart; the "can" is elliptical—"I can speak no more." The bold ellipsis indicates the rush to have it all said before death, and the final simplicity, the acceptance of the common enemy who will be, one day, Caesar's conqueror also. Antony's silence marks the departure.

In her dying speech Cleopatra claims triumph not only over Caesar, but over death as well:

> I am fire and air; my other elements
> I give to baser life. So, have you done?
> Come then, and take the last warmth of my lips.
>
> (5.2.289-91)

She identifies herself with the elements of the vital spirit that leave the body in the breath of life, not with those that remain bound to the cold, mortal image. Thus she overcomes death by becoming one with it, as she had overcome the vagaries of human passion by being "infinite variety" (2.2.235). Her words, in fact, describe the death of anyone, but Cleopatra—who can "make defect perfection, / And breathless, pow'r breathe forth" (2.2.231-32)—makes the ordinary an achievement. She does, indeed, leave on Antony's name, fulfilling Mardian's earlier description as a prophecy:

> O Antony!—Nay, I will take thee too:
> What should I stay—
>
> (5.2.312-13)

Like Hotspur, she leaves in the middle of her proverb. Fire and air go with the name of "Antony" and the expression of contempt for a world without him.

To Elizabethans, men and women die by the word as well as by the sword. Loving friends and honor, Shakespearean characters sacrifice life in farewells, counsel, and an accurate account of their lives. Breath goes, but the words do not perish. Others take them up, and under the weight of sad times and the pressure of their hearts, speak what they feel in heart-easing words.

Voice, Expression, and Gesture as Language

"I am no orator, as Brutus is," Antony claims in *Julius Caesar* (3.2.217), and then gives a list of the parts of eloquence that reveals the oratorical training he denies. Antony's list includes not only knowledge, style, and authority of character, but also trained gesture and voice: "For I have neither wit, nor words, nor worth, / Action, not utterance, nor the power of speech / To stir men's blood; I only speak right on" (ll. 21–23). It is the last element, delivery, that concerns us in this section. Significantly, only after delivery does Antony insert the purpose of persuasion, and, leaving out rational conviction, he cites the moving of emotions—"the power of speech / To stir men's blood."

"Tullie saith well," proposes Thomas Wilson in *The Arte of Rhetorique;* "The gesture of man, is the speache of his bodie."[26] Under the last part of rhetoric, pronunciation, Elizabethan and classical rhetoricians treated "voice"—its volume, tone, and rhythm, breathing, and speed of delivery—and "action"—expression, tears, gesture, clothing, even props to point to and expostulate about. Quintilian had observed that "voice adds a force of its own to the matter of which it speaks, while gesture and motion are full of significance,"[27] and Renaissance rhetoricians followed his lead: the body's language adds force to words.

But a particular kind of force. In *The Advancement of Learning,* Bacon reflects on "the Motions of the countenance and parts" of the body that "disclose the present humour and state of the mind & will."[28] Perhaps he, like Wilson, is thinking of Cicero, who states in *De Oratore*, "nature has assigned to every emotion a particular look and tone of voice and bearing of its own; and the whole of a person's frame and every look on his face and utterance of his voice are like the strings of a harp, and sound according as they are struck by each successive emotion."[29] While certain emotions spontaneously evoke certain tones of voice and actions in the speaker, these physical signs naturally move the same emotions in the listener. And so in his commonplace book Francis Meres suggests, "As by the same breath, but sent forth after diuers maners, we heat & coole things, so by the same speech being diuerslie pronounced, wee either stir vp affections, or moue none."[30] Because the body's language comes naturally to everyone, it cuts across the boundaries of race and nation. "Gesture and action," Abraham Fraunce asserts, "is both more excellent and more vniuersall than voice: as belonging not onelie to those that vse the same speach, but generallie to all people, yea to beasts and senceles creatures, as the verie pictures which being dumme, yet speake by gesture and action."[31] He, too, is borrowing from Cicero, who argues that delivery "has most effect on the ignorant and the mob and lastly on barbarians; for . . . clever ideas frequently outfly the understanding of people who are not clever, whereas delivery, which gives the emotion of the mind expression, influences everybody."[32] The orator who persuades effectively must thus feel in himself the emotions he wishes to move in his audience; he must "from his harte fetche his complaintes, in suche sort," concludes Thomas Wilson, "that the matter maie appere . . . more greeuous to the eare, and . . . so heinous, that it requires . . . a spedy reformacion."[33] It is with the body's language, what Montaigne calls "the proper and peculier speech of humane nature," and Du Bartas a "dumbe discourse," that speech achieves this emotional power.[34]

The physical part of language is naturally forceful, it is universal and affective, and it speaks particularly to the vulgar: most of these ideas are heard from the mouth of one or another of Shakespeare's characters, as well as from Elizabethan rhetoricians. In *Love's Labor's Lost* Boyet calls this affective power of speech "the heart's still rhetoric, disclosed with the eyes" (2.1.229). Ulysses hears this language in Cressida's movements—"There's language in her eye, her cheek, her lip, / Nay, her foot speaks; her wanton spirits look out / At every joint and motive of her body" (*Tro.* 4.5.55–57); he concludes that only the animal in woman speaks so clearly from her body. "Action is eloquence," Volumnia instructs Coriolanus, "and the eyes of th' ignorant / More learned than the ears" (*Cor.* 3.2.76–77). "The power of speech / To stir men's blood," Antony calls it, exploiting it while he denies it. Holding out Caesar's will, his eyes red from weeping, coming down from the public chair to point to the rents in Caesar's cloak, throwing it aside to show the wounds, Antony takes over the stage with his delivery. Brutus had remained in the pulpit, and his lines do not explicitly call for gesture. While the citizens miss the point of Brutus's speech, crying to make him "Caesar" when he has offered them "a place in the commonwealth" by Caesar's death (*JC* 3.2.43–52), they are moved to violence by Antony's emotional voice, expression, and gesture. The text thus implies an even more dramatic contrast between the two orators than the differing styles of language suggest: while Brutus's clever ideas outfly the understanding of the mob, Antony's impassioned delivery stirs their blood.

The mob in this scene respond to Antony's delivery, even when it speaks the opposite of his words: after hearing his praise of Caesar's virtues, and his increasingly bitter nomination of the conspirators as "honorable men," the citizens take the meaning of Antony's voice against the significance of his words: "They were traitors; honorable men!" (l. 153). Henry Peacham defines irony, as do all classical and Renaissance rhetoricians, with respect to delivery: "when a sentence is vnderstood by the contrary, or thus, when our meaning is contrary to our saying, not so well perceaued by the wordes, as eyther by the pronunciation, by the behauyour of the person, or by the nature of the thing."[35] Adding the body's language to words, Shakespeare may even make his characters speak against themselves. In the *Henry VI* plays, Richard of Gloucester had been straightforwardly choleric, eliciting from us a simple response to his anger. In *Richard III* he plays this melodramatic Richard in several public scenes, but Shakespeare has given him, as well, a new ironic voice in private—in asides, in soliloquies, and in speeches to his confidant, Buckingham. With this voice Richard sets himself against himself, making us uncomfortable with his words: crowing that he must be handsome since Anne has succumbed to him, when he shows his knowledge that he is not in his voice (1.2.252–63); urging Buckingham to tell the citizens only indirectly that Edward was a bastard, "Because . . . you know my mother lives" (3.5.94), when his tone shows that he cares nothing for his mother's dishonor. We cannot give a simple response to this Richard, who mocks his own despair at never being a man equal to others, and who lies even to himself in his ironic voice. Richard's frightened soliloquy at the end of the play grows naturally from the personality shaped by delivery and words at odds:

> Then fly. What, from myself? Great reason why—
> Lest I revenge. What, myself upon myself?
> Alack, I love myself. Wherefore? For any good
> That I myself have done unto myself?
> O no! Alas, I rather hate myself.
>
> (5.3.185–89)

We have seen these many selves of Richard earlier in his ironies, setting voice against significance, part of his personality against another. Perhaps this is why the soliloquy finally seems flat: clearly stating the division makes it less interesting, lacking in the tenseness and complexity of the earlier ironic voice.

Only in prison does Richard II acknowledge that he sets "the word itself / Against the word" (*R2* 5.5.13–14), but he does so often between his fall and his death. His speeches are at times what we would call irony, the intention opposite from what is said; thus he greets Bolingbroke, "Fair cousin, you debase your princely knee / To make the base earth proud with kissing it" (3.3.190–91). At other times his words speak acceptance of his fall, but his voice speaks anger turned inward to self-pity:

>   I hardly yet have learn'd
> To insinuate, flatter, bow, and bend my knee.
> Give sorrow leave a while to tutor me
> To this submission. Yet I well remember
> The favors of these men. Were they not mine?
>
> (4.1.164–68)

Had Shakespeare written this play earlier, Richard might have been like Marlowe's Bajazeth, more directly asserting his royalty, cursing and beating his head against the cage. Instead, Richard's voice builds his own prison of self-love and resentment around his assertion of kingship. Unlike the orator, who wishes to move a particular emotion in the audience and so must use his delivery to the same end as his words, the dramatist, who wishes to make his audience feel the complexities of human experience, may use the actor's voice and action against his words, to speak the opposition that men give themselves.[36]

This complexity is a lesson that Shakespeare only gradually learns; in his later plays, even the blunt and choleric characters become ironic, and thus complex. Coriolanus, for example, that straightforward hacker of men and hater of flattery, yet sophisticates himself with ironical words. In Shakespeare's source, Plutarch had ascribed Coriolanus's failure at his trial to his proud speech disappointing the people's expectation of humility.[37] Shakespeare, in contrast, depicts Coriolanus's failure as issuing from the difference between his humble words and his contemptuous delivery when he asks the people for the consulship. Coriolanus can bring himself to stand in the gown of humility and speak the required formulae, but he cannot keep the natural language of voice and gesture from showing his contempt:

> Your voices? For your voices I have fought;
> Watch'd for your voices; for your voices bear
> Of wounds two dozen odd; battles thrice six
> I have seen, and heard of; for your voices have
> Done many things, some less, some more. Your voices?
> Indeed I would be consul.
>
> (*Cor.* 2.3.126-31)

By disgust in the utterance of "voices," growing more bitter as the word is repeated, and also perhaps by gesture and rigid bearing, Coriolanus denies his own meaning, until his delivery tells the opposite of his words: he cares nothing for the voices that will make him consul. As the man who fled his own earned praise tries to flatter, his delivery also reveals the contempt he feels for himself, as well as for the citizens who require these lies of him. Shakespeare thus provides a motive for the citizens' indecisiveness, which is left unmotivated in the source: in the play the people perceive at first only what Coriolanus spoke, later the attitude expressed by his voice and bearing (2.3.153-63). But there is a further gain in characterization. When Coriolanus rages at the citizens who reject him — "Must these have voices, that can yield them now, / And straight disclaim their tongues?" (3.1.34-35) — we may see that his is the blind anger of a man who has similarly compromised himself.

To study the remaining implications for the drama in Elizabethan ideas about the body's language, we must turn to the debate between painters and poets. Renaissance painters borrowed from the

rhetoricians the idea of the emotional force and universality of gesture to argue that painting communicates better than poetry. "If
poetry describes the functioning of the mind," demands Leonardo
da Vinci, "what does painting consider, except the mind working
through bodily motion?" Although Leonardo claims to paint the
mind, what he in fact catalogues for painters are the expressions and
gestures that accompany each emotion. As a result, he may com-
mend the universal appeal of painting: painting is more expressive
than "mute poetry" because gestures speak without interpretation to
observers.[38] We have already heard the Elizabethan, Abraham
Fraunce, praising the universality of gesture, such that "the verie
pictures which being dumme, yet speak by gesture and action."[39] In
addition, the narrator in *Lucrece* judges the painting of Troy by
these Renaissance standards, listing with admiration what human
expressions and gestures reveal in the work: both Ajax's and Ulysses'
faces "cipher'd either's heart" (l. 1396); the crowd listens to Nestor's
speech "with several graces" (l. 1410), those on the edge showing
"signs of rage" (l. 1419) that they miss Nestor's words; the Trojan
mothers watch their sons go to war with such "odd action" (l. 1433)
that their "fear" shows through their "hope" and "joy" (ll. 1432-34).
The narrator praises the representation of physical form—Hecuba's
aging face, for example—but even more the seeming motion of
human form and what feelings these expressions and gestures reveal.

Implicit in the painters' claims, however, is a broader understanding than that of the rhetoricians of what the action of the body
may communicate. "The good painter," wrote Leonardo early in
the sixteenth century, "has two principal things to paint: that is,
man and the intention of his mind. The first is easy, the second difficult, because it has to be represented by gestures and movements of
the parts of the body."[40] This broader claim, different from the
assertion of the emotional force of gesture, forms the basis of the
poet's praise of the painter's work in *Timon of Athens:*

> Admirable! How this grace
> Speaks his own standing! What a mental power
> This eye shoots forth! How big imagination
> Moves in this lip! To th' dumbness of the gesture
> One might interpret.
>
> (1.1.30-34)

The poet does not judge the painting good because it looks like the man: the painting "tutors nature," he says; it is "livelier than life" (ll. 37–38). He rather praises the power of the painting to communicate the energy of life and the essence of the inner man through the motions of the outward form. By the turn of the century, Thomas Wright makes a similar claim for the orator's delivery: "For action is either a certaine visible eloquence, or an eloquence of the bodei, . . . or an external image of an internall minde, or a shadow of affections."[41]

Elizabethan poets defend their art as equal to painting on this point, for poetry also reveals the inner man through the outer: by description. When Chapman praises, "*Enargia,* or cleerenes of representation" in poetry, he cites the painter, who does not "draw the figure of a face onely to make knowne who it represents," but also "must lymn, giue luster, shaddow, and heightening," which add "motion, spirit and life."[42] In speaking of "exornation" or description, Peacham provides a gloss for Chapman's last phrase: good poetry, like painting, represents the person "by outward countenance of the inward spirite and affection."[43] In *The Defense of Poesy,* Sidney shows not that poetry is superior to painting, as it is to philosophy and history, but that it is equal to it—for "right poets" like "more excellent" painters imitate "what may be and should be." As an example, he gives "the constant, though lamenting, look of Lucretia, when she punished in herself another's fault"; in this expression, Sidney claims, the painter "paints not Lucretia (whom he never saw) but . . . the outward beauty of such a virtue."[44] The lively image that the painter presents to the eye the poet may present to the mind's eye, through words. In both cases, moreover, the artist may make the image livelier than life: both poet and painter may idealize the motions of the human form in order to communicate not only the energy of a particular passion, but also its general essence, and, further, the virtue or quality of the inner person that causes it.

The dramatic implications of the poets' claims are two. First, on a stage where the expressions and gestures of actors may not always be seen,[45] the audience may yet hear the motions of the characters in energetic language; indeed, they might "see" them by suggestion. Characters in the Elizabethan theater describe their own passionate gestures and expressions: from Hieronimo—"O eyes! no eyes, but fountains fraught with tears"—to Mistress Frankford—"Once more thy wife, dies thus embracing thee";[46] from York in *1 Henry VI*— "Mad ire and wrathful fury makes me weep" (4.3.28)—to Ferdinand in *The Tempest*— "Naples . . . does hear me, / And that he does I weep" (1.2.434-35). Shakespeare's use of this technique becomes more realistic: the long descriptions of a character's own voice and gesture (such as Suffolk's of his own expression of anger in *2 Henry VI*, 3.2.310-21) gradually give way to descriptions by others (such as King Henry's of Cranmer's "joyful tears," in *Henry VIII*, 5.2.208). But even when realistic, these descriptions have a purpose other than rendering specific visual detail. The point of them, to borrow da Vinci's distinction, is not to paint the man but the intention of his mind. In this manner, a gentleman describes Leontes' and Camillo's offstage discovery of Perdita: "the changes I perceiv'd in the King and Camillo were very notes of admiration. They seem'd almost, with staring on one another, to tear the cases of their eyes. There was speech in their dumbness, language in their very gesture; they look'd as they had heard of a world ransom'd, or one destroy'd. A notable passion of wonder appear'd in them" (*WT* 5.2.10-16). Through these words we cannot visualize the scene—we do not know, for instance, what they are wearing or where standing—but we have described in great detail what the Renaissance thought especially worthy of picturing in painting or poetry: the expressions and gestures, the "changes" or motions of the affections in the King and Camillo. The description not only invites, but even demands that we interpret the inner men by the outer: the focus quickly shifts from the visual details of their eyes to the significance of their wonder. Moreover, the description moves us further by the hyperbolic comparisons—"as they had heard of a world ransom'd, or one destroy'd"—to see through the particular feelings of Leontes and Camillo to the universal essence of human wonder.

The second implication of the poet's claim to equality with the painters may be inferred from Shakespeare's use of description to eke out the stage picture. Although in *Henry V* the theater may not "hold / The vasty fields of France" (pro.11-12), yet the audience's imagination may, when the poet provides images with his words: "Think, when we talk of horses, that you see them / Printing their proud hoofs i' th' receiving earth; / For 'tis your thoughts that now must deck our kings, / [and] Carry them here and there" (pro.26–29). More limiting than the failure to present setting realistically is the incapacity of the theater to present idealized character. To be sure, Shakespeare does trust his stage to hold Harry walking among his soldiers the eve before Agincourt, almost despairing at his kingly responsibilities. What his stage cannot be trusted to present, but what his language can, is Harry as he should be:

> Then should the warlike Harry, like himself,
> Assume the port of Mars, and at his heels
> (Leash'd in, like hounds) should famine, sword, and fire
> Crouch for employment.
>
> (pro.5–8)

This is the Harry that Shakespeare presents to our imagination through the descriptions in his choruses: "A largess universal, like the sun, / His liberal eye doth give to every one, / Thawing cold fear" (4.cho.43–45). *Enargia* as Chapman explained it, the representation of the motion and spirit of human life, occupies Shakespeare in the choruses of acts 3, 4, and 5. Through this power of poetic language, Sidney observed, we may imagine men better than they are; through the idealized description of the language of expression and gesture, Shakespeare may bring alive in our minds, if not before our eyes, the heroic character of his king.

The Actors' Language

When the lords in *Love's Labor's Lost* prepare Moth to be their prologue, they teach him "Action and accent": " 'Thus must thou speak,' and 'thus thy body bear' " (5.2.99–100). What the poets overlooked in their defense against the painters was the drama, in which actors provide a means other than description of supplying motion and life. The benefits of their medium did not escape the players, however; and they even compared themselves to painters on this score. Thomas Heywood argues the superiority of acting to the "dumbe oratory" of painting; and the author, perhaps John Webster, of the Overburian character of "An excellent Actor" draws an analogy between "playing" and "an exquisite Painter."[47]

Players also compared themselves to orators. "An excellent Actor" is like "the graue Orator . . . for by a ful and significant action of body, he charmes our attention: sit in a full Theater, and you will thinke you see so many lines drawen from the circumference of so many eares, whiles the *Actor* is the *Center.*"[48] That rhetorical delivery and acting depend on the same elements of language — voice and gesture — does not mean, however, that the two arts share all other features.[49] In accord with theatrical practice and in response to Puritan criticism, the players gradually developed a theory of acting as an art distinct from both its model, rhetorical delivery, and its occasion, dramatic poetry. We may trace three overlapping stages in theory, each with a corresponding moral purpose, each borrowing but adapting ideas from rhetoric or poetic: the first emphasizes passion, the second, character, and the last, grace. Whether Shakespeare, as a playwright and player, helped to formulate this theory or merely took up others' interpretations, I do not know; both, I suspect. What is clear is that the developing ideas about the actors' language correspond to changes in Shakespeare's dramatization of emotion and character during his career.[50]

The earliest Elizabethan notion of acting is decidedly rhetorical: the actor, like the orator delivering his speech, adds voice and action to the words, and, so, liveliness and passion. In the prologue to *Damon and Pithias*, in 1571, Richard Edwards assumes that the poet provides character, framing "eche person so, / That by his common talke, you may his nature rightly know"; the actor merely adds voice and gesture, so that the "speeches well pronounste, with action liuely framed," will please the audience.[51] Advising that the orator's "gesture must followe the change and varietie of the voyce, . . . yet not parasiticallie as stage plaiers vse, but grauelie and decentlie as becommeth men of greater calling," Abraham Fraunce assumes that acting and rhetorical delivery differ only in degree, acting being more extravagant and passionate.[52] In *The Faerie Queene*, Spenser portrays Ease as the typical actor:

> And to the vulgar beckning with his hand,
> In signe of silence, as to heare a play,
> By liuely actions he gan bewray
> Some argument of matter passioned.[53]

To Spenser, acting is passion expressed through gesture and aimed at the crowd, who understand this universal language better than

the reasoned message of words. Spenser thus inculcates many commonplaces from classical and Renaissance rhetorical delivery, yet
represents acting as a vulgar art (as is all the art of the House of
Busyrane), separated from the reason and dangerous in its power to
express and move the passions.

Even defenders of the art in the 1590s would not have challenged
Spenser's basic assumptions about acting, although they granted
actors more respect. When Thomas Nashe praises actors in 1592,
for example, it is for their ability to move the audience's emotions:
"How would it haue ioyed braue *Talbot*," he asks, "to thinke that
after he had lyne two hundred years in his Tombe, hee should . . .
haue his bones newe embalmed with the teares of ten thousand spectators?"[54] As late as 1612, in an actor's prologue Dekker enthusiastically describes acting as the artful evocation of feelings:

> That Man giue mee; whose Brest fill'd by the *Muses,*
> With Raptures, Into a second, them infuses:
> Can giue an Actor, Sorrow, Rage, Ioy, Passion,
> Whilst hee againe (by self-same Agitation)
> > Commands the *Hearers,* sometimes drawing out Teares,
> > Then smiles, and fills them both with *Hopes* and *Feares.* [55]

Dekker's idea, another rhetorical commonplace, is yet adapted to
the special purpose of playing. Quintilian had cautioned that the
orator will move his audience only by combining the natural with the
counterfeit in an artful control of true emotions: "excite the appropriate feeling in oneself, . . . form a mental picture of the facts, and
. . . exhibit an emotion that cannot be distinguished from the
truth"; only then will the voice "produce precisely the same emotion
in the judge that we have put into it."[56] In England, Thomas Wilson
had echoed Quintilian's warning in his rhetoric, and Thomas
Wright, in his treatise on the passions, had even offered a scientific
explanation for its necessity: since passion is a physical motion, passing from the heart to external expressions, and so to the eyes and
ears of the audience, the force with which it originates determines
the response; a feigned emotion, lacking force, will get little response.[57] In Dekker's adaptation, the fiction of the poet inspires the
actor with a true emotion, which he then arouses in the audience;
players thus move men by the power of emotions that are fictional
and true at once.[58]

In the plays of the 1590s, Shakespeare's characters similarly speak
of acting as an art of voice and gesture expressing and moving the
passions. "Give me a cup of sack to make my eyes look red," demands Falstaff when he acts Henry IV, "that it may be thought I
have wept, for I must speak in passion, and I will do it in King Cam-
byses' vein" (*1H4* 2.4.384–87). The disguised Julia claims the utmost
success for her presentation of "Ariadne passioning" (*TGV* 4.4.167):
"Which I so lively acted with my tears / That my poor mistress,
moved therewithal, / Wept bitterly" (ll. 169–71). Shakespeare, of
course, is guiding us to feel this same sadness: the Julia who was supposed to have been the audience is actually recounting her "true"
feelings about Proteus, and to the lady who has become his new love
—a lady, moreover, who is herself weeping for the sadness of
Ariadne and Julia (l. 175). One may see that this idea encourages
melodramatic characterization: the playwright must give his actors
the sad or angry speeches that allow them to exercise their craft.
"Come," demands Hamlet when the Players enter, "give us a taste of
your quality, come, a passionate speech" (*Ham.* 2.2.431–32). And if
Shakespeare is modeling the players in *Hamlet* on an earlier age of
acting, it is not too far in the past. "Come," says Richard to Buckingham in *Richard III*, "canst thou quake and change thy color, /
Murther thy breath in middle of a word, / . . . As if thou were dis-
traught and mad with terror?" (3.5.1–4). "Tut," replies Buckingham—

> I can counterfeit the deep tragedian,
> Speak and look back, and pry on every side,
> Tremble and start at wagging of a straw;
> Intending deep suspicion, ghastly looks
> Are at my service, like enforced smiles;
> And both are ready in their offices
> At any time to grace my strategems.
>
> (3.5.5–11)

Scheming to take the crown, Richard creates the fiction of
Hastings's plot against him and the two cousins imagine themselves
as actors, expressing the appropriate passions in voice and action.
Critics have often observed that Richard is an actor; more important by Elizabethan standards, Richard is a bad actor, one who does
not deliver true emotions. In this situation, he is still effective: by his

passionate delivery he moves a fear in the crowd that allows them to accept the execution of Hastings and the necessity of a strong man as king. But later, when he attempts to convince Queen Elizabeth of his love for her daughter, he loses his audience by the insincerity of his art.

Part of the impetus for change in acting theory came from Puritan criticism, part from theatrical practice. The Puritans attacked the English stage in the 1570s and 1580s along three important lines: the immoral content of plays, the lewdness of actors and theatergoers, and the obscenely passionate acting. In the 1580s, responders defended the morality of poetry in general and the good character of most actors, but not the passionate acting, for which they had no moral justification.[59] In 1615, the Puritan John Greene is still warning against the same "wanton gestures" used by players, the "lipping and kissing, . . . clipping and culling," the same presentation of "lustfull passions," and the same results: "Then these goodly Pageants being done, euery one sorteth to his mate, each bring another home-ward of their way: then begin they to repeate the lasciuous acts and speeches they haue heard, and thereby infect their minde with wicked passions, so that in their secret conclaues they play the *Sodomits*, or worse."[60] But, by 1615, the players have a defense.

An early but unsuccessful attempt at such a defense is Henry Chettle's *Kind-Heart's Dream*, in 1592. Through the mouth of Tarleton's ghost, Chettle satirizes the Puritans' own arguments: "Fie . . . vppon players speeches, their wordes are full of wyles; vppon their gestures, that are altogether wanton. Is it not lamentable, that a man should spend his two pence on them . . . and in liuely gesture see trecherie set out, with which euery man now adaies vseth to intrap his brother?" Chettle wonders how the Puritans can miss the point: we players deliver the viciousness of passion before the audience so that they may feel and know its power. Finally, however, Chettle begs the question: "he that at a play will be delighted in the [vice], and not warned by the [punishment], is like him that reads in a booke the description of sinne, and will not looke ouer the leafe for the reward."[61] Chettle thus sidesteps the issue of the actor's responsibility, since he does not distinguish between exploiting and moving passions, and between sentimental and more natural characterizations. What literary historians hesitate to admit is that the Puritans had a valid objection to many early Elizabethan plays: soap opera is not good art, and it does take advantage of susceptible audiences. The early theory of passionate acting must have encouraged melodrama and overacting.

Certainly one is hard put to think of an example from Shakespeare's later plays where gesture is used with such melodramatic force as it is in the early plays: in the Temple Garden scene of *1 Henry VI* (2.4), for example, where the partisans of York and Lancaster punctuate their argument by plucking white and red roses (six of them!), by thrusting them out as they make their vows, and by fastening them to their clothes as a sign of the anger they carry with them. Since the roses are political symbols, the actions are not without significance, and the gestures do give "life" to the scene, in the sense of excitement; but they do not contribute to the individuality of characters, even though they provide energy. In the first scene of *Richard II,* the gestures of Mowbray and Bullingbroke similarly enliven the ceremonial language of ritual address, of long sentences, regular meters, and formal couplets, even triplets: Bullingbroke throws down his gage, Mowbray picks it up, Richard raises his scepter and vows Mowbray may have free speech, Mowbray throws down his gage, Bullingbroke picks it up, and the scene is frozen while Richard and Gaunt request the giving up of gages; then again comes a flurry of action with Mowbray kneeling to lay his life but not his gage at the King's feet, and the King holding out his hand yet again for the gage. But the same challenging gesture is taken up again in a later scene (4.1) and melodramatically exploited, as Aumerle, Fitzwater, Percy, Surrey, and a fifth lord—all heap their gages with extraordinary passion at each other's feet. What this scene requires of actors is not subtlety and variety but merely intensity.

What was required of actors, however, gradually changed. As the players assumed more importance in the theatrical industry, their giving "life" to their characters came to mean more than expressing passions with voice and gesture. The old idea was still there, but overlaid with a new one closer to our idea of characterization. In 1600, Jonson's sketch of his character Puntarvolo, a man who "deales vpon . . . strange performances, resoluing (in despight of publike derision) to sticke to his owne particular fashion, phrase, and gesture,"[62] requires from the actor a presentation through voice and gesture of Puntarvolo's idiosyncratic habits of mind and person-ality. Moreover, in the "Induction" to *Antonio and Mellida,* Marston portrays the players—shown discussing their parts—as independent artists who "personate" the characters. The actor of Matzagente adds "a spruce Attick accent of adulterate Spanish" (with no indica-tion of it in the playwright's text) in order to indicate his "corrupt and mungrel'd" ancestry. The actor of Antonio, who disguises himself as an Amazon, frets over playing both sexes: "when use hath taught me action, to hit the right point of a Ladies part, I shall growe ignorant when I must turne young Prince againe." His con-cern is not rhetorical but natural movement, not passion but realist-ically playing two very different parts at once. Alberto claims that his role, "impossible to be made perspicuous by any utterance," must be acted out "by signes & tokens"; he then conveys, with a series of gestures, the conflicting aspects of his character.[63] Eventu-ally Webster's praise of "the action" of *The White Devil* (1612) in-cludes "the true imitation of life, without striving to make nature a monster"; and Chapman, in 1631, defends playing on the grounds that "the personal and exact life it gives to any history, or other such delineation of human actions, adds to them lustre, spirit, and ap-prehension."[64] No longer merely adding passion to the playwright's words, the actor creates his own imitation of nature in voice and ac-tion: his personation, with its particularity and spirit, gives life to the role that the playwright designs.

This development in acting theory corresponds to a growing real-ism in Shakespeare's characterization. In the tragedies, Shakespeare uses gestures in a more restrained way than in the earlier histories, at the emotional climax of a scene, and to particularize his characters. The kneeling in *Othello*—all the lords, led by Cassio, to greet Des-demona at Cyprus (2.1.84); Othello and Iago "In the due reverence of a sacred vow" to revenge infidelity (3.3.460-63); and Desdemona suing to Othello for explanation of his rage (4.2.31)—comes only with the emotional height of each scene, and in each case em-phasizes character: the courtesy of Cassio, the hypocrisy of Iago, and the submissiveness of Desdemona. Voice is even more an instrument for particularizing character. Kent could have been modeled on the didactic counselor of Shakespeare's early plays, like the Friar in *Romeo and Juliet* or the Lord Chief Justice in *2 Henry IV,* parts calling for a consistent and controlled voice. Or Kent, whose temper is short enough, might have spoken with the voice of Shakespeare's early choleric characters—all run-on sentences and passion. Instead, Kent is given a variety of rhetorical voices,[65] even in the first scene of *King Lear,* where he has relatively few lines. His first voice is conversational and polite, when he is introduced to Edmund (1.1.1–30). Beginning his debate with Lear in a full oratorical voice, rhythmic, still polite, and with an urgency that suggests rapid delivery (ll. 139–42), he is interrupted before he is well into his only elaborate period in the scene. In a changed voice, more abrupt in rhythm, quicker in delivery, with greater emphasis on accented words, he reflects back to Lear his own anger (ll. 144–66). The rhymed endings and balanced clauses of his last speech (ll. 180–87) require yet another voice, this time one of less passion, slower in delivery, restrained in volume, perhaps with a tone of weary defeat. Neither a consistent voice nor a voice conveying only passion provides individuality. It is the quick movement of mind and emotion reflected in vocal changes that particularizes and brings alive a character.

"Life-like" rather than "lively" acting gave rise to a new conception of the moral purpose of acting. To study this development, we must consider Hamlet's advice to the players as a defense of acting, as in part it is. Hamlet's instructions (*Ham.* 3.2.1–45) incorporate many of the commonplaces we have already discussed: the actor's medium is voice ("Speak the speech, I pray you, as I pronounc'd it to you") and gesture ("Nor do not saw the air too much with your hand, thus, but use all gently"); and a major concern is delivering passion ("in the very torrent, tempest, and . . . whirlwind of your passion"). But Hamlet also defines a moral purpose for the art by distinguishing between good and bad actors and audiences. The bad actor "tear[s] a passion to totters" and "spleet[s] the ears of the groundlings"; he performs for those "who for the most part are capable of nothing but inexplicable dumb shows and noise," those who expect only passionate gesture and voice. The good actor, on the other hand, aims his performance at the "judicious" spectator, and he "o'erstep[s] not the modesty of nature." To deliver passion is not the primary purpose of the good actor, whose aim is "to hold as 'twere the mirror up to nature"; he thus assumes a responsibility at once moral and aesthetic "to show virtue her feature, scorn her own image, and the very age and body of the time his form and pressure."

Hamlet includes special instructions for the fool: "And let those that play your clowns speak no more than is set down for them, for there be of them that will themselves laugh to set on some quantity of barren spectators to laugh too, though in the mean time some necessary question of the play be then to be consider'd" (*Ham.* 3.2.38-43). The "barren spectators," who encourage overacting and dishonest delivery, are the opposite of the "judicious" whom Hamlet would have his actors play to. The implication of the passage is not only that the fool must not add lines and stage business (as editors have usually glossed it) but also that he must not laugh or otherwise exaggerate voice, expression, and gesture in his attempt to make his audience laugh; in the body's language he must aim at the ridiculous not the burlesque. In this light, Feste's delivery of Malvolio's letter in *Twelfth Night* (so close in time to *Hamlet*) seems almost a practical exposition of bad acting in a clown:

> *Clown.* Look then to be well edified when the fool delivers the
>   madman. "By the lord, madam," —
> *Olivia.* How now, art thou mad?
> *Clown.* No, madam, I do but read madness. And your ladyship will
>   have it as it ought to be, you must allow *vox.*
>
> (*TN* 5.1.290-96)

Acting out Malvolio's "mad" passion in an exaggerated voice, Feste begins to read the letter; when Olivia objects, he argues that he must adopt a rhetorical voice (*"vox"*) suited to the subject and speaker. But Feste is in fact using the idea that delivery must express the appropriate passion to disguise his real aim: the laughter of the audience at his caricature of Malvolio. Feste is here a bad actor, one who exaggerates Malvolio's anger to give a false imitation of insanity, and thus exploits his audience through his voice. Olivia, a "judicious" spectator, remains unmoved by Feste's burlesque, and demands an honest delivery that will allow her a reasoned evaluation of Malvolio's letter. We have only to imagine Sir Toby's and Maria's response to the clown's reading to see what the result of a bad actor and a bad audience would be: "some necessary question of the play" would indeed be lost in the laughter, for Malvolio would be left in the dark closet, and there would be less justice in the play's ending.

In Thomas Heywood's *An Apology for Actors,* we may see the final stage in the moral defense of acting. Defending the drama for moral content in books 2 and 3, along the traditional lines of the player-Puritan debate,[66] in book 1 Heywood creates a new defense, one based on the power of the aesthetic means of acting to reach a moral end. Hercules, he claims, was moved by a dramatized history of his father Jupiter, "Which being personated with liuely and well-spirited action, wrought such impression on his noble thoughts, that in meere emulation of his fathers valor . . . he perform'd his twelue labours."[67] Heywood weds two ideas: that the actor's language gives "life" to plays, and that delivery moves men. By the substitution of emulating virtue for moving passion in the audience, however, Heywood directly answers the Puritans' objection to acting.

Modeling his defense not on rhetorical theory but on Sidney's *Defense of Poesy,* Heywood argues that acting surpasses both oratory and painting, just as Sidney had argued that poetry surpasses both philosophy and history. He picks up where the painting-poetry debate left off: some say that oratory, "a speaking picture," moves men to emulate virtue; others say that painting, "a dumbe oratory," persuades men to great deeds by their depiction (sig. B3ᵛ). He finds, however, that neither art fully uses human capabilities of expression and moral persuasion: "A Description is only a shadow receiued by the eare but not perceiued by the eye: so liuely portrature is meerely a forme seene by the eye, but can neither shew action, passion, motion, or any other gesture, to mooue the spirits of the beholder to admiration" (sig. B3ᵛ). Heywood turns to English history plays to show that only acting realizes the full potential in the language of delivery: "What English blood seeing the person of any bold English man presented and doth not hugge his fame, and hunnye at his valor, pursuing him in his enterprise with his best wishes, and as beeing wrapt in contemplation, offers to him in his hart all prosperous performance, as if the Personator were the man Personated, so bewitching a thing is liuely and well spirited action, that it hath power to new mold the harts of the spectators and fashion them to the shape of any noble and notable attempt" (sig. B4ʳ). In Heywood's idea of "personation," the actor identifies with the character he plays, and, by the power of his delivery, spectators identify with his personation. Moving the audience to admiration, the actor's imitation becomes a way of releasing the power within spectators to reshape themselves. For Thomas Heywood, acting might provide a Henry V to make other Henry Vs.[68]

Heywood does not require a discerning audience for acting to achieve its moral effect. Attributing the civility of the ancient Greeks partly to acting, he infers that then, as now, "Action was the neerest way to plant vnderstanding in the hearts of the ignorant" (sig. C3^r). Not at all vulgar, acting is the noblest universal art because it moves even the ignorant to ethical and political government.

Shakespeare apparently came to share Heywood's idea of the reforming power of acting. As early as *Hamlet*, Shakespeare had referred to the stories that Heywood later cites of a person being moved by a play to confess a crime.[69] Shakespeare's last reference to acting, in *The Tempest*, grants it even further power. Communicating through music and actions alone, the spirits under Prospero's direction move the King to wonder:

> I cannot too much muse
> Such shapes, such gesture, and such sound expressing
> (Although they want the use of tongue) a kind
> Of excellent dumb discourse.
>
> (3.3.36-39)

The spirits speak the actor's language, a "dumb discourse" in the familiar Renaissance phrasing. The universality of gesture appeals even across the barriers between alien peoples, and Gonzalo is also moved to admire the

> people of the island,
> Who though they are of monstrous shape, yet note
> Their manners are more gentle, kind, than of
> Our human generation you shall find
> Many, nay, almost any.
>
> (3.3.30-34)

The acting has immediate emotional effect, for the men respond with acceptance to the "gentle actions" (l. 20), and then with fear to the violent ones, when Ariel "like a harpy, claps his wings upon the

table and with a quaint device the banquet vanishes" (ll. 52-53).
But the actors arouse emotions only to a moral end, and Ariel begins
his sermon: "You are three men of sin" (l. 53); you must reform
through "heart's sorrow, / And a clear life ensuing" (ll. 81-82).
Prospero praises Ariel—"Bravely the figure of this harpy hast thou /
Perform'd" (ll. 83-84)—and the other spirits as "good" actors in the
highest sense:

> Of my instruction hast thou nothing bated
> In what thou hadst to say; so with good life,
> And observation strange, my meaner ministers
> Their several kinds have done.
>
> (3.3.85-88)

"Instruction" refers primarily to the moral knowledge that Ariel im-
parted, but also to the acting: Ariel and the lesser spirits acted their
roles not melodramatically but "with good life." The word "life"
here suggests "personation," an imitation in action moving the audience to "heart's sorrow." But the actor cannot provide the "clear
life ensuing." Heywood comes close to saying that acting can make
men good against their wills. Not so in *The Tempest:* Alonso is
moved to repentance, Gonzalo to pity, but Antonio and Sebastian
only to fear and anger. Shakespeare's vision suggests that acting has
a force equal to that which Sidney found in poetry: an actor, like the
poet, is a maker whose creation opens a way to re-creation in the audience, "if they will learn aright why and how that maker made
him."[70]

Soon Heywood's idea of the moral power of personation became a
commonplace. In 1616, even the Puritan Thomas Gainsford admits
that in ancient times (though not in modern ones) through "gesture
and personated action" the actor "was euer the life of dead poesie,
. . . so that vice was made odious, [and] vertue set on a throne of im-
mitation."[71] He is refuting the claims for the modern actor made by
the writer of "An excellent Actor": "By his action hee fortifies
morall precepts with example; for what wee see him personate, wee
thinke truely done before vs: a man of a deep thoght might ap-
prehend, the Ghosts of our ancient *Heroes* walk't againe."[72]

The popularity of the theory of personation would seem to encourage further realism in characterization and naturalism in act-

ing. But the emphasis on remaking the man in the audience precludes either development. "To see as I haue seene," exults Heywood, "*Hercules* in his owne shape . . . killing the Centaurs, pashing the Lion, squeezing the Dragon, dragging *Cerberus* in Chaynes, and lastly, on his high Pyramides writing *Nil vltra,* O these were sights to make an *Alexander*" (sig. B4ʳ). But they are not sights to sustain naturalistic acting. At the same time that actors are claiming to make the ghosts of ancient heroes walk again, Shakespeare is drawing the stories of his last plays from myth and legend. The connection is characterization: both the actor who personates well and the moral playwright idealize, presenting men as they ought to be, not as they are. In Prospero's pageant, with its mythical "monstrous shapes" and its symbolic motion and dance, we may see the implications for acting in this last stage of the theory. Although Prospero praises Ariel for the "good life" of his acting, he judges even the violent actions of Ariel's harpy by artistic style: "a grace it had, devouring" (*Tmp.* 3.3.84). "Grace," the final requirement of good acting, represents a qualification of the earlier goal of lifelike character.

The ideal of grace originates with classical rhetoricians, who required an orator to be temperate in gesture, selecting only important words for emphasis and implying the deeper emotion that may not be shown with dignity in public. Quintilian judges the best actors to be equally selective, although most actors employ more frequent and vehement gestures.[73] In the Renaissance, Castiglione's Sir Frederick demands this ideal of the courtier, who must strive for a voice "sweete and well framed with a prompt pronunciation," and "gestures, . . . not affected nor forced, but tempred with a manerly countenance, and with a mouing of the eyes that may giue a grace and accorde with the wordes, and (as much as he can) signifie also with gestures, the intent and affection of the speaker."[74] Grace is partly elegant movement, partly gesture in harmony with the words, so that it signifies the attitude of the speaker.

This rhetorical ideal comes into acting theory only in the seventeenth century. When Hamlet instructs his players to "use all gently" in gesture, his aim is "a temperance that may give [passion] smoothness" (*Ham.* 3.2.4–8); and when he requires that his actors "Suit the action to the word, the word to the action," (3.2.17–18), he is demanding the "accorde" that Castiglione required, the harmony that gives significance as well as dignity to delivery. Heywood adapts this rhetorical ideal to the special purpose of playing. The ideal is the same, "a gratious and bewitching kinde of action" whereby the actor fits "his phrases to his action, and his action to his phrase"; but the purpose is "to qualifie euery thing according to the nature of the person personated: for in ouer-acting trickes, . . . men of the ripest desert . . . may breake into the most violent absurdities" (sig. C4r). Heywood combines what might seem opposed qualities to modern actors: convincing portrayal of character and idealized symbolic gesture. The actor and playwright cooperate to achieve the ideal of grace. In his preface to *The Devil's Law-Case* (1623), Webster admits, "A great part of the grace of this . . . lay in Action; yet can no Action ever be gracious, where the decency of the Language, and Ingenious structure of the Scaene, arrive not to make up a perfect Harmony."[75] Beginning in the sixteenth century, actors defend their art by arguing that in voice, expression, and gesture they portray men as they are, and teach the viciousness of passion. In the seventeenth century they add to this defense another: if the poet portrays men as they should be, the actors, understanding the symbolic force of action, will embody those men in their graceful delivery and remake their audience in heroic shapes.

This last development in acting theory corresponds to a growing effectiveness in Shakespeare's use of voice and action as artistic symbols. The embraces in *Antony and Cleopatra*[76] reflect the passions of the characters, but take on symbolic significance as changing passions cause loyalties to vary; in the final poetic image, we hear of the stage action stilled, ironically also in an embrace: "No grave upon the earth shall clip in it / A pair so famous" (5.2.359–60). Even voice becomes symbolic in the later plays. The voices in *King Lear* are truly "personations," symbolic identities adopted by characters as they grow in knowledge of themselves. The actor of Lear needs the greatest range of voice, not only to deliver Lear's terrible anger and grief, but also to indicate his change in identity, when his voice wanders from mad to sane and his identity from King to Man in the scenes on the moor with Edgar and Gloucester. Kent, whose voice has remarkable variety, needs an entirely new voice for Caius, the disguise he adopts when he borrows "other accents" to carry through his "good intent" (1.4.1–2). Did the actor of Kent, like Marston's player of Matzagente, adopt an accent appropriate to his character, perhaps a homely Kentish accent in place of the courtly London one? Such a change would be appropriate to Kent, the character who from the beginning knows himself and so changes his voice only to keep his old identity: Caius is still the plain-speaker, who "can keep honest counsel, . . . mar a curious tale in telling it, and deliver a plain message bluntly" (1.4.32-34). The actor of Edgar embarks on an odyssey of voices and identities. Sloughing off the old Edgar, he takes on first the lunatic beggar's voice: "Poor Turlygod! poor Tom! / That's something yet: Edgar I nothing am" (2.3.20-22). The "something" he makes of this poor mad identity is "the thing itself: unaccommodated man" (3.4.106-7); and to Lear in the storm his is the voice of the "philosopher," the "learned Theban" (3.4.154-57). During Gloucester's attempted suicide (4.6), Edgar speaks with four voices besides his own: those of Poor Tom, the man at the bottom of the cliff, a gentleman addressing Cordelia's men, and a peasant who aids Gloucester and kills Oswald. His voices are personations that dramatize the gods' miraculous care for Gloucester, thus moving him to remake himself. With his voices, however, Edgar also travels an epic journey, through the entire social hierarchy of his nation. And when he takes up his own identity again, it is something finer, integrating what he has learned from speaking as British beggar, peasant, and gentleman. Edmund does not recognize his voice, but Edgar is so obviously noble that he accepts his challenge: "since thy outside looks so fair and warlike, / And . . . thy tongue some say of breeding breathes" (5.3.143-44). Edgar is a hero, speaking it, says Albany, even in the action of his body: "Methought thy very gait did prophesy / A royal nobleness" (5.3.176-77).

In the later tragedies, and even more in the romances, Shakespeare shapes the actors' voices and gestures into symbols of human growth: in the action of the dumb shows in *Pericles* and of the pageants in *The Tempest;* in the voices of Marina, whose harmonious speech persuades Pericles to speak and return to reality, and of Ariel, whose songs lead the followers on journeys of self-discovery; and in both voice and action in *The Winter's Tale,* when the statue, "Standing like stone" (5.3.42), first takes on the "life" (l. 66) and "motion" (l. 67) of art, and then the action and voice of the real Hermione (ll. 99-121), reborn to herself as Leontes has been to himself. From the early histories to the late romances, it is as if Shakespeare's stage practice developed in the way that Elizabethan ideas on the actors' language developed: from the expression of the life and force of human passions to the communication of men's power to remake themselves.

Notes

1. Peacham, *Garden* (1593), sig. ABiii^r.

2. Mulcaster, *Elementarie*, p. 97, and *Positions [on] the Training up of Children* (London, 1581), pp. 29–34 and 56.

3. Sir Thomas Elyot, *The Castel of Helth* (London, 1541), sigs. Oiiii^v–Pi^r.

4. Classical references to speech as a purge include Hippocrates, "Humours," x.8–9, and "Regimen," II.1xi.13–17; and A. Cornelius Celsus, *De Medicina*, I.7–8, III.18.10–11, IV.10.1, and IV.13.3. Other English Renaissance references include *Batman vppon Bartholome*, fols. 48^r and 56^r; Thomas Cogan, *The Haven of Health* (London, 1589), sig. A2^r; and Sir John Harington, *The Englishmans Doctor* (London, 1609), sig. Cl^r. On Elizabethan psychology and Shakespeare, see Hardin Craig, "Shakespeare's Depiction of Passions," *PQ*, 4 (1925), 289–301; and Ruth L. Anderson, *Elizabethan Psychology and Shakespeare's Plays*, Univ. of Iowa Humanistic Studies, vol. 3, no. 4 (Iowa City: Univ. of Iowa, 1927).

5. Mulcaster, *Positions*, pp. 55–62.

6. Henry Howard, Earl of Surrey, from "A warning to the louer," in *Tottel's Miscellany*, ed. Hyder Rollins (1928; rpt. Cambridge, Mass.: Harvard Univ. Press, 1965), I, 2.

7. Spenser, Sonnet XLIII, ll. 3–4, in *Amoretti*, quoted from *Spenser: Poetical Works*.

8. See, for example, *The Collected Poems of Sir Thomas Wyatt*, ed. Kenneth Muir and Patricia Thomson (Liverpool: Liverpool Univ. Press, 1969), Poem XX, ll. 10–15, Poem LIII, ll. 9–12, and Poem LXXXIV, ll. 53–60; *Tottel's Miscellany*, I, 239–40, "The louer complaineth"; and Spenser, Sonnet II, *Amoretti*. Cf. Shakespeare's *Ven.*, ll. 334–36.

9. Albert L. Walker, in "Convention in Shakespeare's Description of Emotion," *PQ*, 17 (1938), 26–66, asserts that most physiological concepts in Shakespeare's plays, including the idea of speech as a relief of passion, originate in Elizabethan dramatic conventions, not in Elizabethan science; as proof he lists many examples from earlier Tudor plays. It may well be that Shakespeare was not directly influenced by science, but the idea of speech as a purge is a scientific notion that gradually gains popularity during the century with all sorts of writers, not just with the dramatists.

10. For Richard, Duke of York, see *2H6* 5.1.23-27; for Richard, Duke of Gloucester, *3H6* 2.1.81-86 and 2.2.95-112; for Suffolk, *2H6* 3.2.310-21; and for Hotspur, *1H4* 1.3.125-28. Thomas Wright, in *The Passions of the Minde* (London, 1604), sig. H8r, declares that rashness in speech "proceedeth from lacke of iudgement, a prowd conceit of their owne conceits, [and] a bold, hote and rash affection."

11. Francis Meres, *Palladis Tamia* (London, 1598), sig. Kk4v. See also Peter de la Primaudaye, *The French Academie*, tr. T. B. (London, 1586), pp. 126-36, whose essay, "Of Speech and Speaking," is primarily on control and restraint in speech.

12. Wilson, *Arte of Rhetorique*, sig. aiir. See also Castiglione, *The Courtier*, sig. F2v: "in our owne tongue, whose office is (as all others) to expresse well and clearely the conceites of the minde, we delite in darknesse"; and Meres, *Palladis Tamia*, sig. Kk2v: "speech was giuen to vs to lay open our mindes and matters."

13. Peacham, *Garden* (1577), sig. Aiir.

14. Du Bartas, *Deuine Weekes*, p. 422.

15. Vives, *On Education*, p. 39. Cf. *Timber*, in *Ben Jonson*, VIII, 620-21: "*Speech* is the only benefit man hath to expresse his excellencie of mind above other creatures. It is the Instrument of *Society*."

16. Montaigne, "Of giving the lie," *Essayes*, p. 386.

17. Elyot, *Castel*, sig. Riiiiv. Cf. the doctor's comments on Lady Macbeth, *Mac.* 5.1.71-74:

> Unnatural deeds
> Do breed unnatural troubles; infected minds
> To their deaf pillows will discharge their secrets.
> More needs she the divine than the physician.

18. *3H6* 2.5.21-54; *TGV* 2.3.5-32; *MV* 5.1.1-22; and *Ant.* 5.2.280-90.

19. According to medieval and Renaissance grammarians, interjections do not signify things or thoughts, as do nouns and verbs, but attitudes or passions. Cf. *Ars Minor of Donatus*, p. 55, on "interjection": "A part of speech signifying a state of the mind by an unusual tone of the voice"; and Richard Carew, "Epistle," p. 5: "Again, for expressing our Passions, our Interjections are very apt and forcible."

20. Some recent critics have seen Coriolanus as a man trusting only deeds, not words: see James Calderwood, "Coriolanus: Wordless Meanings and Meaningless Words," *SEL*, 6 (1966), 211-24, esp. 214-15; and Danson, *Tragic Alphabet*, p. 149. Coriolanus is not a silent hero, however much he prefers battle to talking. He does not think that all words are lies, but that words not spoken straight from the heart are lies; and he trusts

only his own heart as judge of sincerity. As Madeleine Doran writes, in *Shakespeare's Dramatic Language* (Madison: Univ. of Wisconsin Press, 1976), p. 207: Coriolanus "does not know that honesty need not be clothed in arrogant pride."

21. Hippocrates, "Aphorisms," VII, fragment, 25-39.

22. Francis Bacon, *The Historie of Life and Death* (London, 1638), sigs. M7^v-M8^r.

23. *Batman vppon Bartholome*, fol. 17^r.

24. See John Henry Wigmore, *A Treatise on the Anglo-American System of Evidence* (Boston: Little, Brown, and Co., 1940 [3rd ed.]), V, 230: "All Courts have agreed . . . that the *approach of death* produces a state of mind in which the utterances of the dying person are to be taken as free from all ordinary motives to mis-state." The dying declaration is thus admissible as hearsay evidence. See also V, 218: as a legal exception to the hearsay rule, the validity of the dying man's declaration came into being in the early eighteenth century when hearsay was first strictly excluded; however, Wigmore notes that the principle was included in the twelfth-century London Custumal, and was invoked in Sir Walter Raleigh's trial in 1603. I owe this reference to my friend, Anthony M. Paul, Atty.

25. On Gaunt's proverbs and their significance for his character, see Maynard Mack, Jr., *Killing the King* (New Haven: Yale Univ. Press, 1973), pp. 16-21.

26. Wilson, *Arte of Rhetorique*, sig. Ggii^v. Cf. the Ramist, Omer Talon [Talaeus], *Rhetorica* (London, 1636), p. 66: "*gestus, sermo corporis & eloquentia recta à Cicerone nominatur.*" The passage in Cicero to which Wilson and Talon refer is probably *De Oratore*, III.lix.222: "by action the body talks." Bertram Joseph documents the influence of *pronuntiatio* on humanist education in *Elizabethan Acting* (London: Oxford Univ. Press, 1951), pp. 1-33. Terence Hawkes approaches the idea of gesture as language from a modern point of view in *Shakespeare's Talking Animals* (London: Edward Arnold, 1973), pp. 15-23.

27. Quintilian, *Institutio Oratoria*, XI.iii.9. Other classical rhetoricians are even more certain of the importance of delivery, arguing that without voice and gesture, a speech makes no impression on the audience: see Isocrates, "To Philip," v.25-26; and *Rhetorica ad Herennium*, III.xi.19. MacDonald Critchley, in *The Language of Gesture* (London: Edward Arnold and Co., 1939), traces ideas of gesture as language through classical sources to support his interjectional theory of the origin of language.

28. Bacon, *Advancement*, sig. Kkl^r. The complete passage distinguishes what physiognomy—"the Lyneaments of the bodie"—reveals (character) from what expression and gesture communicate (emotions). Thus Carroll Camden grants too much to physiognomy when he assigns it

the rhetorical idea of facial expression as language, in "The Mind's Construction in the Face," *PQ*, 20 (1949), 400–412.

29. Cicero, *De Oratore*, III.lvii.216; see also III.lix.221: "For delivery is wholly the concern of the feelings." The same relationship between gesture and emotion is discussed by Quintilian, *Institutio Oratoria*, XI.iii.2–14; and by Wilson, *Arte of Rhetorique*, sig. Ggii^v.

30. Meres, *Palladis Tamia*, sig. Kk6^r.

31. Abraham Fraunce, *The Arcadian Rhetorike* (London, 1588), sig. I7^v. Cf. Quintilian, *Institutio Oratoria*, IX.iii.65–67, for a similar praise of gesture as the universal language, shared by the dumb, animals, dancers, and pictures; and XI.iii.87, for gesture as the language that transcends the "multitude of tongues." References in the sixteenth-century to gesture as a universal language include Wilson, *Arte of Rhetorique*, sig. Ggii^v; Talon, *Rhetorica*, p. 66; Montaigne, "Apologie," *Essayes*, pp. 260–66; and Wright, *Passions of the Minde*, sig. M8^v. The idea is so popular that François Rabelais burlesques it in *Gargantua and Pantagruel*, tr. Sir Thomas Urquhart and Peter Le Motteaux (London: Oxford Univ. Press, 1934), I, 249–53. Thus James R. Knowlson mistakenly attributes the discovery of gesture as a universal language to the teachers of the deaf from 1600–1800, in "The Idea of Gesture," *JHI*, 26 (1965), 495–508.

32. Cicero, *De Oratore*, III.lix.223.

33. Wilson, *Arte of Rhetorique*, sig. ti^v.

34. Montaigne, "Apologie," *Essayes*, p. 261; Du Bartas, *Deuine Weekes*, p. 422.

35. Peacham, *Garden* (1577), sig. Diii^r. See also Fraunce, *Arcadian Rhetorike*, sig. H7^r. Bertram Joseph discusses irony in the rhetorical treatises on gesture, in *Elizabethan Acting*, p. 67.

36. Robert Y. Turner, in *Shakespeare's Apprenticeship* (Chicago: Univ. of Chicago Press, 1974), p. 92, outlines the general effect of rhetorical delivery on Shakespeare's characterization: "The playwright who adapts the assumptions of the rhetorician conceives of a one-to-one relation between how the character feels and how the audience responds. The character who feels passion must deliver a speech to stimulate the audience to feel the same way." Although Turner's analysis is generally true of Shakespeare's early characters, the trope of irony, as defined in the rhetorics, offered the dramatist a means of evoking more than this simple response in the audience.

37. *Shakespeare's Plutarch*, tr. Sir Thomas North, ed. C. F. Tucker Brooke (London: Chatto and Windus, 1909), II, 168–69: "But where [the people] thought to have heard very humble and lowly words come from him, he began not only to use his wonted boldness of speaking (which of itself was very rough and unpleasant, and did more to aggravate his ac-

cusation, than purge his innocency) but also gave himself in his words to thunder, and look therewithal so grimly, as though he made no reckoning of the matter."

38. Leonardo da Vinci, *Treatise on Painting* [Codex Urbinas Latinus 1270], tr. A. Philip MacMahon (Princeton: Princeton Univ. Press, 1956), I, 13–19 and I, 149–57. Rensselaer Lee suggests the influence of Cicero and Quintilian on Renaissance painting aesthetic, but gives it little weight, in *Ut Pictura Poesis* (1940; rpt., New York: W. W. Norton & Co., 1967), p. 25. To W. G. Howard, speaking of Leon Battista Alberti's *Della Pictura* (1436), classical rhetoric seems an important influence; in *"Ut Pictura Poesis,"* *PMLA*, 24 (1909), 45–46. On Leonardo's influence throughout the Renaissance, see Lee, *Ut Pictura*, pp. 60–61.

39. See n. 31.

40. Leonardo da Vinci, *Treatise on Painting*, I, 104.

41. Wright, *Passions of the Minde*, sig. M8[v].

42. George Chapman, prefatory letter to *Ovids Banquet of Sence* (London, 1595), sig. A2[r].

43. Peacham, *Garden* (1593), sig. Tiii[v].

44. Sidney, *Defense*, p. 12.

45. See Bernard Beckerman, *Shakespeare at the Globe 1599–1609* (New York: Macmillan Co., 1962), p. 129; "The sightlines of the [Elizabethan public] theater also had an effect upon the acting. Essentially they were poor. We are dealing with an aural theater, not a visual one. . . . Gesture for specific communication rather than general reinforcement of the speech was not feasible. For example, the comic actor could not rely on a visual gag."

46. The first quotation is Thomas Kyd, *The Spanish Tragedy* (1586–88), ed. Andrew S. Cairncross (Lincoln: Univ. of Nebraska Press, 1967), 3.2.1; the second is Thomas Heywood, *A Woman Killed with Kindness* (1607), ed. R. W. Van Fossen (Cambridge, Mass.: Harvard Univ. Press, 1961), sc. xvii, l. 222.

47. Thomas Heywood, *An Apology for Actors* (London, 1612), sig. B3[v]; and Sir Thomas Overbury et al., *His Wife with . . . New Newes, and diuers more Characters* (London, 1616), sig. M2[v].

48. Overbury, *Characters*, sig. M2[r]. On comparing actors to orators with respect to delivery, see Cicero, *De Oratore*, I.v.18, I.xxviii.130, II.xlvi.193, and III.lvi.214; Quintilian, *Institutio Oratoria*, XI.iii.73–74, 111–12; Agrippa, *Vanitie*, fol. 32[v]; and Talon, *Rhetorica*, p. 66.

49. Those who argue for a formal or idealized style of Elizabethan acting on the basis of the comparison of orators to actors have not recognized that the medium may be the same, while the styles and ends of the arts

differ: see Joseph, *Elizabethan Acting;* Alfred Harbage, *Theatre for Shakespeare* (Toronto: Univ. of Toronto Press, 1955), pp. 92-118; and Lise-Lone Marker, "Nature and Decorum in the Theory of Elizabethan Acting," *The Elizabethan Theatre II,* ed. David Galloway (n.p.: Macmillan Co. of Canada, 1970), pp. 87-107. To point out the non sequitur is not to say that Elizabethan acting was naturalistic, the view of Marvin Rosenberg in "Elizabethan Actors," *PMLA,* 69 (1954), 915-27. What both schools of critics share, however, is the assumption that Elizabethan acting and theory did not change from the opening of Burbage's Theatre in 1576 to the closing of the theaters in 1642; this assumption is improbable if we consider that in the same length of time, sixty years, acting style and theory have varied remarkably in films.

50. I would agree with Daniel Selzer, in "The Actors and Staging," in *A New Companion to Shakespeare Studies,* ed. Kenneth Muir and S. Schoenbaum (Cambridge: Cambridge Univ. Press, 1971), pp. 35-54, that the Elizabethan acting style must have been generally a "large" or fairly formal one, but one that changed over the period with the playwrights' changing techniques of characterization. He, however, does not treat the concomitant change in acting theory.

51. Edwards, *Damon and Pithias,* sig. Aii[r].

52. Fraunce, *Arcadian Rhetorike,* sig. I7[v].

53. *Faerie Queene,* III.xii.4, in *Spenser: Poetical Works.* Cf. *Passions of the Minde,* sig. I6[v], in which Thomas Wright begins his chapter, "The discouery of passions by externall actions," with the example of "Comedies, where dumbe shewes often expresse the whole matter."

54. *Pierce Penilesse His Supplication to the Divell,* in *The Works of Thomas Nashe,* ed. Ronald B. McKerrow (1904; rpt., London: Sidgwick & Jackson, 1910), I, 212. Cf. John Marston, "To the Reader" of *The Malcontent* (1604), in *The Plays of John Marston,* ed. H. Harvey Wood (Edinburgh: Oliver & Boyd, 1934-39), I, 139, who speaks of his play as "it was presented with the soule of liuely action."

55. "Prologue" to *If This Be Not a Good Play, the Devil Is in It,* in *The Dramatic Works of Thomas Dekker,* ed. Fredson Bowers (Cambridge: Cambridge Univ. Press, 1953-61), III, 122. When Shakespeare speaks generally of the effect of delivery, or "action," in *Lucrece,* ll. 1317-28, he sounds very much like Dekker and the other celebrators of passionate acting: "To see sad sights moves more than hear them told, / For then the eye interprets to the ear / The heavy motion that it doth behold."

56. Quintilian, *Institutio Oratoria,* XI.iii.61-62. See also *Rhetorica ad Herennium,* III.xv.27: "good delivery ensures that what the orator is saying seems to come from his heart."

57. See *Arte of Rhetorique,* sig. ti[v], where Wilson warns that an orator will persuade only if "from his harte" he "fetche his complaintes"; and Wright, *Passions of the Minde,* sigs. M7[v]-M8[r].

58. See Andrew Gurr, "Elizabethan Action," *SP*, 63 (1966), 144–56; his thesis, that Elizabethans thought the orator delivered "real" and the player "feigned" passions, is disproved by Dekker's prologue and Elizabethan rhetoricians: in these cases, both player and orator are supposed to deliver fictional, true emotions.

59. Examples of such Puritan attacks are Stephen Gosson, *The Schoole of Abuse* (London, 1579), and Philip Stubbes, *The Anatomie of Abuses* (London, 1583). See Elbert Thompson's analysis of their arguments in *The Controversy between the Puritans and the Stage* (New York: Henry Holt and Co., 1903). Examples of such defenses are Thomas Lodge, *A Defence of Poetry, Music, and Stage Plaies* (London, 1579), and Sir Philip Sidney, *The Defense of Poesy.*

60. John Greene, *A Refutation of the Apology for Actors* (London, 1615), sig. H4[r].

61. Chettle, *Kind-Heart's Dream,* pp. 35–38.

62. *Euery Man out of His Humour,* in *Ben Jonson,* III, 423. Robert Y. Turner, in *Shakespeare's Apprenticeship,* p. 92, attributes the passionate theory of acting and characterization to the early Shakespeare. About the time of *R2* and *Rom.,* he perceives a change: "Rejecting his rhetorical principle that sound patterns should stimulate feelings in the audience similar to feelings in the speaker. . . . [Shakespeare] devises contortions of feelings in the character without regard for producing comparable responses in the audience" (p. 103). Concentrating on voice and gesture, rather than on speeches of emotion, I would place the change later, around 1600.

63. Marston, "Induction" to *Antonio and Mellida,* in *Plays,* I, 7–8.

64. John Webster, *The White Devil,* in *The Complete Works of John Webster,* ed. F. L. Lucas (London: Chatto & Windus, 1927), I, 192; and George Chapman, "Dedication" to *The Tragedy of Caesar and Pompey,* in *The Plays and Poems of George Chapman,* ed. Thomas Marc Parrott (London: George Routledge & Sons, 1910), I, 341.

65. Abraham Fraunce, in *Arcadian Rhetorike,* sig. H7[r], describes the range of rhetorical voice, from the "delicate tuning of the voyce," to the "voyce . . . more manly, yet diuersly, according to the varietie of passions that are to bee expressed." See also the analysis of rhetorical voice into the "Conversational Tone," the "Tone of Debate," and the "Tone of Amplification," in *Rhetorica ad Herennium,* III.xiii.23–xv.27. Especially pertinent to Kent's second and third voices are the subdivisions of the tone of debate: "In the Tone of Debate are distinguishable the Sustained and the

Broken. The Sustained is full-voiced and accelerated delivery. The Broken Tone of Debate is punctuated repeatedly with short, intermittent pauses, and is vociferated sharply" (III.xii.23).

66. See Arthur Clark, *Thomas Heywood* (Oxford: Basil Blackwell, 1931), pp. 70-79, for Heywood's borrowings from previous defenses and condemnations of plays.

67. Thomas Heywood, *Apology*, sig. B3ʳ. Heywood's *Apology for Actors* was not published until 1612, but E. K. Chambers argues that it may have been written as early as 1607; see *The Elizabethan Stage* (Oxford: Clarendon Press, 1923), IV, 250. The references for the rest of the quotations from Heywood's *Apology* will be in the text.

68. Heywood mentions the acting of Henry V, *Apology*, sig. B4ʳ. The phrasing of my sentence, however, is Sidney's, in the *Defense*, p. 10: the poet's "Idea" works "substantially . . . to bestow a Cyrus upon the world to make many Cyruses."

69. See *Ham.* 2.2.588-605; and Heywood, *Apology*, sigs. G1ᵛ-G2ᵛ.

70. Sidney, *Defense*, p. 10.

71. T. G. [Thomas Gainsford], *The Rich Cabinet* (London, 1616), sig. Q4ʳ.

72. Overbury, *Characters*, sig. M2ᵛ.

73. Quintilian, *Institutio Oratoria*, XI.iii.88-91 and XI.iii.181-84; see also Cicero, *De Oratore*, III.xxvi.101-2.

74. Castiglione, *The Courtier*, sig. E8ʳ.

75. Webster, *The Devil's Law-Case*, in *Complete Works*, II, 236. In his dedication to *Caesar and Pompey*, Chapman similarly says that his style may add to "elocution some assistance to the acceptation and grace of it," in *Plays and Poems*, I, 341.

76. The kisses and embraces occur between Antony and Cleopatra (1.1); Antony and Caesar (2.2); Antony, Caesar, Pompey, and their followers in the drunken dance (2.7); Antony and Cleopatra (3.11); Tyreus and Cleopatra (3.12); Antony and Cleopatra (4.4, 4.8, and 4.15); and Cleopatra, Iras, and Charmian (5.2). Their placing in the play thus reflects not only the passionate indecisiveness of the lovers, but also the political vacillations of the major characters.

CHAPTER 3

.·꠶·.

"To Grow and Bear":
Attitudes toward Language

In *De Inventione Dialectica,* a treatise on invention fundamental to
the sixteenth-century teaching of both rhetoric and logic, Rudolph
Agricola describes thus the purpose of speech: "all speech . . . has
this for its end, that one person make another the sharer of his
mind."[1] Having considered in the first two chapters the nature of
speech, its origins and powers, and the contributions of the body's
language, we now turn to attitudes toward speech: how confident
are Elizabethans that language is a medium capable of achieving its
noble purpose? Agricola's attitude is complex. Successful discourse,
he continues in the same passage, requires three things, each corresponding to the end of one of the arts of language — grammar, rhetoric, and dialectic, respectively: "that the speaker be understood,
that the hearer be eager to listen, and that what is said be rendered
convincingly and be accorded belief." As a result, discourse has
degrees of effectiveness as communication according to Agricola. A
grammarian, for example, may share facts and ideas with a listener
without communicating his values. Only the master of all the arts of
language may share his mind fully; in Agricola's hierarchical
system, he is the dialectician, "who teaches in such a way as to desire
to produce belief by his speech, and by speaking to draw the mind of
the hearer to himself."[2]

In the past two chapters we have also explored the ends to which
Shakespeare uses ideas about language, and the changes that occur
in his dramaturgy as he learns better to turn them to dramatic account. In this chapter we shall see that a consideration of attitudes
toward language will lend credence to what we have already discovered. Shakespeare's characters do not share a single attitude toward
language; nor does Shakespeare develop either faith in words or dis-

trust of them as a major theme of his plays. Instead, attitudes toward language, like ideas about language, help to render characters as individuals in outlook, to convey the values of the distinctive worlds of each play, and to emphasize the dialectic of the story — either the conflicts between characters or the vocal sharing of events and ideas that enable characters to resolve their conflicts. This exploration will lead us to a final statement on the nature of the dramatic medium as Shakespeare and other Elizabethans must generally have understood it. It may aid clarity, however, to anticipate this final statement by looking at two descriptions of effective discourse in Shakespeare's plays and by comparing them with Agricola's theory of discourse.

At the end of *The Comedy of Errors,* after briefly summarizing the events of the play, the Abbess invites all present "to a gossips' feast": "To go with us . . . / And hear at large discoursed all our fortunes" (5.1.395–96). Despite the fact that words have been one of the causes of misunderstanding and conflict in the play — both "Antipholus" and "Dromio" are confusing names that point to more than one person — all the characters agree to talk out the confusion. "With all my heart," the Duke replies, "I'll gossip at this feast" (l. 408). Thus, in this simple way, *The Comedy of Errors* may be said to offer a range of attitudes toward language: from doubt that words always mean what they seem to mean, to faith that further words will resolve the confusion when willing speakers and eager listeners eventually share their minds through language. By analogy, we may say that Shakespeare's plays invite us to such a feast, wherein many characters offer to share their minds with the audience. As in the Abbess's feast, the point in Shakespeare's plays is not to limit our experience to a single interpretation, but to enlarge our knowledge by sharing many perspectives, and to join in the feast by responding to what we feel and learn.

The Abbess's invitation emphasizes the listener; if we turn to another passage, although still one associating speech and sustenance, we may concentrate on the speaker:

> his plausive words
> He scatter'd not in ears, but grafted them
> To grow there and to bear.
>
> (*AWW* 1.2.53–55)

In his description of the eloquence of Bertram's father, the King of *All's Well That Ends Well* includes, however briefly, many of the characteristics of Agricola's theory of discourse. Communication depends not simply on language, but rather on all the elements of discourse: speaker, listener, words, and the effect on the listeners' minds. As with *The Comedy of Errors* or Agricola's theory, a range of attitudes toward language is implied: words may be effective or not, "scatter'd" or "grafted." Most important, however, the King's description brings into focus a love of language that informs all three references we have looked at. Not merely a love of words, this love of language includes a love for the facts and ideas communicated, as well as for the human interaction that language entails. What we shall see in this chapter is the complexity of Elizabethan response to language: however Elizabethans may distrust the confusions of words, the intent of the speaker, and the receptivity of the listener, they nevertheless retain a love of language—the interaction by which a speaker may draw the mind of the listener to himself and share his own thoughts and beliefs with him, the exchange not simply of words but also of ideas that will grow and bear fruit in the minds and actions of others.

Doubtful Words and Trust in Language

Shakespeare's characters express a range of attitudes toward language. Juliet, Cordelia, and Antony, for example, doubt that words can express the depths of love, while Armado, Orlando, and Lear trust that words can.[3] Nor is one group "right" and the other "wrong": in context we respond with some degree of sympathy to the beliefs of all these characters. The current critical debate on Shakespeare's view of language does not help much in elucidating these various attitudes in his characters. One group of critics, trying to determine Shakespeare's view through a close reading of individual plays, argues that Shakespeare anticipates a modern distrust of language, and that his plays bear the mark of his recognizing "the limits of language."[4] Another group, approaching the issue through a study of Shakespeare's historical context, almost universally holds that Shakespeare, like most educated Elizabethans, trusted that words amply express thoughts and feelings and so fully achieve the end of communication between human beings.[5] By looking again at

Shakespeare's plays in their historical context, I hope to show in this section that they reflect the variety of attitudes toward language that Elizabethans held: from doubt that words clearly express ideas, to faith in the expressive power of language. If there is a characteristic Elizabethan attitude toward language, it is not one or the other, but an amalgamation of doubt and trust: many Elizabethans feared that words do not clearly express ideas, and so may deceive people by their ambiguities; at the same time, they also trusted that knowledgeable speakers and listeners could avoid deception and even gain insight from the many unexpected meanings of words.

Before considering Elizabethan attitudes toward language, which is best done by looking at the contrasting views of logicians and rhetoricians, we need to consider a basic principle of verbal expression as Elizabethan writers formulated it. Richard Mulcaster, the English educator, typifies the Elizabethan approach: "The number of things, whereof we write and speak is infinite, the words wherewith we write and speake, be definite and within number. Whereupon we are driuen to vse one, and the same word in verie manie, naie, somtime in verie contrarie senses."[6] Although it is impossible to create a name for every thing or idea that needs expressing, people have overcome the problem by simply and ingeniously decreeing that the finite system of language shall stand for infinite things and thoughts. Borrowing this idea from Aristotle, Elizabethans yet made it their own. In the preface to his logic, Ralph Lever cites his source and then elaborates on Aristotle in ways that have little to do with the philosopher, and a great deal to do with English nationalism and the humanist arts of language:

I see and confesse, that there be *Plura rerum, quam verborum genera,* (that is, moe things, then there are words to expresse things by) and do know withall, that Aristotle founde that want in the Greeke tongue, whiche for finenesse of speache, and store of woordes, farre excelleth all other languages. Yet is there this helpe in speache, that we ofte vse manye wordes to expresse one thing: yea & sometimes one word is vsed to signifie sundry matters. Moreouer, one language boroweth of another, and where there is want, men sometimes deuise newe names and compounded termes. So that after a man hath conceyved anye newe deuise in hys heade, and is desirous to haue the same published, and made common to manye, he findeth euer some shifte, by one meane or other, to make the same knowen.[7]

Lever's optimism in the expressive power of language is not a simple faith. Language as any speaker receives it is incomplete — potentially, but not actually, capable of expressing all one wants to express, a mere starting point for improvisation. Despite acknowledging the limits of language, Lever sees that through some compromises (circumlocution and using one word to express many things) and with a great deal of creativity (compounding, inventing, and borrowing words) people manage to use language to achieve full communication. Finite themselves, human beings reach toward infinity in their thoughts and shape language in their own double image.

The question of attitude toward language is not fully answered, however, by knowing that Elizabethans trusted the expressive potential of language. Full communication is more than potential expressiveness, as Margreta de Grazia recognizes in her discussion of Shakespeare's attitude when she introduces another element: the charity of the speaker. Only the good man speaks well: Elizabethans found support for this belief in the rhetorical theory of Quintilian and in the works of the early humanists, as well as in the biblical theory of language.[8] Besides speaker and medium, we must consider two other elements necessary to communication: the listener and the end to be achieved by the communication. Taking all these into account, we may say that educated Elizabethans were generally skeptical that words are clear and precise, and so an adequate medium for reasoning and arguing; at the same time, they were optimistic that words are rich and expressive, and so an adequate medium for delighting and moving an audience. Although the two attitudes often coexist, we may see the skepticism more clearly in the logicians and the optimism more clearly in the rhetoricians.

"The cause of all controuersie," declares Thomas Wilson in his logic, *The Rule of Reason,* "is either the not well vnderstandyng, or els the wilie vsyng of woordes, that in sence haue double meanyng. Aristotle chiefe scholemaister to all scholers geueth good warnynge that all menne be right ware in anie wise to haue the right vnderstandyng of euerie seuerall worde."[9] The very richness of language becomes a handicap to the logician, who desires clarity in reasoning: words mean too many things at once to convey truth clearly. Wilson is echoing the same passage in Aristotle that Mulcaster and Lever allude to. In *On Sophistical Refutations,* Aristotle explains that be-

cause we use words as symbols for things, we expect what happens
with the words to happen also with the things; since one word may
represent many things, however, linguistic operations are not exactly analogous to real transactions, or even to rational ones. The consequence is inadvertent confusion in thought; and so "those who are
unacquainted with the power of names are the victims of false reasoning, both when they are themselves arguing and when they are
listening to others."[10] Words may express everything there is to express, but for just this reason logicians must distrust them: owing to
the multiple significations of words, a foolish speaker may mislead
himself, and a dishonest speaker may deceive others.

As a consequence of this attitude toward language, Elizabethans
thought one of the main purposes of logic to be the providing of
techniques for overcoming the confusions caused by words; it is especially in this sense that logic to them was an art of language.[11]
Many English writers—Seton, Lever, and Blundeville, for example
—began their logics by discussing several different categories of
terms. "First learne by the Storehouses the force of euery worde that
is in your question: and if there bee woordes of double vnderstanding in it, laye forth their sundrie and diuers significations, leaste the
speaker meane the word in one sense, and the hearer take it in another"; thus Lever explains the use of the categories of terms.[12]
While the first step in rational inquiry is asking a question, the second step is finding out what the question means: the process is one of
distilling the appropriate meaning from all the false and irrelevant
meanings that obscure it. At the beginning of the seventeenth century, Bacon is elaborating a typically Elizabethan conception of
logic when he maintains that many logical operations, including the
use of the predicaments, "are but wise Cautions againste the Am-
biguityes of Speech."[13]

Just as many English logics begin with a discussion of the equivocal nature of terms, many of them end, as do Wilson's, Fenner's, and
Blundeville's, with a discussion of the sophistical fallacies—half of
them fallacies of diction. The fallacies of diction, Wilson explains,
are "deceipthful argumentes, when a doubtfull worde is vsed, or the
kinde of speache is straunge, and maie be taken .ii. waies, and that
the fault is rather in the kind and maner of speaking, then in the
matter or very thing it self."[14] Once one has answers to an inquiry,

one must run another check on the language, in order to make certain that the answers are precise statements of the truth and that one has not been misled by words into falsehoods.

Misleading through words, of course, often characterizes the action of Elizabethan drama. Many are the stage villains and cheats who accomplish their purposes through the use of "doubtful" words, from the vices of the early interludes to Volpone and Mosca. Richard III, in fact, likens himself to "the formal Vice, Iniquity," not because he lies, but because he equivocates: "I moralize two meanings in one word" (*R3* 3.1.82–83). And one of Richard's striking characteristics is his ability to make evil seem good, or at least expedient, through his sophistical words. Thus Richard makes it seem that Anne has caused the deaths of Edward and Henry: "Your beauty was the cause . . . / Your beauty, that did haunt me in my sleep / To undertake the death of all the world" (1.2.121–23). Anne fails to see that her beauty can be blamed for death *only in a manner of speaking*. Fearing the guilt of another death, Anne will not kill Richard. By the way that Richard then phrases her choices—"Take up the sword again, or take up me" (l. 183)—she appears to have only two: murdering Richard or marrying him. Not possessing great moral strength, ignorant of the confusions caused by words, Anne becomes the victim of Richard's false persuasions.

Anne intends not to, but still succumbs to Richard. Because of the ambiguous nature of language, more is required of a speaker and listener than good intentions. What Elizabethan logicians recommend, with the force of a moral imperative, is education: "Therefore those that be good Grammarians, & knowe the propreties of wordes, and are skilfull in the toungwes, can gaily well solute soche errors as be made by the mistakyng of wordes, or by false vnderstanding of phrases, wherof in very deede many heresies, and moche false doctrine haue had their first begynning."[15] Without wisdom in the ways of words, even the well-intentioned listener may be misled, and even the good man may become a bad speaker, causing moral harm.

Although language is not by nature suitably precise to be used in reasoning, it may be made so through art. Making language clear requires, according to Wilson, first, that "all wordes be wel noted according to their natures," and second, that the speaker choose only univocal words—Lever calls them "plainmeaning words" (p. 3)

—or equivocal words that have been precisely defined. Defining a word is restricting it to one clear meaning: "restreigne the largenesse thereof," advises Wilson, "and declare how you will haue it taken."[16] In the mouth of a knowledgeable and cautious speaker, language may be what it is when Fluellen tells Pistol that he must eat the leek: "Yes, certainly, and out of doubt and out of question too, and ambiguities" (*H5* 5.1.45–46).

These English logicians are concerned that people will be drawn into false convictions by their own ignorance of words or by immoral speakers. Even more, they are concerned that confused language will cause unnecessary conflict. This fear finds its way into other writers: unless language is clear, men cannot see through it to the truth of the matter; unless they understand the meaning of the terms in an argument, they cannot resolve their differences. To Montaigne, the result is tragic: "Our speech hath his infirmities and defects, as all things else have. Most of the occasions of this worlds troubles are Grammatical. Our sutes and processes proceed but from the canvasing and debating the interpretation of the Lawes, and most of our wars from the want of knowledge in state-counsellors, that could not clearly distinguish and fully expresse the Covenants, and Conditions of accords, betweene Prince and Prince. How many weighty strifes, and important quarrels, hath the doubt of this one silable, *Hoc*, brought forth in the world?"[17] It is not the evil man but the ignorant man whom Montaigne fears. The French essayist's analysis of the ambiguities of language must have rung true to the people of his century, whose most vicious wars were fought over the varying interpretations of sacred words. Because of "the false appearances, that are imposed vpon vs by words," warns Bacon, and without precise definitions at the beginning of a dispute, "we are sure to end there where wee ought to haue begun, which is in questions & differences about words."[18] Language, which should be the means of drawing men together in society, may be the opposite: an opportunity for discord.

The idea that words may confuse men not intending evil invites development as tragic irony. In a scene in *Julius Caesar*, Cinna the poet is killed because his name has two meanings. When Cinna tells the mob that he is not the conspirator, one of them replies, "It is no matter, his name's Cinna" (3.3.33). The motive is shocking: Cinna dies because of an accident of naming. His fault is not bad actions, not even opposition to the mob. "I am Cinna the poet," Cinna pleads; "I am Cinna the poet" (l. 29). "Tear him for his bad verses," shouts one plebeian; "Pluck but his name out of his heart" (ll. 30–34). The plebeians, violent men, but not as knowingly evil as Richard III, refuse to consider the facts and settle for the name as sufficient reason to kill. Nor is this unfamiliar behavior in the play. With similar techniques, Cassius persuades both Brutus and Casca to join the conspiracy: any man who would bear the title "king" is a tyrant, whom true lovers of freedom must destroy (1.2.150–61; 1.3.72–111); and any bearer of the name "Brutus" should be a slayer of kings (1.2.158–61). The motive of the murderers of Cinna — a confusion of names — thus compels us to reconsider the motives of the "sacrificers" (2.1.166) of Caesar. As even Brutus admits, Caesar is not yet a tyrant in his government. Yet the words Brutus uses allow him to justify Caesar's murder: to crown Caesar will be to "put a sting in him," to make him like the "adder" that "may do danger" (2.1.14–17). The distinguishing differences between the adder and the man — volition and moral sense — are obscured by Brutus's false analogy. And with Caesar's death, not even history can answer the question that Cinna's murder forces on us: what if Caesar the king would no more be Caesar the tyrant than Cinna the poet is Cinna the conspirator? In the first scene of *King Lear*, the old King, similarly confused by words, asks Cordelia, "what can you say to draw / A third more opulent than your sisters'?" (1.1.85–86). Lear thinks that he is asking, "Do you love me?" Cordelia's answer — "Nothing, my lord" (1.1.87) — addresses Lear's actual request: to flatter, to misuse words and reason by obscuring realities and fussing over ignorance. In neither the scene from *Julius Caesar* nor in this one from *King Lear* is language an instrument of evil in the hands of the consciously deceptive; in both scenes, however, words ensnare those who willfully or weakly refuse the moral responsibility to know.

   In Elizabethan writers, alongside the fear that language may deceive men into unintended conflict runs the conviction that human understanding may resolve it. Thomas Wilson vividly describes the conflict that may arise from words, and the peace that comes with insight into their many meanings: "Of no one thyng riseth so moche controuersie, as of the doubtfulnesse, and double takyng of a worde. Scholars dispute, wise menne fall out, Lawiers agree not, Preachers waxe hotte, gentlemen striue, the people mutter, good men giue counsaile, women haue their wordes, this man affirmeth, thother denieth and yet at length, the double meanyng being ones knowen (when all thynges are quiete) endes the whole matter."[19] The controversy over doubtful words that Montaigne, Bacon, and Wilson describe has extraordinary dramatic potential: the seemingly insoluble problem, the irony of unintended conflict, and the surprising resolution that has been there, unrecognized, all the time.

Nor is this dramatic potential lost on Shakespeare: as Montaigne observed generally of mankind, many of the troubles of Shakespeare's men and women are grammatical. In *Richard II,* when York reports a conspiracy against the new king—his own son, Aumerle, a traitor in it, deserving death—Henry praises York profusely: "O loyal father of a treacherous son! / Thou sheer, immaculate, and silver fountain" (5.3.60-61)—from which flows muddy Aumerle. We, however, are made uncomfortable by the change of referents of the words "loyal" and "treacherous" so soon after Richard's deposition; we have not forgotten York's own betrayal of a king. When the Duchess rushes in to beg "pardon" for Aumerle, the issue of doubtful words becomes explicit. York reverses her meaning—"Speak it in French, King, say '*pardonne moy*' " (5.3.119)—and the Duchess turns on her husband:

> Dost thou teach pardon pardon to destroy?
> Ah, my sour husband, my hard-hearted lord,
> That sets the word itself against the word!
> Speak "pardon" as 'tis current in our land.
>
> (ll. 120-23)

Accusing her husband of equivocation, loyal to the true English meaning, the Duchess succeeds in her plea to the King. Nevertheless, we can see the effects of national division continuing in these verbal disputes. Setting one meaning of a word against another, one member of a family against another, the conflict epitomizes the incestuous destruction of civil war. Hovering over the scene is our recognition that one equivocal word will cause Henry problems the rest of his life: the word "king," signifying both Richard and Henry. From the ambiguous sentence uttered to Exeter—"Have I no friend will rid me of this living fear?" (*R2* 5.4.2)—to John's cold sophistries at Gaultree Forest, from York's request of his son's death with a pun to Falstaff's wordplay entertaining the prodigal heir, equivocation in

jest and earnest is a staple of Shakespeare's dramatization of the
troubled times of Henry IV. Even Henry's death is an occasion for
doubtful words; but in this case we hear, finally, a resolution into
clarity, the peace resulting from ambiguity resolved. Having learned
that he first fainted in the Jerusalem Chamber, Henry returns there
to die:

> Laud be to God! even there my life must end.
> It hath been prophesied to me many years,
> I should not die but in Jerusalem,
> Which vainly I suppos'd the Holy Land.
> But bear me to that chamber, there I'll lie,
> In that Jerusalem shall Harry die.
>
> (2H4 4.5.235–40)

Unable to fulfill his promise to wash off Richard's blood in the Holy
Land, Henry yet dies in Jerusalem. With the explanation of the double meaning of "Jerusalem" comes recognition and acceptance of
death, and the hope of divine forgiveness for the troubled king. Far
from limiting the dramatist, the Elizabethan distrust of the clarity of
words freed him to develop in a complex way the ethical problems of
history and the moral dilemmas of tragedy.

Distrust of language, however, was not the dramatist's only op-
tion. Unlike the logicians, who sought to make words univocal, Elizabethan rhetoricians saw no need to change the nature of language
to suit their ends. Instead, they studied to take advantage of what is
already there: richness of meaning. In his rhetoric, Thomas Wilson
does stop, as he did in his logic, to discuss the dangers of doubtful
words: "Sometymes a doubt is made, vpon some woorde or sentence,
when it signifieth diuerse thynges, or maie diuersly be taken, wher-
upon ful oft ariseth muche contencion." He is considering judicial
rhetoric, and he continues with an attack on immoral lawyers, those
who, "rather then faile, . . . will make doubtes often tymes, where
no doubt should be at all."[20] But generally, as Wilson shows in his
list of arguments to be used in interpreting laws, the ambiguity of
language is a benefit to the lawyer: the many meanings of the words
of the law make it flexible enough to fit a specific case, and humane
enough to bring about an equitable settlement. This advantage of
the ambiguity of language we shall return to in the chapter on *The*

Merchant of Venice, for Portia's success at the trial depends on the fact that laws may have many meanings.

Even more in the rhetoricians' discussion of figurative language, we may see their optimism about the expressiveness of language. Men invented tropes, Elizabethans theorized, to make up for the scarcity of names. "When learned and wise menne gan firste to enlarge their tongue," Thomas Wilson explains, ". . . they founde full ofte muche wante of wordes to set out their meanynge. And therfore remembrynge thinges of like nature vnto those wherof they spake: they vsed suche wordes to expresse their minde, as were most like vnto other."[21] Wilson finds in tropes, especially in metaphors based on the likeness between two things, a means of expressing the idea that would otherwise remain unnamed. He speaks with the best rhetorical authorities behind him: Aristotle mentions in his rhetoric that metaphors "give names to things that have none"; and Quintilian surmises that metaphor "adds to the copiousness of language by the interchange of words and by borrowing, and finally succeeds in accomplishing the supremely difficult task of providing a name for everything."[22] When words seem unable to express his rancor after the drunken quarrel, Cassio turns to metaphor: "O thou invisible spirit of wine, if thou hast no name to be known by, let us call thee devil!" (*Oth.* 2.3.281–83). This much Elizabethan rhetoricians and logicians share: they both believe that language expresses everything because we use one word to signify many things.

Tropes, however, have an advantage over other forms of new names: they teach their own meaning. Cicero had noted that tropes are easily accessible to everyone's understanding: "when something that can scarcely be conveyed by the proper term is expressed metaphorically, the meaning we desire to convey is made clear by the resemblance of the thing that we have expressed to the word that does not belong."[23] Only the metaphor "devil" expresses the disappointment Cassio has in himself because it unites two meanings in one word: the urge to drink and the moral consequences.

In the case of tropes, the poets follow the rhetoricians' lead. In *The Arte of English Poesie,* Puttenham tells the would-be poet that metaphor makes "the word more significatiue," that synecdoche "encombers the minde with a certaine imagination what it may be that is meant, and not expressed."[24] Tropes express what is otherwise inexpressible because they lead the audience, on the bridge of a relationship, from a known to an unknown thing. When Cleopatra demands of Antony, "If it be love indeed, tell me how much" (*Ant.* 1.1.14), Antony knows enough not to set limits on his love by expressing it: "There's beggary in the love that can be reckon'd" (1.1.15). But when Cleopatra takes him at his words—"I'll set a bourn how far to be belov'd" (1.1.16)—Antony finds a hyperbolic figure to say what ordinary words will not: "Then must thou needs find out new heaven, new earth" (l. 17). Faced with the inexpressible in human anger, horror, grief, and love, the characters in this play speak of "The shirt of Nessus" (4.12.43), "time . . . at his period" (4.14.107), the "darkling . . . shore o' th' world" (4.15.10–11), and "fire and air" (5.2.289). Even if tropes are obscure, the difficulty in grasping them adds to our appreciation of the vastness of human thought and feeling: the imagination has cast itself beyond its ordinary bounds, and we have thought and named what we have never thought or named before. If the poet must give "to aery nothing / A local habitation and a name," tropes are the means in language that most often enable him to do so. "As figures be the instruments of ornament in euery language," explains Puttenham, "so be they also in a sorte abuses or rather trespasses in speach, because they passe the ordinary limits of common vtterance, and be occupied of purpose to deceiue the eare and also the minde, drawing it from plainnesse and simplicitie to a certaine doublenesse, whereby our talke is the more guilefull & abusing."[25] The richness in meaning of language that causes confusion for the logician provides the poet with clarity: through the double meanings of tropes, he may lead his audience from the familiar to the scarcely imaginable. If Elizabethan rhetoricians and poets recognize the limits of language, they do so only to exult in overcoming them.

The rhetoricians find ambiguous words to be essential for communication, not only in legal interpretation and in tropes, but also in wit and wordplay. The doubtful words that must be excluded from logical arguments, according to Thomas Wilson, must be courted in rhetorical persuasions: "Wordes doubtfully spoken, geue often iust occasion of muche laughter. Ah (quoth a certain man) do you se yonder felowe, & do you knowe him? Yea, (quod the other) I knowe him verye well. I shall tell you sir (saide the gentilman) there is not a manne of greater vnderstandinge within this Citye then he is. Tushe it is not so (quod he). No? (said the other) marcke well the bought of his legge, and you shall see hys vnderstandinge worthye to be compared with the beste, and greatest of them all."[26] This sort of wit depends on our surprised recognition that words mean more than we thought: where we had expected one meaning, another magically appears in its place. Because it makes the familiar seem fresh, such ambiguity calls back the child in us, when we wondered at each new word and its meaning, and relied on intuition more often than information as a guide to experience. This ability to see the unexpected meaning is a special one according to Crassus, Cicero's spokesman in *De Oratore:* "the power to divert the force of a word in a sense quite different from that in which other folk understand it, seems to indicate a man of talent."[27]

The grim fallacies of the logician thus become the verbal games of the rhetorician. Wilson's catalogue of the places of wit, borrowed from Cicero and Quintilian, includes not only play upon doubtful words (equivocation), but also wit from change in spelling or pronunciation (the fallacy of accent), wit from interpretation of a word (equivocation), and wit from a literal understanding of another's words (equivocation or ambiguity).[28] Launce engages in the last sort of wit in *Two Gentlemen of Verona:*

> *Speed.* How now, Signior Launce? what news with your mastership?
> *Launce.* With my master's ship? why, it is at sea.
> *Speed.* Well, your old vice still: mistake the word.
>
> (3.1.280–84)

Our pleasure in mistaking a word is only possible because language is ambiguous, and because the speaker releases it from its ordinary business of clarity. "The essence of all wit," Quintilian explains, "lies in the distortion of the true and natural meaning of words."[29] Wit is thus sophistry rescued from the ignorant and villainous, intended not to convince but to delight.

Even witty use of the many meanings of words, however, has its dangers. Elizabethan boys in grammar school must have given their complete attention, although for the wrong reason, to Quintilian's discussion of "language to which perverted usage has given an obscene meaning": "take, for example, phrases such as *ductare exercitus* and *patrare bellum,* which were employed by Sallust in their old and irreproachable sense, but, I regret to say, cause amusement in certain quarters to-day."[30] In schoolmasterly fashion Quintilian shakes his head over the many good words gone bad. He has an improbable ally in Doll Tearsheet, who loses her temper at Pistol's usurpation of the title "captain": "A captain! God's light, these villains will make the word as odious as the word 'occupy,' which was an excellent good word before it was ill sorted" (2H4 2.4.147-50). Words, it seems, like prodigal sons, can be corrupted by the company they keep.

Quintilian fears the word with obscene significance that may slip unnoticed into a sentence and take control away from the speaker: "But you will find, unless you exercise the greatest care, that there are a number of persons who take pleasure in putting an indecent interpretation on words. . . . Nay, an obscene meaning may be extracted even from words which are as far removed from indecency as possible. . . . But if this point of view be accepted, it will be risky to say anything at all."[31] "To see this age!" sighs Feste in *Twelfth Night*, "A sentence is but a chev'ril glove to a good wit. How quickly the wrong side may be turn'd outward!" (3.1.11-13). Viola agrees — "They that dally nicely with words may quickly make them wanton" (ll. 14-15) — and Feste immediately takes up the challenge, exploring the sexual implications of her words, proving that it were better his sister had no name, since he who dallies with her name may make his sister wanton. Words, after all, are "wanton" because they are habitually joined to more than one thing, and so Feste assumes a position like Quintilian's, fearing to say anything at all: "words are grown so false, I am loath to prove reason with them" (3.1.24-25). The play with doubtful words in Shakespeare's middle comedies stimulates a delight in confusion analogous to that issuing from the comic confusions of plot: in *Twelfth Night*, for example, Olivia wantonly takes Sebastian for her husband because he is Cesario's "homonym" — he looks and sounds the same.

In rhetorical theory, wit is thus a communication, like praise or persuasion, that involves speaker, medium, and listener. Quintilian advises that wit must be appropriate to the speaker's topic; it must contain no obscenity; and it must show respect for the audience. If the play on words of the speaker is unintended or inappropriate, he will be regarded as foolish, not witty. If his jokes are at the expense of the audience, not at his own expense, he will seem inelegant.[32] Guided by Quintilian's observations, we may see that the witty exchanges of Shakespeare's characters fall into classes according to the speaker's knowledge of his medium and his relation to his audience. A foolish speaker, who does not know the double meanings of his own words, may face a witty audience, who perceive the unintended meanings. The actors of the Nine Worthies in *Love's Labor's Lost* and the constable Elbow in *Measure for Measure* are such speakers, while the aristocrats hearing them out are such audiences. In a second type of exchange, a cynical fool may use his knowledge of words to trick the audience into appearing foolish. Feste, Lavache, and the fool in *King Lear* are such speakers. Feste, in fact, refuses to be called the Lady Olivia's "fool": "I am indeed not her fool, but her corrupter of words" (*TN* 3.1.35–36). In a final type of exchange, speaker and audience, equally sensitive to ambiguities, may share the insight that comes from the unintended meanings of words. Into this category fall the many pairs of equivocating friends in Shakespeare's plays, those such as the Princess and Boyet in *Love's Labor's Lost*, Romeo and Mercutio in *Romeo and Juliet*, and Rosalind and Celia in *As You Like It*.

In all these types of exchanges, wit exercises the generosity and appreciation of speakers and listeners because it requires them to welcome the abundant meanings of words. When Hippolyta worries that the mechanicals presenting the play "can do nothing in this kind" (*MND* 5.1.88), Theseus reassures her:

> The kinder we, to give them thanks for nothing.
> Our sport shall be to take what they mistake;
> And what poor duty cannot do, noble respect
> Takes it in might, not merit.
>
> (5.1.89–92)

What if they do not give the gift they intend, argues Theseus, when the desire to give and a gift are there? Part of what the mechanicals mistake is the language of their play, and the aristocrats take delight in perceiving the appropriateness of the unintended meanings. At the end of the play, the mechanicals show their own generosity: they are as pleased as if their tragedy had elicited tears, not laughter. Thus, if the speaker is to be generous, he must realize that wit derives from the whole process of communication, not simply from his own creativity. "A jest's prosperity lies in the ear / Of him that hears it," Rosaline tells Berowne, "never in the tongue / Of him that makes it" (*LLL* 5.2.861–63). If the audience is to be generous, they must appreciate the insight that wit gives them, even when it is a revelation of their own foolishness. Malvolio criticizes Olivia's pleasure in Feste's wit, and Olivia retorts, "O, you are sick of self-love, Malvolio, and taste with a distemper'd appetite. To be generous, guiltless, and of free disposition, is to take those things for bird-bolts that you deem cannon-bullets" (*TN* 1.5.90–93). Insofar as it is civil and gracious, wit consequently takes on a serious purpose. After discussing some of the classical principles of wit from Cicero and Quintilian, Castiglione makes this fine distinction: "But because those doubtfull wordes haue a pretie sharpeness of wit in them, it appeareth . . . that they rather prouoke a man to wonder than to laugh."[33] Wit evokes wonder by enabling us to appreciate the abundance of meaning in language as a gift unlooked for.

At its best, wit also surprises us into fresh perceptions. If nothing more, we take back from this holiday of language the knowledge that we must watch our words carefully, or they will wantonly beget their own illicit meanings and prove us fools. Ideally, the unexpected meaning jolts us out of our mechanical habits of language, and so out of our equally mechanical habits of thought. In the fool's equivocations in *King Lear*, we can see this process at work:

> *Fool.* Thou canst tell why one's nose stands i' th' middle on 's face?
> *Lear.* No.
> *Fool.* Why, to keep one's eyes of either side 's nose, that what a man
>   cannot smell out, he may spy into.
> *Lear.* I did her wrong.
>
> (1.5.19–24)

The fool's wordplay presses out new knowledge from Lear's grief and sets the old King seeking for yet other new meanings. Wit takes our ordinary meanings from us, and allows us to discover the freedoms of questioning our assumptions and choosing new meanings. By this means it redeems us from our linguistic defects—from our willingness to hear only our own meaning, from our careless speaking of the inappropriate word, and from our preference for the old mechanical phrases over the fresh ones that require us to think. Wordplay forces us to recognize that even in our own speech we make ourselves part of a human community, which listened to will provide us insight. Gonzalo, the old man in *The Tempest* willing to play the fool, is also willing to see miracles on the desert island and to hear unexpected significance in the words of Sebastian:

> *Gon.* When every grief is entertain'd that's offer'd,
>   Comes to th' entertainer —
> *Seb.* A dollar.
> *Gon.* Dolor comes to him indeed, you have spoken truer than you
>   purpos'd.
> *Seb.* You have taken it wiselier than I meant you should.
>
> (2.1.16–22)

Wit takes man's foolish habit of confusing names with things, and generously turns it to the service of truth.

The Elizabethans' fear of wily sophistries and their delight in wordplay thus arise from the same source: a fascination with "doubtful" words. "Yea, so significant are our Words," crows Richard Carew in his praise of the English language, "that amongst them sundry single ones serve to express divers things; as by the word *Bill* is meant a Weapon, a Scrowle, and a Bird's beak; by *Grave* may be understood, sober, burial-place, and to carve; and so by light, marke, match, file, sore, and pray, the Semblables."[34] Carew continues with illustrations of the wonderful possibilities of meaning in English sentences, citing the letter having one meaning with one set of punctuation, an entirely different meaning with another set, which Thomas Wilson had used in his logic to exemplify the "ambiguitee . . . when the construccion bringeth error,"[35] and which Nicholas Udall had originally composed for his witty comedy, *Ralph Roister Doister*. How close to each other are the mean sophistries of the vice and the free disposition of the wit may be seen in Falstaff, whose equivocations strike us as self-serving and delightful at once.

Just as sentimentality and cynicism are often but two sides of the same personality, so the Elizabethans' distrust of the clarity of language and their faith in its expressiveness turn out to be related parts of the same tendency. This unity of two seeming opposites is most clear in the characteristic style of the period. It is obvious that the Elizabethan taste for endless variation, amplification, circumlocutions, and synonyms is a result of delight in the expressiveness of words. But these stylistic devices illustrate, as well, the doubt that an idea will be communicated unless it is held in by a hedge of words, as the Elizabethan garden was held in its tame and artful state by

the inevitable hedge and bowers. "Restreigne the largeness" of meaning in a word, Wilson had suggested, "and declare how you will
haue it taken." The remedy for confusion caused by words is more
words.

The ample Elizabethan style, the wit, and the sophistry may still
delight us. More limited to the age, but showing the same faith in
the richness of language and the same distrust of its clarity, are the
ubiquitous verbal puzzles: sentences read forward to mean one
thing, read backward to mean the opposite, puns, riddles, codes,
and acrostics. Such a love of the capacity of language to both puzzle
and astound must have led Shakespeare to include the acrostic
forming Titania's name in the speech where she woos Bottom (*MND*
3.1.153–57). In addition, such a paradoxical faith and distrust allowed the prophecies of oracles to serve in Elizabethan logics as examples of ambiguity and in Elizabethan stories and plays as a means
of resolving conflict with a neat and surprising insight. Even the
seeming clarity of Apollo's oracle in *The Winter's Tale* is properly
ambiguous: "Hermione is chaste, Polixenes blameless, Camillo a
true subject, Leontes a jealous tyrant, his innocent babe truly begotten, and the King shall live without an heir, if that which is lost be
not found" (3.2.132–36).

In Robert Greene's *Pandosto,* Shakespeare's source, the oracle, an
exception to the general rule, means simply what it seems to mean,
and only the Princess is found. Shakespeare closely follows the word-
ing of the oracle, except for the names; but he does change the
story, with the result that the same words, unambiguous in *Pandosto,* are richly ambiguous in *The Winter's Tale.*[36] It is Paulina who
leads us to recognize the many meanings of "that which is lost," for
she continually reminds Leontes that not only Perdita, but also his
son, his wife, Paulina's husband, and the friendship of Camillo and
Polixenes were lost through his jealousy. While Leontes was assuming only one meaning to the oracle, the finding of his lost heir, the
providential universe was arranging an outcome to accommodate
many meanings. By the end of the play, the audience has been
shown the restoration of Perdita, a "son" in Florizel, Hermione,
Polixenes, and even, in Camillo, a husband for Paulina. That words
mean many things at once may be a happy confusion: the richness of
language may remind us, as it does in *The Winter's Tale,* that truth
has as many faces as falsehood. The Elizabethan playwright may

thus have been skeptical, like Sebastian, that words will always convey what he intends; but he may also have hoped with Gonzalo that words will convey much more, that one may speak truer than he purposed and be taken wiselier than he meant.

The Elizabethan Love of Words: Res et Verba

Elizabethans loved words. We have only to think of Lyly's piles of proverbs, Jonson's biting catalogues of insults, and Sidney's exuberant, alliterative amplifications on love in Arcadia to know that this is true. The love of words shows itself in more than style of language: in the many books on the arts of language, in the proliferation of dictionaries, in the speculation on the history of English, even in the sermons, in which preachers like Bishop Jewel and, later, John Donne pressed the last bit of significance out of a dozen words of holy text before enthusiastic congregations who stamped their feet in appreciation.

The sixteenth-century passion for language is so characteristic of the culture that it is difficult not to see its implications everywhere. Indeed, historians of literature have argued that the humanists' attention to the language of the classics, rather than to their stories and spirit, resulted in the death of the Latin they sought to preserve; that the verbal excess, as well as exuberance, of Elizabethan styles is to be explained by their love of words; that Shakespeare's concern for language caused him to write plays about it; and that Bacon, at the beginning of the seventeenth century, gave impetus to the plain style and science at once in his revolutionary idea that one must love things and not words.[37] If Elizabethans did care for words more than sense or story (the assumption on which these conclusions depend) then we are hard put to explain the achievements of their literature, and we have no explanation at all for one aspect of Shakespeare's plays: the satire aimed at characters like Armado, Osric, and Parolles, who love words for themselves.

That this interpretation of the Elizabethan love of words descends to us from the seventeenth-century writers who rejected it should make us suspect it the more. In The History of the Royal Society (1667), Thomas Sprat congratulates the members on their "constant Resolution, to reject all the amplifications, digressions, and swellings of style: to return back to the primitive purity and shortness, when men deliver'd so many *things,* almost in an equal number of *words.*"[38] What he is rejecting is the literary style of the previous century, the amplitude, gorgeousness, and swelling periods of Elizabethan writings. All he will grant to English thinkers before Bacon is philology: by their love of language, they rescued the ancients and gave modern scientists a place to start. In the same spirit, in a poem prefacing Sprat's *History,* Abraham Cowley praises Bacon — and himself — for overthrowing the idol of their ancestors:

> From Words, which are but Pictures of the Thought,
> (Though we our Thoughts from them perversly drew)
> To Things, the Minds right Object, he it brought.

Remembering the Elizabethan advances in mathematics and the technical sciences, the tumble of knowledge in any good Elizabethan period, and the moral seriousness — even the moral playfulness — of the best literature, we may pause at Cowley's satisfaction in the progress of his age. Were Elizabethans as certain as Sprat and Cowley that they loved words alone?

Not at all. The origin of the Elizabethan love of words lay in the humanist education, which was indeed dominated by the languages and the arts of language. "I would I had bestow'd that time in the tongues that I have in fencing, dancing, and bear-baiting," mourns Sir Andrew in *Twelfth Night;* "O had I but follow'd the arts!" (1.3.92–94). But this care for language was fostered by humanist educators for a purpose that Sir Andrew does not perceive: the preservation of knowledge and, even more, the making of wise and virtuous adults from young students. Erasmus, the most influential propounder of this scheme of education, explains the principle entailed: "Language, indeed, is not simply an end in itself, as we see when we reflect that through its neglect whole disciplines have been lost, or, at least, corrupted."[39] The reason that studying a language is part of education (as Vives, Erasmus's contemporary and another ardent educator, sees) is to give the young a chance at the ideas in it:

> So far we have dealt with the knowledge of languages, which are the gates of all sciences and arts, at all events, those languages in which the works of great minds are handed down to us. . . . But let those who study remember, that if nothing is added to their knowledge by

the study of language, they have only arrived at the gates of knowledge. . . . And that no language is in itself worth the trouble of learning, if nothing is sought beyond the linguistic aspect. Rather let students gain as much of the language as will enable them to penetrate to those facts and ideas, which are contained in these languages, like beautiful and valuable things are locked up in treasuries.[40]

One studies a language to learn what is expressed in it. The humanist ideal is not love of words alone, but love of *res et verba,* words and the facts, ideas, and truths that come from them.[41]

The ideal does not degenerate in the sixteenth century in England. In *A Ritch Storehouse* by Johann Sturm, translated by Thomas Browne in 1570, we are reminded of this ideal of humanist education: "Now in reading we ought specially to follow the same order, which we vse in writing and speaking: that first, we care for things and matter: then after for words."[42] In the 1580s, the English educator, Richard Mulcaster, is still requiring that a main purpose of grammar school be "the understanding of writers," to which the study of language is subordinated: "grammar helpeth to the knowledge of tungs, whereby we vnderstand the arguments hid in them."[43] If the student stops with his grammar and does not continue to moral Seneca, patriotic Cicero, and pious Vergil, he has stopped as short of knowledge as if he had not begun his studies.

When Erasmus divides all knowledge into two categories—knowledge of *res* and knowledge of *verba*—it is the first that is the more important to him. This does not mean that words are to be ignored. Quite the contrary: "They are not to be commended who, in their anxiety to increase their store of truths, neglect the necessary art of expressing them. For ideas are only intelligible to us by means of the words which describe them; wherefore defective knowledge of language reacts upon our apprehension of the truths expressed." If we do not understand words, we will not understand ideas because we acquire them through words. And so, Erasmus continues, a love of words is justified only by a love of ideas: "No one is so apt to lose himself in verbal arguments as the man who boasts that facts, not words, are the only things that interest him. This goes to prove that true education includes what is *best* in both kinds of knowledge."[44] The modern emphasis on scientific facts, as Erasmus could have foretold, has not made communication of knowledge any easier: the inarticulate lovers of facts alone still present vague ideas in specious arguments. According to Tudor humanists, one must love words *because* one loves facts and ideas, in order to get the ideas straight and express them precisely. "Many not perceiuing the nigh and necessary coniunction of these two precious Iewels," observes Henry Peacham, "doe eyther affect fynenesse of speeche, and neglect the knowledge of thinges, or contrarywise couet vnderstanding, & contemne the arte of Eloquence. . . . The one sorte of these speake much to small purpose, and the other (though they be wise) are not able aptly to express their meaning."[45] The speaker who loves only words has nothing to say; the speaker who loves only things has no way to tell his knowledge. Loving both, the speaker becomes the ideal Renaissance man, wise and eloquent.

We misunderstand Ascham, who is often advanced as the spokesman for the Elizabethan addiction to words, if we do not place him in this humanist context. The English educator is not praising words above matter; he is praising words as the major instruments to knowledge and virtue:

> Ye know not, what hurt ye do to learning, that care not for wordes, but for matter, and so make a deuorse betwixt the tong and the hart. For marke all aiges: looke vpon the whole course of both the Greeke and Latin tongue, and ye shall surelie finde, whan apte and good wordes began to be neglected, and properties of those two tonges to be confounded, than also began ill deedes to spring: strange maners to oppresse good orders, newe and fond opinions to striue with olde and trewe doctrine, first in Philosophie, and after in Religion; right iudgement of all thinges to be peruerted, so vertue with learning is contemned, and studie left of.[46]

Ascham thinks that words are neglected at the risk of anarchy and damnation, but only because knowledge of words leads to more important knowledge and so to virtue. Ascham's narrowness shows itself in his religious bias: "Stoickes, Anabaptistes, and Friers: with Epicures, Libertines and Monkes, being most like in learning and life, are no fonder and pernicious in their opinions, than they be rude and barbarous in their writinges."[47] But there is nothing narrow in his ideal. Those who do not love words, he argues, will never love ideas because they will never perceive them clearly; nor will they be moral, for moral action comes from hard thought and knowledge, not simply from intuition. For Tudor humanists, speech, truth, and right action are linked in a generative process: knowledge of one stage opens the way for progress at the next stage.

Even Bacon, in fact, in his passage on the dangers of loving words alone, is expressing the humanist ideal with only a slight change of emphasis:

> Here therefore, [is] the first distemper of learning, when men studie words, and not matter. . . . It seemes to me that Pigmalions frenzie is a good embleme or portraiture of this vanitie: for wordes are but the Images of matter, and except they haue life of reason and inuention: to fall in loue with them, is all one, as to fall in loue with a Picture. But yet notwithstanding, it is a thing not hastily to be condemned, to cloath and adorne the obscuritie even of Philosophie it selfe, with sensible and plausible elocution. For hereof we haue great examples in *Xenophon, Cicero, Seneca, Plutarch,* and of *Plato* also in some degree.[48]

It is an acute irony that the members of the Royal Society rejected the style of language of the previous generation on the basis of one of that generation's favorite ideas.

Having defined the Elizabethan love of words further, what can we say about the implications for the history of literature? The love of words as instruments of knowledge encouraged in the second generation of English humanists a rage of translation; as they poured the knowledge of ancient authors into their own English words, Latin became less important as the learned language. The philosophy of education encouraged the many expressive Elizabethan styles of language, but equally important to the forms taken by Elizabethan literature is the love of exotic facts and ideas: sentences turn into dictionaries of words and encyclopedias of knowledge. The best Elizabethan literature still delights us because we enjoy in it the quick movement of ideas and the full development of story revealed in the amplifications, digressions, and swelling periods. For Shakespeare, the man who loved words alone became a favorite character, but one to be mocked by the wiser sort in his plays: it is the dearth of knowledge in Armado, Osric, and Parolles, as well as their multitudinous words, that makes them splendid fools.

Elizabethan drama, moreover, has a special model for the humanist philosophy because the educators had expressed their ideas in dialogues and dramatized debates. Erasmus devotes a whole dialogue to the ideal of *res et verba* in *The Colloquies:*

> *Beatus.* Greetings to Boniface.
> *Boniface.* Greetings and more greetings to Beatus. But I wish we were each what we're called—you rich and I handsome.
> *Beatus.* So you think it's unimportant to have a splendid name?
> *Boniface.* Very unimportant indeed unless the substance be added.
> *Beatus.* But many mortals feel otherwise.
> *Boniface.* They may be mortals, but I don't think they're men.

The dialogue begins with a pleasant playing on the names of the characters that leads naturally to Erasmus's first point: words are not things, names do not necessarily reflect the characteristics of the people behind them, and so words and names are relatively unimportant. These witticisms eventually bring Beatus and Boniface to some earnest conclusions:

> *Beatus.* But if man is a rational animal, how extremely unreasonable it is that in bodily comforts (a more accurate name than "goods") and in external things granted and snatched away by the whim of Fortune, we should prefer the substance to the name; in the true goods of the mind, should make more of the name than of the reality.
> *Boniface.* A ridiculous choice, by Hercules, if you consider it.[49]

Here they puzzle over the facts of human materialism: that men prefer wealth to the reputation for it, but a good reputation to goodness itself. In high-minded fashion, the boys decide to prefer realities to words in all things, but especially in "the true goods of the mind." Erasmus's dialogue does not teach neglect of words: the schoolboy is learning his Latin words by reading them, and Erasmus helps the student along by his own delight in wordplay. Instead, the dialogue teaches that one must seek the realities behind words, and that one must care only for words that express truths.

The same point is made by Vives in one of his schoolboy dialogues, *"Educatio."* In this dialogue, a rude young nobleman, Grympherantes, who claims that he is "better" than others, is told by an older man, Flexibulus, that he does not have true knowledge: "The circumstance that you do not understand the significance of words leads you far from the knowledge of truth." After they have proved false Grympherantes' first definition of "good" as "being the offspring of good parents," Flexibulus, in humanist fashion, begins to teach the young man the meaning of the word in order that he may know what the thing itself is and so aspire to it: "This, therefore, is not yet known to thee, what it is to be good, and yet you talk about what being 'better' means." Having discarded "worldly goods" as a definition, as did Beatus and Boniface, they choose as a proper definition the true goods of the mind:

> *Flex.* Is there not something good in a keen intellect, a wise, mature judgment, whole and sound; in a varied knowledge about all kinds of great and useful affairs; in wisdom; and in carrying into practice these qualities; in determination; in dexterity in pursuing one's business. What do you say of these things?
> *Grym.* The very names of these qualities seem to me beautiful and magnificent. So much more are the things themselves great!
> *Flex.* Well, then, what shall we say of wisdom, what of religion, piety towards God, to one's country, parents, dependants, of justice, temperance, liberality, magnanimity, equability of mind towards calamity in human affairs, and brave minds in adversity?[50]

By the end of the dialogue, Flexibulus has taught Grympherantes a word, "good," and its meaning; he has also taught him that he is not particularly good, despite his title, and that he must seek to become so. The dialogue dramatizes the progress of a humanist education, from words to things, from speech to knowledge to moral action, especially since, in the remaining dialogues, Grympherantes is a pleasant young man, eager to learn more. Flexibulus, "an instrument for bending or changing," lives up to his name. And Grympherantes, "one who reveals rubbish," has changed: having studied the name for it, he is on his way to becoming "good."

These two dialogues are remarkably similar in form and content to some of the Tudor interludes, perhaps because most writers of the early interludes were part of the humanist circle. For example, the main action of the earliest extant interlude, Henry Medwall's *Fulgens and Lucres,* which was performed at Cardinal Morton's household, where Sir Thomas More grew up, and later was published by John Rastell, the husband of More's sister, is a debate between Lucres's two suitors, Publius Cornelius and Gaius Flaminius, on which is "the more noble man."[51] Lucres decides on this method of choosing a husband because she does not trust the method of ordinary wooing, the "dyssemblynge nowadaye / There is conuayed vnder wordes gaye" (I.475-76). The debate opens with Cornelius, like Vives's Grympherantes, advancing himself as "noble" because he has noble ancestors and worldly goods. Flaminius refutes Cornelius by proving that he does not understand what "noblenes" means, and by offering his own definition: "Nay the title of noblenes wyll not ensue / . . . But it groweth of longe continued vertu" (II.642-44). Flaminius proves himself noble according to this new meaning of the word, and Lucres, like the students of the dialogues, chooses the better meaning and, so, Flaminius as a husband. The main action thus moves from false definitions of the word "noblenes" to knowledge of the thing itself and, in the epilogue, to hope for moral action resulting from the new knowledge: "that suche as be gentilmen of name / May . . . eschew / The wey of vyce and fauour vertue" (II.891-94). This interlude, like the dialogues, seeks to make its audience better by searching into the meaning behind a name.

Gentleness and Nobility, written by John Heywood (who was also a member of More and Rastell's circle), is another interlude that is a debate, this time on the meaning of the words of the title. Again the action, a dialogue between Knight, Merchant, and Plowman, moves through several false definitions, finally arriving at a true one: the Philosopher comes in at the end to define "gentylnes" as "vertew," and "nobylyte" as "suffycyencye."[52] In this play the main characters, who cannot resolve their debate, also illustrate the difficulty of seeing through words to the realities behind them. Owing to their personal biases, that each wants to be called "gentle" and "noble," they distort the truth and cause conflict. The Plowman finally gives up in disgust:

> For exortacyons techyng and prechyng
> Gestyng & raylyng they mend no thyng
> For the amendement of the world is not in me
> Nor all the grete argumente that we thre
> Haue made syth we resonyd here to gedyr
> Do not preuayle the weyght of a fether
> For the helpyng of any thyng that is amys.
>
> (ll. 1014-20)

It is a moment of wonderful humility, on the part of the playwright as well as the Plowman. But the playwright does not give up, for he ends his play exhorting his gentle and noble audience to consider the meaning of these words, to be moved in their consciences by natural reason, and to adopt reform in government.

The schoolboy dialogues and the interludes of the humanists are direct ancestors of the later drama. In particular, as I shall argue in a later chapter, their form is a model for the structure with which Shakespeare shapes the story of *All's Well That Ends Well*. More generally, the early humanist writers point the way to the function of ideas about language in later plays. As language is a means to an end — the expression of ideas — exploring ideas about language is a means to an end: knowledge and moral action. This Renaissance humanist attitude is expressed succinctly in Castiglione's dialogue, *The Courtier:* bored by the extended argument on the nature of speech, the Lady Emilia breaks off the discussion in order to return to the more important question — the shaping of the ideal courtier.[53]

The one play of Shakespeare's age undeniably "about" language seems the exception proving the rule. *Lingua*, a play by Thomas Tomkins published anonymously in London in 1607, is an allegory about language. Lingua, the tongue, desiring to become the sixth sense, plots to set the other five wits at odds so that she may govern. Presented as a woman, and thus overemotional, she even goes against the judgment of Common Sense in the court of Queen Psyche and forms a second plot, this time to take by force the position she was denied by reason. Sleep, the deus ex machina, averts a disordered Microcosm. The play is a delightful satire on the professions, the arts and sciences, and the way human appetites get out of hand, a pageant to be acted by boys in flamboyant costumes. Yet the allegory finally discards its premise that language is worthy of being a subject important in itself: the point is the disastrous consequence of divorcing one human faculty, especially speech, from its integrated context and reasonable control. Even in this play, ideas about language serve as elements of characterization and plot, but not as theme: the moral necessity to subordinate speech to reason is the theme.

To argue that Shakespeare wrote plays about words is to ignore this humanistic context, to interpret his plays as would Armado or Osric, who have no sense of the proper end of language. Although ideas about language are not tied in Shakespeare's plays to the strictly didactic purposes of the interludes, they are subordinated to the proper end of a play: holding a moral mirror up to nature. Each of Shakespeare's plays has its special emphasis. In *Richard II*, ideas about language center on its powers: the bitter power of the words of a king to effect banishment, the power in dying words that Gaunt hopes will make Richard a true king, the power of words that Richard mistakenly calls on to overcome his enemies, and the power Exton finds in ambiguous words to mislead the hearer. In context, the ideas about language lead us naturally to the central issue of political power, as it is used and abused by two kings, their counselors and flatterers, even their assassins. If we consider only the ideas about language, taken out of context, we have a contemplative play about art that is not at all Shakespeare's play about political action. In *Much Ado about Nothing,* the interest in language is focused on slander and rumor: Hero's life almost destroyed by the one, Beatrice and Benedick's love growing out of the other. In *King Lear,* of course, the paramount linguistic idea is the difference between flattery and plain truth. In all these cases, the ideas about language are not the main interest but a means of dramatizing human character and the stories of the faults and triumphs of human judgment and passion.

In the remainder of this book, in chapters on five plays, we shall explore the ideas about language in Shakespeare's plays that are a means of characterization, of shaping the imagined worlds of the plays, and of making the experience of the stories intelligible to us. In the earlier plays, ideas about language do not change much from character to character: a few related ideas are repeated and varied, helping to form a coherent and appropriate world for a play. In *Love's Labor's Lost* ideas about language as a creative system of meaning underline the freedom of a holiday world, where young lovers experiment with human generation in words before it must be turned to a serious purpose in adult love. In *King John* ideas about language as voice emphasize the destruction and transience of the world where a weak king fails and passes. In later plays, ideas about language serve more to particularize characters and to link incidents in the story. In *The Merchant of Venice,* a play focusing on judgment, characters are distinguished not only by their styles of language, through which we judge them, but also by their attitudes toward language, which affect their judgment. In *All's Well That Ends Well* the humanist ideal of education through language becomes a means of structuring the story: the older characters must teach the younger ones to see past names to the realities beneath them; Bertram must learn to give up mere words (Parolles) and choose what is truly valuable (Helena). I have put *All's Well That Ends Well* before *Hamlet* because it may have been written before it, but, more important, because it is a simpler play. In *Hamlet* Shakespeare realizes fully the dramatic potential of ideas about language. In this tragic world, all men and women distrust words, yet acquire individuality as they inadvertently express their passions in voice and action; Hamlet gradually subordinates his own emotions to the ends of acting, and in the process learns to transform his fear into courage — the true fiction that finally allows him to play the hero. In *Hamlet* ideas about language at once help to particularize characters and, also, to shape the world and story of the play into an organic whole. Although these plays cover only part of Shakespeare's career as a playwright, they exemplify all the genres and periods, except for the late romances, and illustrate his growth in handling ideas about language to dramatic ends. With *Hamlet* we may conveniently end, because in it Shakespeare reveals his mastery of this aspect of his dramatic medium.

The Elizabethan playwright who loved words found language his medium, but only his medium, not his message. Words and studying words were of passionate interest to the Elizabethans, but in order that they might use them well, as a means to knowledge and honorable actions. It is a noble passion, and one far older than Elizabethan times: "Serious discourse . . . is far nobler, when one employs the dialectic method and plants and sows in a fitting soul intelligent words which are able to help themselves and him who planted them, which are not fruitless, but yield seed from which there spring up in other minds other words capable of continuing the process for ever, and which make their possessor happy, to the farthest possible limit of human happiness."[54] These are Socrates' words in Plato's dialogue, *The Phaedrus.* Shakespeare uses an image similar to Plato's in *All's Well That Ends Well,* when the King praises Bertram's dead father for his yet living eloquence:

> his plausive words
> He scatter'd not in ears, but grafted them,
> To grow there and to bear.
>
> (1.2.53-55)

"Plausive" means both "persuasive," words with a purpose, and also "worthy of applause," words such as the dramatist might hope to write: ones that bear ideas and help men to grow. Twelve of Shakespeare's plays end with the promise of the characters to tell each other the story we have just heard.[55] Surely this must have been the hope of the dramatist who did not see his plays through publication: that his words would bear others by provoking his audience to go home telling the stories, making the experience their own. These are the words that last, continuing the dialogue in the minds of others.

Notes

1. "Rudolph Agricola's *De Inventione Dialectica Libri Tres:* A Translation of Selected Chapters," tr. J. R. McNally, *Speech Monographs,* 34 (1967), 407. For a fuller discussion of Agricola's theory of language and its context, place logic, see Trousdale, *Shakespeare and the Rhetoricians,* pp. 33–38 and 55–56.

2. "Agricola's *De Inventione Dialectica,*" pp. 407–8.

3. On Juliet's, Cordelia's, and Antony's doubts, see *Rom.* 2.6.30–34; *Lr.* 1.1.76–78 and 91–92; and *Ant.* 1.1.15. Armado's and Orlando's trust is exemplified by their proliferation of love poems (*LLL* 1.2.183–85; *AYL* 3.2.1–8), while Lear's is manifest in his questions for his daughters (*Lr.* 1.1.48–54 and 85–86).

4. See, for example, Richard Altick, "Symphonic Imagery in *Richard II,*" *PMLA,* 62 (1947), 339–65; Leonard Dean, "Voice and Deed in *Coriolanus,*" *University of Kansas City Review,* 21 (1955), 177–84; Michel Grivelet, "Shakespeare as 'Corrupter of Words,' " *ShS,* 16 (1963), 70–76; W. T. Jewkes, " 'Excellent Dumb Discourse': The Limits of Language in *The Tempest,*" in *Essays on Shakespeare,* ed. Gordon Smith (University Park: Pennsylvania State Univ. Press, 1965), pp. 196–210; Sigurd Burckhardt, *Shakespearean Meanings* (Princeton: Princeton Univ. Press, 1968), esp. pp. 138 and 256; Anne Barton, "Shakespeare and the Limits of Language," *ShS,* 24 (1971), 19–30; Inga-Stina Ewbank, " 'More Pregnantly Than Words,' " *ShS,* 24 (1971), 13–18; James L. Calderwood, *Shakespearean Metadrama* (Minneapolis: Univ. of Minnesota Press, 1971), esp. pp. 13 and 185; and Danson, *Tragic Alphabet,* esp. p. 5.

5. See Willcock, *Shakespeare as Critic of Language;* Mahood, *Shakespeare's Wordplay,* pp. 164–88; de Grazia, "Shakespeare's View of Language"; and Calderwood, *Metadrama in Shakespeare's Henriad,* pp. 183–220. Although all these critics agree that educated Elizabethans

trusted language for full communication, they differ in their opinions on Shakespeare: Willcock argues that he trusted words but not linguistic fashions; Mahood, that he moved from skepticism in the early plays to a firm belief in the power and truth of words in the late romances; de Grazia, that he trusted language but not speakers—unless they have the charity that redeems words from their corruption at Babel; Calderwood, that he anticipated a later skepticism in an age of faith in language.

6. Mulcaster, *Elementarie*, p. 92. An exception to the two groups of critics discussed in nn. 4 and 5 is Marion Trousdale, who argues from the Elizabethan distinction between words and things to an aesthetic where the play is not representational but rather consciously artful and intellectual, and where the audience is encouraged to exercise its own invention by exploring the many possible meanings of the words and the actions of the play. See especially her discussion of words and things, pp. 24–31 and 41.

7. Lever, *Arte of Reason*, pp. iiii[v]-v[r].

8. On de Grazia's theory of the influence of biblical history on the Elizabethan attitude toward language, see "Shakespeare's View of Language," pp. 375–79. On the good man as the good speaker, see also Quintilian, *Institutio Oratoria*, I.Pr.9–12; Erasmus, *Concerning the Aim and Method of Education*, tr. W. H. Howard (1904; rpt. New York: Columbia Univ. Teachers College Bureau of Publications, 1964), p. 198; and Vives, *On Education*, p. 185.

9. Thomas Wilson, *The Rule of Reason* (London, 1563), sig. Ciiii[r].

10. Aristotle, *On Sophistical Refutations*, 165a, 17–19.

11. This understanding of logic as an art of language is an inheritance from the late Middle Ages: see William Kneale and Martha Kneale, *The Development of Logic* (Oxford: Clarendon Press, 1962), p. 226. The treatise most important to the twelfth-century renaissance in logic was the recently discovered *On Sophistical Refutations* of Aristotle; the Kneales cite the *Ars Disserendi* (1132) of Adam of Balsham as an example: "According to this author . . . one of our main aims in studying logic is to gain a mastery of language so that we cannot be deceived by sophisms" (p. 227). See also John of Salisbury, *The Metalogicon*, pp. 80–81: "Just as grammar . . . is concerned with ways of saying things, dialectic is concerned with what is said. While grammar chiefly examines the words that express meanings, dialectic investigates the meanings expressed by words."

12. Lever, *Arte of Reason*, pp. 231–32. Logics other than Lever's that begin with a discussion of the classes of terms are Seton's *Dialectica* and Thomas Blundeville's *The Art of Logike* (London, 1599).

13. Bacon, *Advancement*, sig. Oo3[r].

14. Wilson, *Rule of Reason*, sig. Riv[v]. Aristotle lists the fallacies of diction as "equivocation, ambiguity, combination, division, accent and

form of expression," in *On Sophistical Refutations*, 165b, 25–28. Elizabethan logics other than Wilson's that include a discussion of the fallacies are Dudley Fenner's *The Artes of Logike and Rethorike* (London, 1584) and Blundeville's *Art of Logike*.

15. Wilson, *Rule of Reason*, sig. Riv[v].

16. Ibid., sig. Civ[v].

17. Montaigne, "Apologie," *Essayes*, p. 305.

18. Bacon, *Advancement*, sig. Ppl[r].

19. Wilson, *Rule of Reason*, sig. Sii[r].

20. Wilson, *Arte of Rhetorique*, sig. Oi[r].

21. Ibid., sig. Zii[v]. Cf. Peacham, *Garden* (1577), sig. Bi[v]: "Necessity was the cause that Tropes were fyrst inuented, for when there wanted words to express your nature of diuers thinges, wise men remembring that many thinges were very like one to an other, thought it good, to borrow the name of one thing, to expresse another, that did in something much resemble it." Similar ideas on the origin of tropes appear in Fenner, *Artes*, sig. C4[r]; and Fraunce, *Arcadian Rhetorike*, sig. A2[v].

22. Aristotle, *The "Art" of Rhetoric*, 1405a; and Quintilian, *Institutio Oratoria*, VIII.vi.5. Cf. Cicero, *Orator*, lxii.211.

23. Cicero, *De Oratore*, III.xxxviii.155. See also Peacham, *Garden* (1577), sig. Bi[v]. Cf. Rosemond Tuve, *Elizabethan and Metaphysical Imagery* (Chicago: Chicago Univ. Press, 1947), p. 101: "The rhetoricians from Quintilian on persistently note that metaphor is *necessary*, because there are no words for naming things, and that it *enhances* by including more of the significance of things. One may not name the 'leg' even of a rustic bench by saying 'stick of wood'; the supportingness is left out. Metaphor directs the mind inward to supply from remembered experience what is unstated. Tropes were not commended as suitable to clear visualizing of object, act, place, person; they were commended as a means of getting around the inadequacies of language economically, of making the reader think connections which language does not actually say."

24. Puttenham, *Arte of English Poesie*, pp. 150 and 163.

25. Ibid., p. 128.

26. Wilson, *Arte of Rhetorique*, sigs. tiv[v]-tv[r].

27. Cicero, *De Oratore*, II.lxi.254. *"Ingeniosi"* is the Latin word translated as "a man of talent"; it might as well be translated as "a man of natural genius" or as "a man of intuition."

28. For Wilson's borrowings, see Cicero, *De Oratore*, II.lxi.250-lxii.254, lxiii.256-57, and lxiv.259-60; and Quintilian, *Institutio Oratoria*, VI.ii.48-52, iii.53-56, and iii.84-88.

29. Quintilian, *Institutio Oratoria*, VI.ii.89.

30. Ibid., VIII.iii.44.

31. Ibid., VIII.iii.47.

32. Ibid., VI.ii.23–iii.57.

33. Castiglione, *The Courtier*, sig. R1^r. In *De Oratore*, Cicero makes the points that wit may be serious, as well as comic in effect (II.lxi.248–49), and that even the comic jest must further the serious purpose of the whole discourse (II.lx.247).

34. Carew, "Epistle," p. 6.

35. Thomas Wilson, *The Rule of Reason*, sigs. Sii^v-Siv^r.

36. See Robert Greene, *Pandosto* (1588), in *Elizabethan Prose Fiction*, ed. Merritt Lawlis (New York: Odyssey Press, 1967), p. 245: "Suspicion is no proof. Jealousy is an unequal judge. Bellaria is chaste, Egistus blameless, Franion a true subject, Pandosto treacherous, his babe an innocent. And the king shall live without an heir if that which is lost be not found." In Greene's romance there is no surprising return of Queen Bellaria, no fruitful reconciliation with Egistus (Pandosto kills himself in despair at his former actions), no return of the counselor Franion, no emphasis upon Dorastus as a replacement for Pandosto's lost son. The oracle is fulfilled in one sense only: the lost daughter is found.

37. On the humanists and Latin, see Lewis, *English Literature in the Sixteenth Century*, pp. 20–22. On love of words and style, see Willcock, *Shakespeare as Critic of Language* and "Shakespeare and Rhetoric," *E&S*, 29 (1943), 50–61. On Shakespeare's writing plays about language, see, for example, Jewkes, " 'Excellent Dumb Discourse' "; Calderwood, *Shakespearean Metadrama* and *Metadrama in Shakespeare's Henriad;* Danson, *Tragic Alphabet;* and Porter, *Drama of Speech Acts.* On Bacon's revolutionary loving of things not words, see Willcock, *Shakespeare as Critic of Language*, pp. 26–27; and Calderwood, *Metadrama in Shakespeare's Henriad*, pp. 212–18.

38. Sprat, *History of the Royal Society*, p. 113.

39. Erasmus, *Concerning . . . Education*, p. 199.

40. Vives, *On Education*, p. 163.

41. For an application of this ideal to the way a Renaissance audience might have viewed a play, see Trousdale, *Shakespeare and the Rhetoricians*, esp. pp. 125–28.

42. Johann Sturm, *A Ritch Storehouse*, tr. Thomas Browne (London, 1570), sigs. Diiii^{r-v}.

43. Mulcaster, *Elementarie*, p. 228. Cf. p. 51: "But in the second vse of grammer, we are enforced of necessitie . . . to deall with the tungs, ear we passe to anie matter, which help of tungs, tho it be most necessarie for the thing, . . . yet it hindreth vs in time . . . naie it hindreth vs in knowledge a thing of more price."

44. Erasmus, *Concerning . . . Education*, p. 162. Erasmus's argument

for the importance of studying words probably derives from Aristotle, *Topica,* 108a: "It is useful to have examined the various meanings of a term both with a view to clarity (for a man would know better what he is stating if the various senses in which it can be used had been made clear), and also in order that his reasonings may be directed to the actual thing and not to the name by which it is called."

45. Peacham, *Garden* (1577), sig. Aii^v.

46. Roger Ascham, *The Scholemaster,* sig. Oii^v.

47. Ibid., sig. Oii^r.

48. Bacon, *Advancement,* sigs. E3^v-E4^r.

49. Erasmus, "Things and Names [1527]," *The Colloquies,* tr. Craig R. Thompson (Chicago: Chicago Univ. Press, 1965), pp. 383–85.

50. Vives, *"Educatio,"* in *Tudor School-Boy Life,* pp. 227–29.

51. Henry Medwall, *Fulgens and Lucres* (1497?), ed. F. S. Boas and A. W. Reed (Oxford: Clarendon Press, 1926), *Pars* II, l. 57.

52. John Heywood, *Gentleness and Nobility* (1529?), ed. A. C. Partridge and F. P. Wilson (Oxford: Malone Society, 1950), ll. 1113–33.

53. Castiglione, *The Courtier,* sig. F8^v.

54. Plato, *Phaedrus,* 276e–277a. Cf. Seneca, *Epistulae Morales,* XXXVIII.

55. The plays ending with the characters about to tell each other the story are *Err., TGV, MV, Wiv., Ham., AWW, MM, Oth., Cor., Per., WT,* and *Tmp.*

꒜

Love's Labor's Lost:
Creative Words

It is easy to see that in the early plays, until at least 1595, Shake-speare is experimenting with styles of language appropriate for dramatizing his various kinds of stories. The Roman revenge plot of *Titus Andronicus* is embodied in an appropriate style: the hyper-boles, gratuitous moralizing, and cosmic metaphors of the Englished Seneca of the 1580s. *The Taming of the Shrew,* a farce, has a com-paratively plain style, taking advantage of prose rhythm, English colloquialisms, and racy banter. In *Two Gentlemen of Verona* and *Comedy of Errors,* the clowns are set apart somewhat by their styles, but the former play, with its sources in Italian romance, is generally more lyric than the latter play, which draws on the witty cross talk, as well as the confusions in plot, of Plautine comedy. By *A Midsum-mer Night's Dream,* Shakespeare is distinguishing groups of charac-ters by style, if not yet always individuals: prose and malapropisms for the mechanicals, blank verse and longer sentences for the court, chiming couplets and lyric images for the young lovers, and nature imagery and occasional ballad meter for the fairies.

At first glance there seems to be no period when Shakespeare ex-perimented with the dramatic power of ideas about language, as he did with styles in language. In the Shakespearean examples in the preceding chapters, drawn from all the plays, we may see that Shakespeare gave attention to ideas about language throughout his career. Furthermore, by the relative frequency of seventeen key words concerning language—speak(s), speech(es), language(s), word(s), name(s), voice(s), tongue(s), mouth(s), throat(s), ear(s), breath, air, airy, pen, paper(s), ink, and parchment—we may say that there is no appreciable change in Shakespeare's interest in language between the early and the middle plays, or between these and the plays of the tragic period, although there is a slightly

lowered interest in the late plays.[1] Nor is there a significant difference between the comedies and the histories, or between these
and the tragedies, although the romances show a slightly lowered interest.[2] There are, of course, plays of each period that fall well
below the average, but clearly Shakespeare's interest in ideas about
language remained steady throughout his plays.[3]

Turning from groups of plays to particular ones, however, we
come to a different conclusion: five of the eleven plays having the
greatest frequency of key terms concerning language were written
during a three-year period, from about 1594 to 1596: *Titus Andronicus, Love's Labor's Lost, King John, Richard II,* and *Romeo and
Juliet.* The other plays showing such high interest in language
stretch across Shakespeare's years of writing plays from *2 Henry IV*
in 1598 to *Coriolanus* in 1607-8.[4] Actually, it should come as no
surprise to find that near the end of the early period, when Shakespeare is experimenting with styles of expression, he also shows a
correspondingly heightened interest in ideas about language. In
fact, the correspondence between styles and ideas about language
obtains, I think, throughout the plays: just as Shakespeare learns
gradually to individualize characters by their styles in language, so
he learns over the course of several years to particularize characters
by their ideas on language. In the early plays, however, both style
and ideas work at a more general level, helping to create an appropriate atmosphere for the story presented. In this and the next
chapter, we shall consider two of the plays from this period of high
interest in language: *Love's Labor's Lost* and *The Life and Death of
King John.* In these early plays, Shakespeare uses ideas about
language as the players used signs with "Thebes" written on them, to
let us know what kind of world we are in. Like imagery or allusions,
ideas about language tell us what kind of people inhabit this world,
and what regulations and forms of society obtain.

In *Love's Labor's Lost* the controlling conception of language is
that of an ordered system of rational symbols through which speakers generate meaning. Admittedly my statement is abstract, but so,
too, are the terms for language used by the characters in this play.
Speech is not "tongue," "mouth," and "breath," as we shall see it is
in *King John.* The names for speech in *Love's Labor's Lost* are derived not from its physical means, but rather from its intellectual effects. Berowne, for instance, complains that the King's academy will

provide no useful knowledge, only a knowledge of the names of things—"And every godfather can give a name" (1.1.92). Learning his own lesson, Berowne later promises to give up "Taffeta phrases, silken terms precise" (5.2.406). Armado explains "l'envoy" as "an epilogue or discourse, to make plain / Some obscure precedence that hath tofore been sain" (3.1.81–82), and Nathaniel praises Holofernes, whose "epithites are sweetly varied, like a scholar at the least" (4.2.8–9). Satirizing the pedants, Moth tells us, "They have been at a great feast of languages, and stol'n the scraps" (5.1.36–37). Speech in *Love's Labor's Lost* is thus referred to in intellectual terms, but ones as abundant and varied as Holofernes' "epithites": language, discourse, names, terms, phrases, and everywhere *words* —"high-borne words" (1.1.172), "fire-new words," (1.1.178), "apt and gracious words" (2.1.73), "foul words" (4.1.19), "*pauca verba*" (4.2.165), an "alms-basket of words" (5.1.38–39), a "word . . . well cull'd, chose, sweet, and apt" (5.1.93), "a good word" (5.2.274), a "happy word" (5.2.370), "a brace of words" (5.2.523), "Honest plain words" (5.2.753), and finally, "The words of Mercury" (5.2.930).[5] While the terms for speech remain abstract, Shakespeare gains liveliness from their variety and from the concrete descriptive metaphors attached to them—"taffeta," "fire-new," "feast," and "alms-basket."

The intellectual quality of the terms used to describe language in the play is matched by the bookish nature of the wordplay. Much has been written, of course, about the wordplay of *Love's Labor's Lost*,[6] but not as much about the ideas informing it. Lords and ladies, pedants and peasants—all are fascinated with language as an ordered system of meaning. Equally important, they are delighted with their own knowledge of this system. In his *First Part of the Elementarie*, Richard Mulcaster writes that grammar "serueth in the natur of an anatomie,"[7] and, in Renaissance primers, language was taught as an accumulative and hierarchical system of letters, then syllables, then words, and finally sentences. All parts of the system operate in the wordplay in *Love's Labor's Lost*, exploited, mocked, admired, and wondered at, as if humanity were put on earth solely to indulge itself in the great gift of speech. In addition, the characters indicate their formal knowledge of grammatical anatomy, as they take apart their own and others' words and sentences for the pure fun of looking at the pieces.

When Holofernes ventures some verse, for example, he announces, "I will something affect the letter, for it argues facility" (4.2.55); and he does show off his ease with alliteration in his poem on "The preyful Princess" and "a pretty pleasing pricket" (l. 56). But he also plays with the grammatical idea of letters making up words, not just with the rhetorical figure:

> The dogs did yell: put *l* to sore, then sorel jumps from thicket,
> Or pricket sore, or else sorel; the people fall a-hooting.
> If sore be sore, then L to sore makes fifty sores o' sorel:
> Of one sore I an hundred make by adding but one more L.
>
> (4.2.58-61)

By adding one letter to "sore" (a deer of four years) he makes it a "sorel" (a deer of three years), and then, identifying *L* as the Latin numeral for "fifty," he makes fifty sores (sore-L), or with another *L*, one hundred (sore-LL). Now this is silly stuff, but it is also play with language as a generative system of meaning: by adding on letters, one makes, and then changes, the meaning of words.

Moth similarly delights in the vowels as parts of speech that may generate a meaning. When he accuses one present of being a "most silly sheep, with a horn," Holofernes demands, "*Quis, quis,* thou consonant?" (5.1.50–52). The schoolmaster has his joke at the expense of one part of language: like a consonant, which is unpronounceable without a vowel, the diminutive page is nothing in the world of words. But Moth outdoes the pedant with vowels:

> *Moth.* The last of the five vowels, if "you" repeat them; or the fift, if I.
> *Hol.* I will repeat them—*a, e, I*—
> *Moth.* The sheep: the other two concludes it—*o, U.*
>
> (5.1.53-57)

In the course of his riddle, Moth has Holofernes three times a sheep: if Holofernes repeats the vowels, he is the sheep since Moth has named him "you" (*u*); if Moth repeats the vowels, the last, *u* ("you"), is Holofernes; and finally, when Holofernes recites "I," Moth inserts "sheep" as a synonym, and Holofernes is yet again the dumb animal. Moth's wordplay here is punning, substituting the words for pronouns for the names of the letters. But it is also play with language as a sequence of sounds that are at the same time rational symbols; Moth simply traps Holofernes in the rules of meaning for the system.

After learning the table of letters, Renaissance boys went on not to words but to a table of syllables. As we have seen, Priscian carefully distinguished for Latin students the difference between a syllable as a meaningless unit of sound, and a word of one syllable that yet has meaning. This formal distinction Moth plays with, also at Holofernes' expense. Asking "What is *a, b,* spell'd backward, with the horn on his head?" (5.1.47–48), Moth elicits from Holofernes, proud to show off his little learning, "*Ba, pueritia,* with a horn added" (5.1.49). Holofernes, caught in his table of syllables, does not get the joke, and Moth must add, "*Ba,* most silly sheep with a horn" (l. 50). The page thus snares the schoolmaster in the system of making meaning (the word for the sound of a sheep) from meaningless sounds (the syllable "*Ba*").

Aristocrats also play with this system, which may work by division as well as by addition: dividing a word, one expects to get a meaningless sound, but one may get instead a shorter word, and consequently a new meaning. By the division of Longaville's name, Katherine engenders a new word; "ville" becomes " 'Veal,' quoth the Dutchman. Is not veal a calf?" (5.2.247). Puzzled by an apparent non sequitur, Longaville exclaims, "A calf, fair lady!" and has his words rearranged to form new significance: "No, a fair lord calf!" (l. 248). Thinking to play the game of syllables to his own advantage, Longaville offers another division —"Let's part the word"— but Katherine anticipates the outcome —"No, I'll not be your half" (i.e., " 'alf" or part of "calf," l. 249). Similarly, Boyet and Dumaine part a word for the further discomfiture of Holofernes, already "o'erparted" (as Nathaniel was in his role) in representing the worthy Judas Machabeus:

> *Boyet.* Therefore as he is, an ass, let him go.
>   And so adieu, sweet Jude! Nay, why dost thou stay?
> *Dumaine.* For the latter end of his name.
> *Boyet.* For the ass to the Jude; give it him. Jud-as, away!
>
> (5.2.625–28)

The lords' delight in the routing of Holofernes may be, as he says, "not generous, not gentle, not humble" (5.2.629), but their delight in a system of sounds that take on meaning in surprising ways remains untainted, a festive joy in the opportunities for invention language offers them.

Not only syllables but words themselves come in for mockery and admiration as both sound and sense. The grammatical concept of "word" provides Costard's taunt for Moth: "I marvel thy master hath not eaten thee for a word, for thou art not so long by the head as *honorificabilitudinitatibus*" (5.1.39-41). As the word is the smallest part of meaningful discourse, so Moth is the smallest member in the dialogue of the minor characters. Still, the Latin word is a mouthful for the actor: words, being sound, have "*corpus*," material body with length, breadth, and width, and so Moth is not as long as many of the words mouthed (though hardly digested) by the garrulous knight his master. The idea of words gaining significance only in the context of the whole sentence becomes, for Boyet and the ladies, the means of deriding Berowne:

> *Maria.* That last is Berowne, the merry madcap lord.
>   Not a word with him but a jest.
> *Boyet.*   And every jest but a word.
> *Princess.* It was well done of you to take him at his word.
> *Boyet.* I was as willing to grapple as he was to board.
>
>   (2.1.215-18)

Boyet overturns Maria's admiration for Berowne's wit by reordering her words: Berowne's jests are mere words, the least important part of ordered significance in language. The Princess then mockingly praises Boyet for giving back only what he got, mere word for mere word. Finally, Boyet turns her mockery into a compliment to him and a slur on Berowne, simply by understanding her words as a military metaphor: he has overcome Berowne in the verbal battle occasioned by the intruder's flirtatious assault on the ladies. The extended play on "word," moreover, allows all three to delight in the fact that context lends a word its significance, and so a single word is rich with many possible meanings.

The ideas about language that the characters of *Love's Labor's Lost* play with are most often the simple ones of beginning language studies: letters, syllables, and words, the double nature of language as sounds and symbols. Consequently, as many of the original audience as had a year or two of Latin grammar school might have understood the wit and felt learned; the sophistication comes not from the concepts, but from the wit of the speakers. The society of the play is defined by these ideas about language as educated but not old. None of these characters has worn the gloss off even simple ideas by too many years of study; the lords and ladies seem young and the pedants, parochial. The discussion of language invites us to enter a nostalgic world when knowledge was simpler and acquiring it easier. If the story of the play looks back to a time when falling in love was easy and (as Celia in *As You Like It* has it) only "to make sport withal" (1.2.26), then the ideas on language in the play look back to a time when learning was a child's game and not earnest business.[8]

Indeed, the wits of this play spend a great deal of time proving that the world is *like* a grammar book. The King and his lords are "book-men" (2.1.227) and "book-mates" (4.1.100); and Nathaniel and Holofernes as well are "book-men" (4.2.34). In this literate world the King's expression is a "margent" that comments on his face like a printed gloss (2.1.246); Rosaline's eyes are Berowne's "book" (4.2.109); and women's eyes in general are "books" and "academes" (4.3.299). Mocking the lords' grammatical metaphors, the women have it that Rosaline's face is as "Beauteous as ink," as "Fair as a text B in a copy-book" (5.2.41-42), and the Princess's face, also like a copy-book page, is "full of O's" (5.2.45). Implying that he and Holofernes have well digested their grammar books, Nathaniel mourns that Dull "hath never fed of the dainties that are bred in a book; / He hath not eat paper, . . . he hath not drunk ink" (4.2.24-26).[9] For love of Jaquenetta, Armado will "turn sonnet" (1.2.184), and like a "Negligent student" must be reminded to "learn her by heart" (3.1.35). Moth is almost "eaten . . . for a word" (5.1.39-40); and Costard, asked to deliver a letter, promises to "do it . . . in print" (3.1.172). Both lords and pedants are preoccupied with doing things by the book and to the letter, as if gaining wisdom and giving love were matters of learning correct paradigms and using a plenteous vocabulary.

Those critics of the last twenty years who have written on *Love's Labor's Lost* have generally argued that language is a major theme of the play; certainly linguistic affectation, as one of many vanities exposed in the play, is a major issue.[10] I would suggest, instead, that ideas about language are less thematic than dramatic; they help to create an imagined world that is an appropriate setting for this particular love story. The story is one of young people in transition from youth to adulthood. None of the characters of this play is married, and the parents of the other comedies are lacking. By the end of the play ten characters are contemplating marriage: they have begun to grow up. The society Shakespeare shapes in this play is as artificial as a grammar school, where learning the names for things and the rules of grammar is all there is to achievement, and where girls are exotic visitors from an entirely different world. The young people are still experimenting with love as a social art or game; they are not entirely certain that they wish to take up the work of adult love. The ideas about language reinforce this sense of a society in transition: the young men and women are playing with their generative powers in words before they accept the responsibilities that human generation entails.

Although ideas about language do not particularize each character in *Love's Labor's Lost,* they do distinguish the major groups of characters. The pedants and servants, more often than the lords and ladies, assume that order in language is merely pattern. Because language and wordplay are more mechanical to these lower characters, their speech is less witty. Many critics have pointed out the affected patterns of Armado's synonyms, Holofernes' alliteration, and Nathaniel's proverbs.[11] But a more general observation has not, I think, been stated: by letting pattern shape their sentences and their responses, the pedants lose the opportunity for increased significance that spontaneity in speech affords. Thus Holofernes simply repeats his play with "L"—first fifty, then one hundred sores (4.2.60-61)—and he is caught twice by Moth's play with vowels because he cannot quickly respond to the sounds as both vowels and words for pronouns. Wit depends on the surprises to which order lends overall significance: in an unusual context, a word shows a new face. The mechanical patterns of the pedants offer little surprise, and so less wit.

In this sense, the pedants share more than they would ever admit with Costard. His malapropisms get the wrong words in the right places, comically creating meanings he does not intend: like the pedants, he pays more attention to the patterns of his sentences than to the significance of the words in them. And we laugh at him, rather than with him, because the surprises are in language anyway, even though he does not see them. In this learned society, Costard labors to grasp the meaning of a word simply by its context, as if language were only rigid pattern. Guessing by context that Armado offers him a "salve" when he offers his "l'envoy" (3.1.72-80), Costard concludes, even after Armado's long explanation, that "l'envoy" means "goose" (3.1.104-10). Similarly, from what Armado and Berowne say when they pay him for delivering their letters—and from what he can count in his hand—Costard deduces that "remuneration" is "the Latin word for three farthings" (3.1.136-37), and "guerdon" is "better than remuneration, aleven-pence-farthing better" (3.1.170-71). Although he marvels at strange new words, Costard does not share with the pedants linguistic affectation; what he shares with them is the assumption that pattern is the most important feature of language. In the lower characters of *Love's Labor's Lost,* the only animal who speaks is caught in his most ridiculous form. Mistaking mechanical arrangement for ordered significance, Costard and the pedants are as comical as—and an important parallel to—the lords, who mistake the wooing games and arts of love for love itself. The two sets of characters pretentiously take the significance and creative powers of language and love to be what they themselves have contributed by way of the *arts* of language and love.

The King and his men, and the Princess and her court, also play with language as pattern, but they do so more self-consciously, knowing the limitations of such patterns. One of their most common devices—although there are many—is that of matching the rhythm or rhyme of a former speaker. When the King and his lords are sealing their vows, for instance, Berowne objects that all their studies will lead them only to blindness to larger truths; in shutting themselves off from the world, they also shut out truth, and especially the begetters' of men's truths, women. The King's reply is a sententious denial of Berowne's authority to speak: "How well he's read, to reason against reading!" (1.1.94). Dumaine and Longaville pick up the King's pattern—his sentence structure, meter, and rhyme—and mock Berowne as well:

> *Dum.* Proceeded well, to stop all good proceeding!
> *Long.* He weeds the corn and still lets grow the weeding!
> (1.1.95-96)

This repetition of patterns was itself a scholars' game, although

generally played in Latin: the completion or matching of lines of
Latin poetry.[12] Here the King and his lords indicate, by means of
the linguistic game, a solidarity in the goals of the academe. But
Berowne adds his own matching line: "The spring is near when green
geese are a-breeding" (l. 97). Although predictive of later flirtations,
this sentence makes no sense in context; Berowne is criticizing the
lords for loving pattern over the more important order of significance:

> *Dum.* How follows that?
> *Ber.*   Fit in his place and time.
> *Dum.* In reason nothing.
> *Ber.*   Something then in rhyme.
>
> (ll. 98–99)

Berowne mocks the lords who let sound and mere pattern—"place,"
"time," and "rhyme"—replace sense and the deeper order of significance.

This passage alerts us not only to the self-consciousness of the
lords, who generally do remember that language is more than pattern, but also to the fact that we may take the unusual matchings of
rhythms and rhymes in the play as the artful games of the aristocrats, not just the medium of the dramatist who writes his play in
verse. Here in *Love's Labor's Lost,* as in *As You Like It,* when Jaques
objects, "Nay then God buy you, and you talk in blank verse"
(4.1.31–32), we are enabled to take the verse forms of the lovers as
part of their *own* style and character, not simply as part of Shakespeare's "developing" style. As he often does, Shakespeare makes a
virtue of what might otherwise be mere dramatic convention. Since
the lords and ladies are conscious of speaking in time with each
other, the convention becomes a means of giving life to the characters. It also defines the world of the play as different from ours, an
idealization of it in at least this respect: the characters of *Love's
Labor's Lost* actually hear the harmonies of love and friendship that
we only sense.

In a later scene, the court of the Princess engages in the same sort
of self-conscious play with matching rhythms when Rosaline chal-
lenges Boyet:

> *Ros.* Shall I come upon thee with an old saying, that was a man when
>   King Pippen of France was a little boy, as touching the hit it?
> *Boy.* So I may answer thee with one as old, that was a woman when

Queen Guinover of Britain was a little wench, as touching the
  hit it.
Ros. Thou canst not hit it, hit it, hit it,
  Thou canst not hit it, my good man.
Boy. And I cannot, cannot, cannot,
  And I cannot, another can.

(4.1.119-28)

Here the matching is done first in prose rhythms and sentence structure, and then in ballad meter, schemes, and rhyme. The praise by the onlookers further indicates the difference between lower and higher wits in the play:

Costard. By my troth, most pleasant. How both did fit it!
Maria. A mark marvellous well shot, for they both did hit it.

(4.1.129-30)

Costard praises the pattern, the fitting of answer to rhythm and rhyme of the challenge, whereas Maria praises the significance, the scoring of witty scoffs that both Rosaline and Boyet drive home at each other. And, too, Maria continues the game by matching her meter and rhyme to Costard's. Costard, however, cannot let go his delight in the pattern of the game, and his hyperbolic praise of it, filled with malapropisms—"most incony vulgar wit! / When it comes so smoothly off, so obscenely as it were, so fit!" (4.1.142-43)— reinforces our sense of the difference between the games of language played by the lower characters and those played by the aristocrats. The lower characters delight in language as sound and pattern; the higher characters, especially the women, see that the order of language becomes a way of generating surprising meanings: mankind is guest, not host, at the great feast of language.

What we have so far ignored in the exchange of Rosaline and Boyet, picked up in Costard's malapropisms, are the sexual innuendos. They remind us that this game of matching rhythms is a social game that betokens affection, like catching the rhythm in the stride of another person while walking together. In most cases the game is a flirting game, a way of pairing off. This is certainly true when the lords and ladies play it at the finish of their first meeting. Rosaline and Berowne begin:

Ber. I would you heard it [my heart] groan.
Ros. Is the fool sick?

Ber. Sick at the heart.
Ros. Alack, let it blood.
Ber. Would that do it good?
Ros. My physic says ay.
Ber. Will you prick't with your eye?
Ros. No point, with my knife.
Ber. Now God save thy life!
Ros. And yours from long living!
Ber. I cannot stay thanksgiving.

(2.1.183-93)

Despite Rosaline's insults, these three-beat couplets are a way of using the creative order of language to bring two together. The others follow, pairing off, too (ll. 194-213).[13] This aural experience of coupling occurs again when the lords match lines of iambic pentameter with alternating rhymes in a competitive praising of mistresses (4.3.262-77). The King implies the social purpose of the game when he ends it: "But what of this, are we not all in love?" (l. 278). The delight in language as an ordered system becomes a representation of the imitative quality of love: one way we match ourselves to a friend or lover is by imitating his or her linguistic habits, thus modifying our independence into a harmony with another.

This coupling in rhyme and rhythm occurs only among lords and ladies. The one minor character who falls in love is Armado, and he emphasizes the differences between himself and Jaquenetta by his kind of patterned speeches. Referring to King Cophetua and his love for a beggar maid, Armado argues: "I am the king, for so stands the comparison; thou the beggar, for so witnesseth thy lowliness. . . . What shalt thou exchange for rags? robes; for tittles? titles; for thyself? me" (4.1.78-83). This is not the matching of rhythm and rhyme to another person's, but the declaring of the differences in narcissistic patterns. The style tells the opposite of the words: Armado is not offering to give himself; he is offering, by his alliterative antinomies, to transform Jaquenetta into a mirror of himself, or at least of the self he would like to be. The King spots such self-love in Armado early in the play. Armado is "One who the music of his own vain tongue / Doth ravish like enchanting harmony" (1.1.166-67). Caught up in his own music, Armado cannot hear the music of another, or make the harmony that is love.

The witty characters of *Love's Labor's Lost* use the order of language not only to match themselves to each other, but also to make something of the union. Armado complains to his page, "I love not to be cross'd" (1.2.32), and Moth undercuts his bravado by reversing his words: "He speaks the mere contrary, crosses [i.e., coins] love not him" (1.2.33-34). By turning the order of his sentence around, Moth lets Armado's own words speak against him, thereby diminishing the soldier's pretense to noble wrath. This sort of verbal play minimizes the importance of individual words and emphasizes the importance of the whole structure of language to significance. In addition, it celebrates the communal dialogue required in language: one man's meaning is not necessarily another man's, and the two together may make something greater than either alone.

The structure of a sentence as it contributes to significance is exploited in other forms of wordplay. Often a speaker begins a sentence, by its order setting up expectations for the completion of meaning, whereupon a second speaker interrupts, completing the pattern of the sentence, but with words that reverse the intended significance. Thus Moth begins his prologue, "All hail, the richest beauties on the earth!" (5.2.158), and we expect from the conventions of praise, but also from sentence structure, that he will continue with noun phrases heaped up in elaboration of the ladies and their beauties. Instead, however, Boyet interrupts—"Beauties no richer than rich taffata" (5.2.159)—completing the expected structure of the sentence but reversing the intended significance: the only beauties visible to the lords are the taffeta masks covering the ladies' faces. This sort of play with the significance of the structure of speech occurs more often in the shows (5.2.548, 655), where the restrictions of literary style and meter allow one to guess the intended meaning more easily from the pattern, and where wit depends upon denying and mocking the expected, conventional meaning. Despite the denial of the original intention, two people together make the sentence, and the sharing of new meaning works as a social bond.

In a similar form of wordplay, the speaker delivers a sentence completed in structure and significance, but a second speaker follows with a phrase or clause that, added on to the previous sentence, makes a new structure and reverses or denies the original significance. Thus when Boyet teases her about the infatuation of Navarre, the

Princess tries to dismiss him: "Come to our pavilion—Boyet is dispos'd" (2.1.250). Boyet, however, picks up her sentence, adds a phrase, and makes a sentence and a meaning she did not intend: "But to speak that in words which his [Navarre's] eye hath disclos'd" (2.1.251). By adding to her simple sentence an infinitive phrase, Boyet reverses her suggestion that his observations of the King are insignificant; and, more important, by matching her rhythm and completing the couplet, he implies that he only speaks the other half of the whole truth, the half that the Princess would leave unspoken.

This second pattern occurs often in the wooing games. Berowne at first pairs off with Katherine, but, finding her wit too insulting, he complains, "Your wit's too hot, it speeds too fast, 'twill tire"; Katherine, seeing through his criticism to his fear of her, taunts him, "Not till it leave the rider in the mire" (2.1.119–20). In taking over his sentence structure by rhyme, meter, and the addition of a subordinate clause, Katherine invites herself verbally into Berowne's world, but also asserts herself by reversing the significance and, through making explicit Berowne's fear, the intended insult. These games and many more—patterned questions and refuting answers that yet maintain the pattern, borrowing the words of another to fit them into an order that reverses their meaning—indicate that lords and ladies in their wooing are making language more often than making love. The arts of language reflect, in fact, the arts of love, but not love itself: this play implies that the first step in loving another person is speaking with him, but it confines itself to the first step. Still this world is one of promise: those who manage to share a sentence may be able some day to share their lives.

The ideas about language reveal people very conscious of themselves and their own powers, willing to orchestrate themselves and their verbal skills into patterns of social celebration, but not willing to give themselves over entirely to others. As a result, the games do not require a particular partner: the lords try out a lady or two before they settle on a favorite partner for their wit; the women practice their flirting games with Boyet; when the ladies change favors and put on masks, the lords enthusiastically vow their souls and weave their patterns with the wrong ladies; occasionally even men with men and women with women play the games that signify affection and social harmony. "For society, saith the text, is the happiness of life," crows Nathaniel, forgetting that the Bible is not as explicit as his spirit of good fellowship would require.[14] The elaborate play with the interaction of order and significance in language thus reflects the communal order, and happily expresses the psychology of love as a social art: the matching of pattern indicates mutual attraction and acceptance; the denial or refutation of intended significance represents self-assertion and the attempt to maintain control of the interaction; and, finally, the entire exchange—two meanings made something weightier by the bond of order—indicates the generative possibilities of putting two together.

"Words are the Peoples" in *Love's Labor's Lost,* as Ben Jonson maintained that words generally are. Although individuals are not differentiated by their ideas on language, social groups are. This is a play exploring love as a social experience, not as a unique experience for each different lover (as in *The Taming of the Shrew* or *Much Ado about Nothing*). Delighting in what they have already learned, the young men and women make rhymes and rhythms and sentences together, and, doing so, prepare themselves to make love: they are learning to share, and to find joy in the sharing. By flirting and venturing toward love all together, at the same time and in the same way, they overcome their fears of the opposite sex and this new experience. The play celebrates love as a necessary social custom above love as a personal need. Appropriately, then, Shakespeare has found many ways in this play, both in style and in ideas about language, to embody the commonplace that language is a means of civilizing men and women and of binding them together in society.

Love's Labor's Lost is certainly not a play about philosophy of language. But Shakespeare does make comedy out of philosophical grammar. The characters are as in love with ideas as they are with words, or, more accurately, in love with their own creativity when they play with ideas. They treat even the most ponderous question, the meaning of meaning, as matter for a "light" joke. Katherine and Rosaline, bantering about Cupid and a sister who "died" of love, suddenly find themselves exploring the maze of meaning in words:

> *Kath.* Had she been light, like you,
>   Of such a merry, nimble, stirring spirit,
>   She might 'a' been a grandam ere she died.
>   And so may you; for a light heart lives long.

Ros. What's your dark meaning, mouse, of this light word?
Kath. A light condition in a beauty dark.
Ros. We need more light to find your meaning out.
Kath. You'll mar the light by taking it in snuff;
        Therefore I'll darkly end the argument.
Ros. Look what you do, you do it still i' th' dark.
Kath. So do not you, for you are a light wench.

(5.2.15-25)

For the sake of doing business through speech, one must pretend
that a word has only one meaning, and that both speaker and listener know what it is. Not content to let language go its businesslike
way, the two women are fascinated by the fact that words are units
of meaning, and, unlike things, not predictable entities; words have
"dark" and "light" sides, shades of meaning that need to be colored
by the intention of the speaker. Words are subjective: they may
change their meanings as often as people change their minds. When
Shakespeare's contemporary, Richard Carew, exults in the significance of English words—"Yea, so significant are our Words, that
amongst them sundry single ones serve to express divers things"—
"light" is one of the words he lists that have many meanings.[15]
Intrigued by a system that holds such abundant possibilities of
meaning, Rosaline asks a question so equivocal that it cannot be answered: she requests a clear statement of the "dark meaning" (hidden or evil meaning?) of the "light word" (the word *light,* or the
merry word, or the vulgar word?). As meanings multiply and each
speaker in turn adds new ones, we recognize in this love of symbols a
love of the generative capacity of the human spirit. Not only do people invent ideas, but language, made by people, is so creative a system that it will beget ideas for us. The control of this fecundity is
intention, as Rosaline understands when she begs for more "light" to
find out "your meaning" (not, apparently, her own). But the fun of
language is to let go control and see where it takes us. By the end of
the exchange a "dark" meaning is the same as a "light" meaning—
for both eventually indicate sexual appetite—and we, too, are in
love, as these characters are, with the ambiguity of language, its
vitality and power to generate meaning. By her last insult—"light
wench"—Katherine makes clear that her original intention was to
insult Rosaline with an implication of sexual looseness. But her orig-

inal intention, channeled into the symbolic system of language, is amplified into a variety of meanings and a higher level of energy. The energy of interaction with language, this wordplay seems to suggest, is like the energy of sexual interaction.

This energy from interacting with language, something all the characters of *Love's Labor's Lost* delight in, makes us feel the world to be even more a holiday one, not one for ordinary and everyday affairs. In *The Merry Wives of Windsor,* the Host praises the qualities of Master Fenton above those of Anne's other suitors because, he says, "he speaks holiday" (3.2.68). In *Love's Labor's Lost* all characters, whether or not they are wooing, speak holiday. Not only do they have special and exotic vocabularies, not appropriate to everyday experience, but also, if in ordinary society the plain truth is the end of language, in this society on holiday the expectation is reversed: one takes pleasure not in clarity, but in the richness of many meanings, and one does not subordinate delight in the means of expression, the sound and shape of words and the pattern of sentences, to the message conveyed. Thus, when the Princess on holiday meets the Forester arranging the business of hunting, they literally can make nothing of each other's words:

> *Prin.* Then, forester, my friend, where is the bush
> That we must stand and play the murtherer in?
> *For.* Hereby, upon the edge of yonder coppice,
> A stand where you may make the fairest shoot.
> *Prin.* I thank my beauty, I am fair that shoot,
> And thereupon thou speak'st the fairest shoot.
> *For.* Pardon me, madam, for I meant not so.
> *Prin.* What, what? First praise me, and again say no?
> O short-liv'd pride! Not fair? alack for woe!
> *For.* Yes, madam, fair.
> *Prin.*   Nay, never paint me now;
> Where fair is not, praise cannot mend the brow.
> Here (good my glass), take this for telling true:
> Fair payment for foul words is more than due.
> *For.* Nothing but fair is that which you inherit.
> *Prin.* See, see, my beauty will be sav'd by merit.
> O heresy in fair, fit for these days!
> A giving hand, though foul, shall have fair praise.
>   (4.1.7-23)

Unlike the Princess in holiday mood, the Forester will not let go his control of his words: they signify what he intends they shall; they are only a means to the end of truth. The Princess pays him for his words, for truth is valuable, but she points out that they are still "foul words," because, yoked only to purpose, words are not merely and completely beautiful as they are in play (just as the Princess's beauty, if connected to merit, is no longer merely and completely beautiful). The Princess tries to make new meaning from the generative order of language, but the Forester denies her that meaning, able to hear only his own, and unable to listen to the unintended gifts of significance in language.

Just as Dull's language lets us see by contrast the creativity as well as the affectation of the styles of the other characters, the Forester's comments let us see the creativity as well as the pedantry of the ideas about language of the other characters. Indeed, the people of *Love's Labor's Lost,* excepting the Forester and Marcade, break the rules that make language work well for ordinary business in order to try it out as a system, as children take apart a clock, fascinated by the mechanism, not caring that they can no longer tell time with it, delighted in the clock as sculpture—or mystery—not as tool.[16]

In enjoying language merely for itself, however, the characters find it working still, perhaps even on a higher level, as a system of giving, as well as transferring, meaning. Despite his narcissistic control over the patterns of language, even Armado cannot escape its generative powers. Wearing the grand words of Hector, as he has worn the boasting words of the knight throughout the play, Armado finds himself forced to see, in his own words, the essential man beneath:

> *Arm.* "This Hector far surmounted Hannibal.
>   The party is gone"—
> *Cost.* Fellow Hector, she is gone; she is two months on her way.
> *Arm.* What meanest thou?
> *Cost.* Faith, unless you play the honest Troyan, the poor wench is cast away. She's quick, the child brags in her belly already. 'Tis yours.
>   (5.2.670–77)

Costard's literal understanding of Armado's words apprehends a true meaning, even if it is not the intended one: under the proud words, Armado is only a man, driven by dishonorable appetites and afraid to face his faults honestly. But Armado welcomes the unlooked for meaning in words, even though it proves him a fool: "I breathe free breath. I have seen the day of wrong through the little hole of discretion, and I will right myself like a soldier" (5.2.722–25). In this play, words are indeed generative: the meaning that Costard finds for Armado in words describing Hector is like the astonishing surprise of Jaquenetta's pregnancy. Love and language both give back more than we put into them.

With the entrance of Marcade, the world of the play is transformed as abruptly as Armado, who leaves the stage vowing to hold the plow for Jaquenetta. The natural facts of Jaquenetta's pregnancy and the death of the Princess's father replace the festivities, and the simple song celebrating the passing of seasons and the rhythms of human industry replaces the artifice of earlier pageantry.[17] The holiday of love played as a game is over, too, because the Princess is called into her grown-up role by her father's death. The men have already offered to take the game seriously, to give up the arts of language—wooing in rhymes, taffeta phrases, figures pedantical—for something simpler: honest, plain noes and yeses. The women, however, will not trust their vows:

> We have receiv'd your letters full of love;
> Your favors, embassadors of love;
> And in our maiden council rated them
> At courtship, pleasant jest, and courtesy,
> As bombast and as lining to the time;
> But more devout than this in our respects
> Have we not been, and therefore met your loves
> In their own fashion, like a merriment.
>
> (5.2.777–84)

The women do not reject the love of the men: they take it as it was offered, a graceful gift of wit and courtesy. But love as a social art is too delicate a form to last: "A time methinks too short / To make a world-without-end bargain in" (ll. 788–89). And so the men are given the trial of time, a twelve-month and a day, to see if their love is made of sterner stuff. The King, in fact, is given a special penance: an "austere insociable life" (l. 799). If his personal love will en-

dure, cut off from all the pleasant sociability of being young, with
friends, and doing what is fashionable, then perhaps it is strong
enough to hold out against time. The young men and women have
shared games and words together, and joy; they have yet to share
suffering. And that experience is, as Berowne observes, "too long for
a play" (l. 878).

With the entrance of Marcade, the dominant ideas about language—the grammar book units of letter, syllable, and word, the
concept of language as an ordered system of rational symbols—are
transformed as well. Marcade tells his news slowly, for it is "heavy in
[his] tongue" (5.2.719); the Princess apologizes for her bold "opposition" to the King, "In the converse of breath" (ll. 733–35); but she
does not elaborate, since "A heavy heart bears not a humble tongue"
(l. 737). Speech becomes "tongue" and "breath," the simple, natural fact. Rosaline assigns Berowne his penance to perform if he will
have her to wife in a year: to "Visit the speechless sick, and still converse / With groaning wretches" (ll. 851–52). It is a melancholy vision, as is the ending of the play, when "Jack hath not Gill" (l. 875).
Marcade's message, Berowne's penance, and perhaps also the
change in ideas about language—from generative words to thoughts
sounded on the tongue, as transient as breath—remind us that all
things human, including the gift of speech, partake of mortality.
The world of youth and holiday has fallen to pieces, and verbal
games will not do to make a new one. The feast of language has
vanished.

Although the words "tongue" and "breath" replace "language"
and "word," indicating a shift toward the more natural idea of language as voice, we yet see no loss in the creativity associated with language. Language becomes something else in the world of the play,
not something less. Rosaline wants, in a year, a Berowne made
whole, not only within himself, but integrated into his community.
She expects him to accomplish this change by speaking:

>   A jest's prosperity lies in the ear
>   Of him that hears it, never in the tongue
>   Of him that makes it; then if sickly ears,
>   Deaf'd with the clamors of their own dear groans,
>   Will hear your idle scorns, continue then,
>   And I will have you and that fault withal;
>   But if they will not, throw away that spirit,

And I shall find you empty of that fault,
Right joyful of your reformation.

(ll. 861-69)

Rosaline asks Berowne to use his jesting words to alleviate suffering, or else to give them up for words that may. Berowne has said something like this himself: "Honest plain words best pierce the ear of grief" (l. 753). From this larger perspective, Berowne's words are meant not for his own delight but for the nurturing of others. Wit, like love, only comes into being when it is given away. Beauty, after all, is connected to merit, and words merely beautiful are not strong enough to bear the weight of mortality.

If, as has been suggested, there are three orders of human experience—the mechanical and isolated one, lacking spontaneity; the narcissistic but lively delight in one's own powers; and, finally, the livelier joy in spontaneity, experience of the world, and intimacy with others[18]—then *Love's Labor's Lost* celebrates the second and points to the third, especially in ideas about language. Certainly the primary meaning of the final words of the play—"The words of Mercury are harsh after the songs of Apollo" (5.2.930-31)—is that youthful festivity is interrupted by death and the call of life's earnest business. But perhaps a secondary meaning is a change in the conception of language, indicating a growth in humanity in the characters of the play: language as a creative system wondered at simply for its order and significance is finally harnessed to the ends of social purpose and the intimacy of truths.

Notes

1. The counts of the seventeen key words are based on Marvin Spevack's *A Complete and Systematic Concordance to the Works of Shakespeare*, 6 vols. (Hildesheim: Georg Olms, 1968-70). Not every listing of the words is counted, but only those with linguistic significance. According to these counts, the early plays (1590-95) average one reference per twenty-four lines; the middle plays (1596-99), one per twenty-five lines; the plays of the tragic period (1600-1607), one per twenty-four lines; and the plays of the late period (1608-13), one per thirty lines; the average for all plays is one reference per twenty-six lines. Dating, of course, is a difficult matter. I have chosen not to enter the controversies, and so simply follow the estimates given in *The Riverside Shakespeare:* in the chronological list-

ing of this edition, I have categorized as early plays *1H6* through *MND*, as middle plays *MV* through *AYL*, as plays of the tragic period *Ham.* through *Tim.*, and as late plays *Per.* through *TNK*.

2. The comedies average one reference per twenty-two lines; the histories, one per twenty-five lines; the tragedies, one per twenty-three lines; the romances, one per thirty-one lines. I have placed *Jn.* and the tragedies that are part of the historical tetralogies in the category of histories, not in the category of tragedies.

3. The plays with lowest frequency of key words concerning language are *TNK*, one reference per forty-five lines; *R3*, one per thirty-three lines; *Tim.*, one per thirty-three lines; *WT*, one per thirty-three lines; *1H6*, one per thirty-two lines; *MV*, one per thirty-one lines; *Cym.*, one per thirty-one lines; *Shr.*, one per thirty lines; and *Ant.*, one per thirty lines.

4. The plays with highest frequency of key words concerning language are *R2*, one reference per sixteen lines; *Cor.*, one per seventeen lines; *LLL*, one per eighteen lines; *Jn.*, one per nineteen lines; *JC*, one per twenty lines; *Ham.*, one per twenty lines; *Tit.*, one per twenty-one lines; *Ado*, one per twenty-one lines; *MM*, one per twenty-one lines; *Rom.*, one per twenty-two lines; and *2H4*, one per twenty-two lines.

5. With a count of forty-eight, *LLL* of all the plays has the greatest number of references to "word(s)"; next is *3H6*, with thirty-eight; the average per play is twenty-four.

6. See especially Bobbyann Roesen, *"Love's Labour's Lost,"* *SQ*, 4 (1953), 416; C. L. Barber, *Shakespeare's Festive Comedy* (Princeton: Princeton Univ. Press, 1959), pp. 99–103; E. M. W. Tillyard, *Shakespeare's Early Comedies* (New York: Barnes & Noble, 1965), pp. 159–64; Thomas McFarland, *Shakespeare's Pastoral Comedy* (Chapel Hill: Univ. of North Carolina Press, 1972), pp. 65–73; and Herbert Ellis, *Shakespeare's Lusty Punning in Love's Labour's Lost* (The Hague: Mouton, 1973).

7. Mulcaster, *Elementarie*, p. 50.

8. Cf. Barber, *Shakespeare's Festive Comedy*, p. 96: "Even the princess and her ladies in waiting, when they talk in terms of copy-book letters, seem just freshly out of school." I am much indebted to Barber's entire essay.

9. By a count of four key terms associated with writing — pen, ink, paper(s), and parchment — *LLL* ranks highest of all plays with fifteen references; the average is four.

10. Critics who have argued that language is a main theme of *LLL* are William Matthews, "Language in 'Love's Labour's Lost,' " *E&S*, n.s. 17 (1964), esp. p. 10; Ralph Berry, "The Words of Mercury," *ShS*, 22 (1969), 69–77; Calderwood, *Shakespearean Metadrama*, pp. 52–84; Thomas M.

Greene, *"Love's Labour's Lost:* The Grace of Society," *SQ,* 22 (1971), esp. p. 315; McFarland, *Shakespeare's Pastoral Comedy,* esp. p. 73; Hawkes, *Shakespeare's Talking Animals,* pp. 53-72; Malcolm Evans, "Mercury vs. Apollo," *SQ,* 26 (1975), 113-27; and William C. Carroll, *The Great Feast of Language* (Princeton: Princeton Univ. Press, 1976), esp. pp. 63-64. In contrast to these critics, I would hold up those who wrote before the idea of language as theme became popular, and who saw in *LLL* language subordinated to larger interests: see O. J. Campbell, *"Love's Labour's Lost* Re-Studied," in *Studies in Shakespeare, Milton and Donne* (1925; rpt. New York: Haskell House, 1964), pp. 3-45; Roesen, *"Love's Labour's Lost,"* pp. 411-26; Barber, *Shakespeare's Festive Comedy,* pp. 87-118; and Tillyard, *Shakespeare's Early Comedies,* pp. 137-81.

11. On the affected styles of the pedants, see Campbell, *"Love's Labour's Lost* Re-Studied," pp. 38-40; Willcock, *Shakespeare as Critic of Language,* pp. 10-17; Matthews, "Language in 'Love's Labour's Lost,'" pp. 3-9; and Carroll, *Great Feast,* pp. 19-51.

12. See Ernst Robert Curtius, *European Literature and the Latin Middle Ages,* tr. Willard R. Trask (Princeton: Princeton Univ. Press, 1953), pp. 58-59, on the games of matching verses in Latin education.

13. The other men pair off by approaching Boyet and talking about the ladies; the pairing is indicated by the questions and answers, each man using his own special meter, which Boyet imitates: Dumaine and Boyet in six-beat lines on the subject of Katherine; Longaville and Boyet in four- and then three-beat lines on Maria; and Berowne and Boyet in two-beat lines on Rosaline. The pairing is indicated by the matching of rhymes and rhythms; a fear of this new experience is indicated by the men's doing it through an intermediary.

14. See my note, "Nathaniel's 'Text' in 'Love's Labour's Lost' IV.ii.161-62," *N&Q,* n. s. 25 (Apr., 1978), 122-24. Nathaniel's allusion is to the Vulgate version of Ecclesiastes 4:8-12, especially verse 9: *"Meli est ergo duos esse simul, quam vnum: habent enim emolumentum societatis suae."* [It is better therefore that there should be two together than one alone: for they have the benefit of their society—my translation.] The passage celebrates society, as the glosses, though not the translations, of this passage in the Geneva Bible and the Bishops' Bible acknowledge; but the passage does not imply quite the festivity that Nathaniel justifies with it. Nevertheless, since *LLL* was performed at court during the Christmas revels in either 1597 or 1598, the allusion was particularly pointed: Elizabeth generally began her theatrical season on St. Stephen's Day, for which this passage from Ecclesiastes was a reading at evening prayer.

15. Carew, "Epistle," p. 6.

16. See Calderwood, *Shakespearean Metadrama,* p. 56: "In perhaps no

other play does language so nearly become an autonomous symbolic system whose value lies less in its relevance to reality than in its intrinsic fascination." But compare G. K. Hunter, "Poems and Context in *Love's Labour's Lost,*" in *Shakespeare's Styles,* ed. Philip Edwards, Inga-Stina Ewbank, and G. K. Hunter (Cambridge: Cambridge Univ. Press, 1980), p. 37: "the whole play moves in a direction which keeps open (at the very least) the possibility that stylishness is a necessity rather than a self-indulgence."

17. This change in mood toward the somber was dramatically taken advantage of in the production of *LLL* directed by David Conville in the open-air theater in Regent's Park in London in 1977: in the evening performances the play began in daylight and ended in darkness (with only artificial lighting). Perhaps in the open-air Globe in the winter season the original performances in the afternoon had much the same effect.

18. See Eric Berne, *Games People Play* (New York: Grove Press, 1964), pp. 178-81.

CHAPTER 5

King John:
Mutable Speech

If we accept the estimates in *The Riverside Shakespeare, The Life and Death of King John* was written within a year or two of *Love's Labor's Lost.*[1] The comedy, moreover, is third of all plays in frequency of key terms concerning language, and the history is fourth.[2] Yet Shakespeare's interest in language in *Love's Labor's Lost* has often been commented on, while that in *King John* has been mentioned only in passing.[3] Part of this difference in critical attention is due, no doubt, to the relative quality of the two plays: *King John* is an unattractive play, rarely produced, criticized for its style, lacking the sharply focused conflict of the successful histories, and wanting the dominant hero or pair of heroes of the more successful tragedies; *Love's Labor's Lost,* on the other hand, is a quite satisfactory comedy, often produced, and sharing the confusions in plot, the witty verse, and the mockery of young love with other successful comedies. Some of the difference in critical attention to language, however, is owing to the nature of Shakespeare's interest in language in the two plays. *King John* is second among the plays in oral speech imagery, while *Love's Labor's Lost* is fifth.[4] *Love's Labor's Lost,* in contrast, overwhelmingly exceeds *King John* in interest in written language and in "word(s)."[5] *Love's Labor's Lost* thus emphasizes what modern critics are especially attentive to, language as a system of meaning. In opposition, *King John* emphasizes language as voice: breath, tongue, mouth, and ears. As several critics and historians have pointed out, Elizabethans were generally more sensitive to this oral aspect of language than we are.[6]

It seems unlikely that Shakespeare fundamentally changed his conception of language in whatever short time passed between the composition of *Love's Labor's Lost* and that of *King John.* In fact, the ideas about language, though radically different in these two

165

plays, achieve the same end: establishing an atmosphere appropriate to the story. The conception of language as voice — physical act and transient breath — is as essential to the world of *King John,* where a weak king fails and passes, as the conception of language as a generative system of meaning is to the holiday world of *Love's Labor's Lost.* Unlike the comedy, however, *King John* is a mediocre play. It lacks the clear motivation and unity of story of its probable source, *The Troublesome Raigne of John, King of England.*[7] While I have seen *Timon of Athens,* despite its tedious vituperation, work admirably on the stage, I have seen *King John* fail in exactly the way one would expect from reading it: the unending confrontations remained stiff, overrhetorical, and difficult to follow; the character of the Bastard stood out as the one lively element in an otherwise dreary play; and the hopeful ending seemed incongruous. Finally, there is critical consensus that *King John* is a poor play.[8] This chapter will suggest another reason for the play's lack of success: Shakespeare's attempt to embody in his style the defects in language that the characters perceive in their world. Part of what makes *Love's Labor's Lost* succeed as a play, the shaping of style and ideas about language into a coherent world, is part of what makes *King John* fail.

In *King John,* as in the definitions of *"vox"* in Elizabethan grammar-school textbooks, speech is air struck by the tongue and sounded in the ears. Sneering, Austria demands the identity of the Bastard: "What cracker is this same that deafs our ears / With this abundance of superfluous breath?" (*Jn.* 2.1.147–48). Blanche addresses the Dauphin — "O husband, hear me! ay, alack, how new / Is 'husband' in my mouth!" — and begs him, "even for that name, / Which till this time my tongue did ne'er pronounce," not to go to war against her uncle (3.1.305–9). Near the end of the play, Hubert apologizes to the Bastard for not recognizing him in the darkness: "pardon me / That any accent breaking from thy tongue / Should scape the true acquaintance of mine ear" (5.6.13–15). The terms used to describe language are as physical in *King John* as they are cerebral in *Love's Labor's Lost.* Moreover, while "word(s)" is the most typical reference to language in *Love's Labor's Lost,* "breath" is the most typical in *King John:*[9] Constance tells a messenger that his news is not to be trusted, for it is "the vain breath of a common man" (3.1.8), and the deserting English lords wait with the French for the papal legate, who will "on [their] actions set the name of right / With holy breath" (5.2.67–68). In fact, people do not so much speak in this play as "breathe" words. Pandulph will "breathe" the Church's curse on John (3.1.256); the lords have "breath'd" their "counsel" to John, who neglects it (4.2.36); Salisbury swears to avenge Arthur's death, "breathing to his breathless excellence / . . . a holy vow" (4.3.66–67); and, at the end of the play, the Bastard comes to "breathe" the news of English defeat in a dead king's "ear" (5.7.65). The emphasis in almost all these passages is on the transience of speech. Words come as easily as breathing to the men and women in *King John,* and with as little consequence; language fails to be a social bond because breath passes and vows are equally transitory.

The imagery of the play, moreover, presents language as a vehicle for man's self-destructive urge toward anarchy, not his enlightened progress toward civilization. The references to speech in *King John* are mimetic, not discursive: vivid descriptions of speakers and the act of speaking. In the examples we have glanced at, speech is depicted as "breath," "mouth," and "tongue," either synecdoches standing for the speaker, or metonymies standing for speech.[10] But the particularity emphasizes fragmentation, not the coming together of individuals into a community: Blanche holds the name of "husband" in her "mouth," not the man in her arms; Hubert does not recognize the "tongue" of his only protector in a suspicious society; the Bastard breathes his news to an "ear" that will not hear him. It is not that there is no mention of the civilizing force of language; rather, the unifying power of words is mentioned, only to be denied. When John denounces the Pope, Philip reconsiders the peace he has just made with England, despairing that the union made by words must be broken:

> The latest breath that gave the sound of words
> Was deep-sworn faith, peace, amity, true love
> Between our kingdoms and our royal selves,
>
> . . . .
>
> And shall these hands, so lately purg'd of blood,
> So newly join'd in love, so strong in both,
> Unyoke this seizure and this kind regreet?
> Play fast and loose with faith? so jest with heaven?
> Make such unconstant children of ourselves,

As now again to snatch our palm from palm,
Unswear faith sworn, and on the marriage-bed
Of smiling peace to march a bloody host,
And make a riot on the gentle brow
Of true sincerity?

(3.1.230–48)

The reference to the binding power of words makes its transience, and the resulting fragmented society, all the more tragic. Just as in their speech men are not whole, but parcels of breath, hands, palms, and brows, so the society is not united, but a mere collection of bloody warring men.[11]

English society is no better in this respect than international society, as we may see in Hubert's description of the citizens' response to Arthur's death:

Young Arthur's death is common in their mouths,
And when they talk of him, they shake their heads,
And whisper one another in the ear;
And he that speaks doth gripe the hearer's wrist,
Whilst he that hears makes fearful action
With wrinkled brows, with nods, with rolling eyes.

(4.2.187–92)

In Hubert's description, the England outside John's palace mirrors the breakdown of the King within, for John is also fearful at this moment, about to patch up an inglorious bargain with the Pope to save his crown. The picture presented is vivid, recalling the color, structure, and grotesquerie in paintings by Brueghel and Cranach: focused details pile up in a busy, almost frenzied scene of intensity and sorrow. But the images also anatomize the men; the participants disintegrate into bright but ominous pieces—mouths, heads, ears, wrists, and rolling eyes—that emphasize the larger falling apart of which Arthur's death is one small piece. Speech operates not to bring men together into civil society, but to break down what little community exists into lonely fragments; and the imagery reflects this moral and social disorder. People do not affirm in *King John;* they only give tongue and hand. England is not a garden, but a "fleshly land, / . . . this confine of blood and breath" (4.2.245–46).

Because of the destructive forces at work in their world, individuals themselves cannot remain whole. Blanche, faced with a choice between uncle and husband, gives part of her loyalty to each, and feels destroyed in the process: "I am with both, each army hath a hand, / And in their rage, I having hold of both, / They whirl asunder and dismember me" (3.1.328-30). When Philip tries to quiet Constance after the capture of her son Arthur, her prayer is as foretelling as Margaret's curses are in *Richard III*:

> No, no, I will not, having breath to cry.
> O that my tongue were in the thunder's mouth!
> Then with a passion would I shake the world,
> And rouse from sleep that fell anatomy
> Which cannot hear a lady's feeble voice,
> Which scorns a modern invocation.
>
> (3.4.37-42)

The fragmenting power of that "fell anatomy," nothing but bones, Shakespeare pictures in the style of the play. If not Constance's voice, then the voices of kings and prelates successfully invoke ruin. While in *Love's Labor's Lost* the power of language is generative, in *King John* it is destructive.

Even more ominous than the preceding images are the military metaphors for speech in the play, for they tell us that words are merely weapons. Thus John woos the townsmen of Angiers and grandly reviles the French:

> Behold, the French amaz'd vouchsafe a parle,
> And now instead of bullets wrapp'd in fire,
> To make a shaking fever in your walls,
> They shoot but calm words folded up in smoke,
> To make a faithless error in your ears.
>
> (2.1.226-30)

Words are figuratively "smoke" because they are literally air; and the metaphor "shoot" captures the potential violence in the grammarians' idea of speech as air struck by the tongue. The metaphors for speech tell us what the men are in the play: like their words, they are violent and destructive. Challenging the spokesman for the besieged city, the Bastard repeats and amplifies John's metaphors:

> Here's a large mouth indeed,
> That spits forth death and mountains, rocks and seas!
>
> . . . . .
>
> He speaks plain cannon-fire, and smoke, and bounce,

> He gives the bastinado with his tongue;
> Our ears are cudgell'd — not a word of his
> But buffets better than a fist of France.
> 'Zounds, I was never so bethump'd with words
> Since I first call'd my brother's father dad.
>
> (2.1.457-67)

Speech is "smoke," "cannon-fire," and "the bastinado," cudgeling, buffeting, and bethumping the listener. Language is not a social bond, but a battle.

Speech is a battle waged within individuals, as well as between them. Persuading Philip to break his vows to England, Pandulph tells him that he is "like a civil war," setting "oath to oath, / Thy tongue against thy tongue" (3.1.264-65), his "later vows" to England against his "first" to the Pope being "in thyself rebellion to thyself" (3.1.288-89). In these violent metaphors Shakespeare embodies the discord of John's England and Christian Europe. The power of words rests not in their significance, but in their physical effects and the force of their speakers. The Bastard had mocked the words of the citizen of Angiers, but with them — and the promise of gain — the citizen arranges a truce between the English and French. Only when Pandulph arrives, a more powerful speaker — with more to offer — does Philip break faith to keep papal support and to seize Arthur's inheritance for his own son. The social order, in language as in government, is based on might, not right.[12]

Speech is powerful for immediate ends, to change men's minds temporarily, but its effects do not last: by this cynical philosophy most of the characters in *King John* operate. Eleanor's comment to John on the betrothal of Blanche to Lewis might serve as a paradigm for the effect of language in this world; urge the French, she admonishes John,

> while their souls
> Are capable of this ambition,
> Lest zeal, now melted by the windy breath
> Of soft petitions, pity, and remorse,
> Cool and congeal again to what it was.
>
> (2.1.475-79)

Negotiate the marriage before the breath of Hubert's words disappears, lest the softening of the French last no longer than his speeches. Language in *King John* has the transience of voice in Robinson's treatise on pronunciation: "it is no sooner vttered but it is dissolued, euery simple sound doth expell and extinguish the sound going before it."[13] Speech, in form and function, seems a reflection of human mutability.

Eleanor's analysis of the effect of speech is tragically accurate: the English accomplish the immediate end of marrying Blanche to Lewis, but fail in their larger purpose, a lasting peace with France. Throughout the play Philip, John, Pandulph, and Lewis speak their vows and break them as soon as it is convenient: treaties are pledges given on the battlefield and denied in the tents soon after, serving mainly as an opportunity for later conflict. It is the same with all sacred words in the play. The holy words of the marriage service achieve their limited function: Blanche must go with Lewis when the battle begins. But Blanche is not made something more than herself by the words uniting her to another person; she is made something less, torn apart by her conflicting loyalties. In like manner, the words of the law are not the foundation of this society, unifying men in order to pursue the larger end of social justice; law is rather the voice of the current interests of the man who has power. Because of the law of primogeniture, John judges Falconbridge's will leaving his lands to his younger son void; yet Eleanor reveals that John's title rests on exactly this kind of will (2.1.192). Legal documents and common law thus have no certain legitimacy; verbal contracts weigh only with what force some judge's voice gives them at the moment.

In the legal and ritual words of this world, the private men usurp the powers of their offices, and speak to their own personal interests. During his most heroic moment, John refuses Pandulph's demand that he justify his actions to the Pope:

> What earthy name to interrogatories
> Can taste the free breath of a sacred king?
> Thou canst not, Cardinal, devise a name
> So slight, unworthy, and ridiculous,
> To charge me to an answer, as the Pope.
> Tell him this tale, and from the mouth of England.
>
> (3.1.147-52)

By reference to "breath," John celebrates the authority of the English king, as freely ranging as voiced sound; by the physical fact that his speech comes from his "mouth," John stands firm on the absoluteness of his decision. Although John swears by his own kingly speech and name not to succumb to papal power, he does so when it is in his own private interest; he assumes that the King's powers are his own. The name "King" thus comes to have no more value than "Pope" to compel loyalty or to serve as a standard of truth because the title is devalued by the man in the office. Pandulph similarly, and blasphemously, assumes that the divine powers of a priest's voice are his own, to be used to personal ends:

> Now hear me speak with a prophetic spirit;
> For even the breath of what I mean to speak
> Shall blow each dust, each straw, each little rub,
> Out of the path which shall directly lead
> Thy foot to England's throne.
>
> (3.4.126–30)

With a play on the word "spirit" (as in Latin, "breath" as well as "inspiration"), Pandulph boasts that his voice is God's. Inciting Lewis to vengeance against John, the Cardinal appeals to Lewis's ambition, and assumes that Lewis will also ignore his princely office to further his personal gain. Lewis's actions ironically bear out the legate's assumption: Lewis listens to Pandulph only as long as he speaks his support of the Dauphin's ambition to England's throne. If in *Love's Labor's Lost* the characters' love of words prepares them to love other people, in *King John* the characters' passion for words indicates their willingness to use people, as they use words, for their own selfish interests.

The ideas about language in *King John* help to shape a world of raw power and violent physical action, but a mutable one, where all power has passing effect. What the Count in Castiglione's *The Courtier* infers from the fact of change in language may equally apply to the dramatic impact of the use of language in *King John:* "time [doth] make those first wordes to fall, and vse maketh other to spring a fresh . . . because at the last both wee and whatsoeuer is ours, are mortall."[14] The ideas about language thus support the larger purpose of the play: in *King John* Shakespeare studies man as a political animal, not in the ideal Renaissance sense of the seeker after glory and knowledge infinite, but in the lesser sense of the vain striver after merely worldly power. All seek after power and fail to hold it: John, the weak king who buys his throne by giving away his lands, who cannot successfully carry off the war in France, the defiance of the Pope, or the murder of Arthur; the haughty French, who yet cannot conquer England; the frantic women, who cannot keep their sons securely in power; even the Bastard, whose heroic acts are frustrated by his weak patron. To be sure, this is a staple of English Renaissance tragedy: great men fall after they rise. But in other of Shakespeare's tragedies, except perhaps in *Timon of Athens,* the imagined world of the play allows us belief in transcendent principles of order despite the fall of individuals. In *King John* Shakespeare has created a society of men and women so intent on augmenting their own powers, and so weak in their inability to see any but their private interests, that when the spokesman for order, Prince Henry, appears at the end of the play, we cannot believe that he actually belongs to this world, or, if he does, that he can create an England suddenly true to itself.[15]

The lack of credibility in the ending is in proportion to Shakespeare's success in creating a believable world in the rest of the play. Most significantly, the style reinforces the effects of the ideas about language in *King John:* how men speak corresponds to what they say about speech. If the power of speech is destructive and transient, it is because the powerful men in *King John* exploit language in their personal interests, using words more often to conceal truth than to reveal it. In the opening scene, for example, Chatillon, the French ambassador, does not simply ask John to give up his kingdom; he desires him in formal jargon, "to lay aside the sword / Which sways usurpingly these several titles" (1.1.12-13). Nor does John simply deny his request; equal to any modern bureaucrat, he instead demands, "What follows if we disallow of this?" (l. 16). Chatillon does not straightforwardly threaten John with war and death, but instead with "The proud control of fierce and bloody war, / To enforce these rights so forcibly withheld" (ll. 17-18). Although his embassy has as its purpose to secure control over John's power and lands, his words make it appear that the French only wish to control John's unjust ambitions to wrongful power. John, moreover, picks up the euphemism in his answering challenge: "Here have we war for war and blood for blood, / Controlment for controlment" (ll. 19-20). What an ugly word "controlment" is! By adding a syllable, John does not get more meaning, as do the characters of *Love's Labor's Lost,* but less. Ignoring Chatillon's meaning, and giving back mere word for mere word, John joins in perverting language from a means of communication to a struggle for power. And by speaking of war as an abstraction and their soldiers as merely "blood," John and Chatillon aid each other in ignoring the fact that they make the decision of war and that other men suffer for it. They refuse moral responsibility in their vague words, as if the decision comes from some relentless logic not their own. Like the American presidents of the 1960s, while the French and English intend war, they agree in not admitting that their aim all along was war: the French fight only for the "rights" of Arthur Plantagenet; the English fight only for John's "rights." The private exchange between John and his mother (who but a mother for these truths of conscience?) sets forth the actualities behind the vague words: John's "possession" speaks more strongly in this war than his "right" (1.1.40–43).

Many rhetorical devices for concealing truth besides euphemisms and vague generalities are employed in this play. John's style is florid, like that of most of the other characters, and his favorite device for obscuring facts is an extended metaphor or conceit, what Elizabethans called an *"allegoria."*[16] John speaks to Philip by way of allegory, for example, when the English king claims Angiers:

> France, hast thou yet more blood to cast away?
> Say, shall the current of our right roam on?
> Whose passage, vex'd with thy impediment,
> Shall leave his native channel and o'erswell
> With course disturb'd even thy confining shores,
> Unless thou let his silver water keep
> A peaceful progress to the ocean.
>
> (2.1.334–40)

John distances himself from the truth of his unjust presence in France first by the euphemism of "our right" for "our army," and then by the metaphor of the flooding river for the destruction of war. His final extension of the conceit carries him even further from the truth: while he describes his intent as a peaceful river flowing away from the lands to the ocean, his actual desire is to confirm his rights to his French lands by a warlike progress through them.

Everyone in this political play has something to hide, and many linguistic devices with which to do it. Speakers often argue side issues, rather than the central issues of power and broken vows. When Philip, for instance, informs Constance that he has made peace with the English, he praises the day, instead of telling Constance that the alliance betrays her son's interests in favor of his own son's gains: today is "this blessed day," (3.1.75), this "holy day," (l. 82), on which

> the glorious sun
> Stays in his course and plays the alchymist,
> Turning with splendor of his gracious eye
> The meagre cloddy earth to glittering gold.
>
> (ll. 77-80)

Presenting himself as Joshua rather than the more appropriate Judas, Philip shifts the argument to the side issue of the day—what Renaissance logicians taught as an "argument from adjuncts" or circumstances[17]—and thus avoids the brutal truth, that his own son will get as dowry many of the lands by right belonging to Arthur. And his ploy works. Caught by his false eloquence, Constance aims her anger at the day, not at Philip: this "wicked day" (3.1.83), "This day of shame, oppression, perjury" (l. 88), when women will bear only cursed children, and all bargains will be broken, until "faith itself to hollow falsehood change!" (l. 95). Constance, moreover, is a willing victim of Philip's obfuscation: she is equally reluctant to speak of her personal ambitions for her son.

Through the style of language of the princes of the play, Shakespeare makes of *King John* a political exposé: the royal and international negotiation is the worst sort of political humbug. The decadence in political speaking seems a manifestation of the corruption in political ambition; the men and women of *King John* cannot afford to tell the truth about themselves. Although the style operates with the ideas about language to form a coherent and credible world, the play is not good theater. Unlike the despicable but strong politicians of *Richard III*, who exult at least to their allies in achieving their selfish interests, the politicians of *King John* appear merely despicable, afraid to express their desires clearly, even to themselves. Consequently, the many characters speaking vague language come together in a play that seems generally turgid, especially in the early acts. The aesthetic problem that Shakespeare fails to solve in *King John* is a crucial one for Elizabethan tragedy: how to depict immoral and obscure speakers—men as they often are—in a play that remains eloquent and forceful.

When the speakers in *King John* do make words clear, they are generally using them to attack others. This aspect of the style does not bring relief, though, for language becomes in this case the ugliest of men's tools: the weapon. One critic has complained that Constance "is the last and most terrible of Shakespeare's wailing women. . . . There is a vicious force in her feeling, an unexplained, untamed intensity which drives her at once into conceits."[18] But what is here said of Constance might be said of most of the characters: of Lady Falconbridge when she attacks her son for telling of her illicit affair, of Eleanor when she insults Constance, of the French and English before Angiers, of John when he turns on Hubert.[19] The monstrous insults and hyperbolic conceits do not make us wonder at these characters for the grandness of their passions, as we wonder at even the evil characters in the earlier histories and tragedies. In the shrill voices of *King John* is heard neither an unexplained feeling, nor the grand anger of vengeful desire, but simply fear: each wants to be on top in the scramble for power, and when each feels himself slipping, losing it all, he strikes out with words. The verbal insults soon weary us because they, too, like the political negotiations, are finally meaningless. As with Austria, who boasts of his courage, these others have no intention of risking their lives to make their words good. The people are small, not large in spirit, and their verbal attacks are merely tantrums: nothing comes of them.

In *King John* Shakespeare has succeeded in making a credible world only to fail in engaging our deeper interest in it; the language is generally vague or mean-spirited, and the characters are rarely likeable and never awesome. The exception is the Bastard, the soldier who speaks straight out, the man willing to act when others prefer politic indirections. I am tempted to call him a "plain speaker," a prototype of Kent and Enobarbus. But his style is not very different from that of other characters in the play, as we have seen in the passage where he picks up John's military metaphors for speech and amplifies them. He differs from the others not so much in style, as in his ideas about language and his intent in speaking. The Bastard is the only character perturbed by the issue of language, addressing it in his two major soliloquies; he is also the only character who means what he says. The others surrender to words, giving up their control over them in order to hide behind them, hoping no one will notice what they are doing behind the smoke screen. The Bastard takes moral responsibility for his words, speaking only what he will perform.

Elizabethans were not unaware of the danger of vague language in politics. The moral and political consequences are Ascham's concerns when he warns, "Ye know not, what hurt ye do to learning, that care not for wordes but for matter, and so make a deuorse betwixt the tong and the hart."[20] And Mulcaster, another educator, postulated that languages have "ascent" and "discent," depending on whether the state grows "to better countenance," or falls off "to the more corrupt."[21] For both Ascham and Mulcaster, corrupt language inevitably accompanies a corrupt age, to some degree causing the corruption.

In *King John* the Bastard makes a similar connection between language and politics. In his soliloquy after his introduction to court, he turns immediately to the corruption of courtly language. Coming from outside the world of the others, he mockingly contemplates learning a different way of speaking in order to keep his place in this new world:

> And if his name be George, I'll call him Peter;
> For new-made honor doth forget men's names;
> 'Tis too respective and too sociable
> For your conversion.
>
> (1.1.186-89)

The Bastard has himself just received a new name and must forget his old one: "Philip? sparrow!" (l. 231). Entering courtly society, he tells himself that he must learn not to call things and people by their right names because names are social bonds; he who rises to power must set himself off from others in aristocratic isolation. In addition, he must practice the "dialogue of compliment" (l. 201), the polite formulas by which men offer their "service" (l. 198) to each other, all the while intending to serve no one except themselves. Finally, he must learn to empty words of all but their most impersonal meanings, "talking of the Alps and Apennines / The Pyrenean and the river Po" (ll. 202-3). Words are not pledges of commitment in this world, but only a way to pass the time until supper. Such language, hiding rather than revealing truth, is "Sweet, sweet, sweet poison for the age's tooth" (l. 213), and the Bastard means to learn it not to de-

ceive, but to avoid deception (ll. 214–15). In his metaphor of
"poison," the Bastard seems to understand that such language
harms not only those taken in by it, but also those who speak it: if
one hides the truth with words too long, one may forget where it is
hidden.

The natural response to this world is opportunism, what the Bastard calls "commodity." France, says the Bastard in his second soliloquy, is

> rounded in the ear
> With that same purpose-changer, that sly devil,
> That broker that still breaks the pate of faith,
> That daily break-vow, he that wins of all,
> Of kings, of beggars, old men, young men, maids,
> Who having no external thing to lose
> But the word "maid," cheats the poor maid of that.
>
> (2.1.566–72)

It is "this same bias, this commodity, / This bawd, this broker, this
all-changing word" (ll. 581–82) that the Bastard, taking the lead
from John and Philip, will have as his guide, too: "Since kings break
faith upon commodity, / Gain, be my lord, for I will worship thee"
(ll. 597–98). To the Bastard, commodity is the devil, who whispers
false promises in men's and women's ears and causes them, in turn,
to break faith and make their own promises false. It is an "all-changing word" not only because it changes human intention, but also because it has no stable meaning itself: one man's commodity is not
another's, since what one gains, the other loses. In response to the
transience of vows and the bad faith of speakers, one must seize the
moment, for nothing lasts. And yet the Bastard does not act on the
cynical philosophy he mockingly espouses here; even in this speech,
he reveals the knowledge that prevents him from taking this way. In
a world where words mean virtually nothing and all promises are
broken, he who gains today will surely lose tomorrow. The only win-
ner is the devil, taking from the poor maid her sole possession—the
title "maid." With this example, the Bastard indicates his esteem for
the title of integrity one awards oneself, rather than for mere reputation. Being true to one's word, one gains a self to rely on: the only
gain that cannot be lost in the passing of commodity from person to
person.

Despite this knowledge, his choice of patron makes it difficult for the Bastard to keep his word true. When Austria blusters at Constance's insult — "O, that a man should speak those words to me!" (3.1.130) — the Bastard takes up the challenge, disgusted by Austria's empty boasts and willing to prove their falsity and his own honor. John's reprimand — "thou dost forget thyself" (l. 134) — ironically frustrates what it purports to foster: the Bastard's being true to himself. This interchange highlights the difficulty of honesty in this society: how can the Bastard be true to his own words when his king's words change the reality around him from moment to moment? John accepts the Bastard's plan to prove his royal right by leveling Angiers and then battling the French, only to take an easier and less honorable way when the marriage is suggested: John's "right" to the French lands becomes another commodity, which he offers in exchange for a truce. Similarly, the English king sets the Bastard the tasks of collecting money from the monasteries and recalling the disaffected lords to face the French, only to make a pact with Pandulph that obviates the necessity of these tasks. Nor is it only human nature that makes this world mutable: John sends the Bastard to bring back the lords because Arthur is still alive; the Bastard finds the lords as they discover the dead prince. In his third and last soliloquy,[22] the Bastard almost despairs at a world where "vast confusion waits, / . . . The imminent decay of wrested pomp" (4.3.152–54). It is a world so changeable that a man is hard put to respond to it and yet remain himself, unchanging: "Now happy he whose cloak and center can / Hold out this tempest" (ll. 155–56). Thus the Bastard has the dramatic strength of a man of integrity, but, like the innocent Arthur, he has no power to impose his own integrity on this all-changing world. At the end of the play, Shakespeare appropriately gives the Bastard the vision of an England true to itself. But because the vision does not seem achievable in this society, we have gradually given up our faith in the Bastard's ability to enact the values he speaks. Even his words lose meaning in this world.

As the Bastard loses credibility in the second half of the play, Shakespeare has better success in dramatizing the characters of John and Pandulph. This success, though, leads to the same failure in the ending: the credibility of their opportunism renders us cynics, incapable of hoping that the values the playwright finally offers as a substitute for commodity may be put into effect. These men without values, to be sure, do fall from power. The ideas about language underline this tragic irony: seeking through vague and immoral language to destroy others, John and Pandulph bring destruction on themselves. But this world, like that envisioned by some other Renaissance writers (Agrippa and Brinsley among them) appears capable only of a falling action: there seems no way to restore words and people to their uncorrupted state.[23] The new generation offers little hope: Arthur dies; Lewis is, if anything, worse than his father; Henry is an unknown; and the lords who offer him fealty have broken vows to two other kings. Despite the final speeches, Shakespeare has written a play that is mainly an elegy for human hope.

And yet, in the latter half of the play, Shakespeare begins to solve some of his aesthetic problems — in particular, the difficulty of representing vague and immoral speech in language that contributes to an eloquent play. John's fall begins with the desertion of the English lords, brought on by the King's attempted murder of Arthur. Calling Hubert to him, John opens the interview with his usual obliqueness. First comes an extended financial conceit, recalling the importance of commodity in the play: John's soul "counts" Hubert his "creditor" and will repay his love with "advantage" (3.3.21-22). The King then elaborates what he has *not* said in a long "argument from adjuncts": John has something to say, but the time ("day"), the place ("the world"), and the mood ("too wanton") are not appropriate: he needs "midnight," a "church-yard" (i.e., a graveyard), and "that surly spirit, melancholy." All this occupies one of the longest speeches (ll. 30-55) in a play of very long speeches, and we are still no nearer to John's real purpose. He concludes by wishing for a new form of communication:

> Or if that thou couldst see me without eyes,
> Hear me without thine ears, and make reply
> Without a tongue, using conceit alone,
> Without eyes, ears, and harmful sound of words —
> Then, in despite of brooded watchful day,
> I would into thy bosom pour my thoughts.
>
> (3.3.48-53)

John's clearest words in the play state his wish to avoid clarity. Wanting his desires to be guessed and carried out, he seeks a language without words so that he will not have to hear what he wants done. Despite his long speeches, John does not love words. Words would be "harmful" because they would declare him a murderer, a truth about himself he is not strong enough to face. How different is this John from the John of *The Troublesome Raigne,* who sends Hubert the order to blind Arthur under his own "hand and seale, / Charging on lives regard to doo the deede."[24]

Shakespeare's John uses his vague words to his immediate advantage: Hubert promises service before he hears what it will be, as do the courtly men in the "dialogue of compliment." And in the elliptical syntax of his exchange with Hubert, John approaches the mode of communication he seeks, leaving Hubert to order his words into a complete thought or meaning:

```
King.     He is a very serpent in my way,
          And wheresoe'er this foot of mine doth tread,
          He lies before me. Dost thou understand me?
          Thou art his keeper.
Hubert.                        And I'll keep him so,
          That he shall not offend your Majesty.
King.                                          Death.
Hubert. My lord?
King.            A grave.
Hubert.                   He shall not live.
King.                                        Enough.
                                    (3.3.61-66)
```

In these chilling insinuations Shakespeare manages a language that obscures the moral issue for the characters while making it clearer to us: as the two convince themselves that being another's "keeper" may mean killing him, we are reminded of the moral opposite. John's refusal of clarity extends even to Hubert's reward: "Well, I'll not say what I intend for thee" (l. 68). In the mouth of Richard III, we would take this statement to mean Hubert's death. In John's mouth, the statement has less significance: he seems only to be afraid of his own meaning, unable to make even this commitment.

The language John speaks, however, requires deception of self, as well as of others. When the lords desert, John discovers the secret he had kept from himself by his vague and distancing words: Arthur's death is not in his interest. Hiding behind his vague words, John finds that the very suspicions he feared to raise are engendered by his hiding. Trust is gone, and so are his barons. John then curses "slaves" like Hubert who "on the winking of authority / . . . understand a law . . . [and] know the meaning / Of dangerous majesty, when perchance it frowns / More upon humor than advis'd respect" (4.2.209–14). If his "humor" and "frown" accidentally insinuated murder, if Hubert interpreted these signs as an order, it is not the fault of John. To Hubert John complains:

> Hadst thou but shook thy head or made a pause
> When I spake darkly what I purposed,
> Or turn'd an eye of doubt upon my face,
> As bid me tell my tale in express words,
> Deep shame had struck me dumb, made me break off,
> And those thy fears might have wrought fears in me.
>
> (4.2.231–36)

John's unclear language had allowed him to request Arthur's death without facing the enormity of his act. Even in his recognition, however, John discards self-knowledge. He still cannot name his sin; it is only "The deed, which both our tongues held vild to name" (l. 241). And his imprecise language now allows him to deny his responsibility for the command and to shrug off his own immorality.

Hubert had attempted to follow his master's model. Preparing to blind Arthur, he had urged himself to do it quickly, for "If I talk to him, with his innocent prate / He will awake my mercy" (4.1.25–26). Similarly, he had urged Arthur to "hold" his "tongue" (4.1.96), fearful that he would name Hubert's act a sin, and so force him to acknowledge its evil. But the Prince speaks on, telling Hubert the truths of love and mercy, and Hubert recognizes the immorality of his act through Arthur's pitiful words. Thus, when John repents and turns on Hubert, the servant may tell his master, "Young Arthur is alive" (4.2.251).

John now denies that he ordered Arthur's death, and Hubert now denies that he did the act. But fortune ironically fulfills the promise of their words when the fulfillment is no longer to their benefit: the lords desert and find the dead prince. No matter now that John and Hubert did no murder; the consequence of their words is the same. It is almost as if some providential Humanist is at work forging the connections between words and events that politicians of every age would deny. And yet it is a grim force that chooses to give words their worst meaning, visiting the sins of the fathers on the children.

Having spoken his murderous words, John has no power to call them back. Hubert had filled John's "dogged spies with false reports" (4.1.128) in order to conceal his reprieve of Arthur. The citizens are now "Possess'd with rumors" (4.2.145); "men's mouths are full" of the French invasion (4.2.161); a prophet is foretelling that John will give up his crown (4.2.147–52); and everywhere goes the report of murder: "Young Arthur's death is common in their [the people's] mouths" (4.2.187). Traditionally, the goddess *Fama* was depicted with a multitude of tongues, mouths, and ears on her garments.[25] John's world is now ruled by this goddess of rumor: her tongues are everywhere, and her ears are those of the common people, "With open mouth swallowing the tailor's news" (4.2.195), close to revolt upon hearing of Arthur's death. John's secret has become breath on the lips of every citizen to blow down his kingdom.

John, finally, is the major victim of his corrupt language. Denying his immorality to himself, he yet hears it spoken in the rumors of his subjects. As Orwell warned our age in his essay, "Politics and the English Language," immoral politics have begotten decadent language, and such language has further corrupted politics.[26] Yet in John's world, if not in Orwell's, there is yet some retributive force that reveals truth and makes men accountable for their words and actions. John remains in the play only to give up his crown to the Pope and to lose his life to a monk's poison. He lost his power earlier through his corrupt words, "sweet, sweet, sweet poison for the age's tooth."

Pandulph, too, hears his own words turned against him. Assuming that his power over the French still holds, Pandulph promises the compromised English king to end the invasion:

> It was my breath that blew this tempest up,
> Upon your stubborn usage of the Pope;
> But since you are a gentle convertite,
> My tongue shall hush again this storm of war,
> And make fair weather in your blust'ring land.
>
> (5.1.17–21)

In Pandulph's bold assertion, metonymies standing for his own speech merge with hyperbolic metaphors of cosmic power, and betray the Cardinal's confusion of his transitory human voice with the powers of his office and the providence he serves. But speech, not having been limited earlier by human moral responsibility, has ceased to be an effectual political control. When Pandulph presents his new plan of peace to Lewis, the French Dauphin rejects it with contempt:

> Your breath first kindled the dead coal of wars
> Between this chastis'd kingdom and myself,
> And brought in matter that should feed this fire;
> And now 'tis far too huge to be blown out
> With that same weak wind which enkindled it.
>
> (5.2.83-87)

Lewis's speech imagery ironically echoes Pandulph's previous assertion of power, but only to reveal that Pandulph is not providence — his speech is merely breath. The Cardinal, like the English king, has become a victim of his corrupt language: his words were powerful only to raise destructive forces that take his power from him.

When the Bastard enters, Lewis refuses to listen any longer:

> *Pandulph.*   Give me leave to speak.
> *Bastard.*   No, I will speak.
> *Lewis.*   We will attend to neither.
> Strike up the drums, and let the tongue of war
> Plead for our interest and our being here.
>
> (5.2.162-65)

Only destruction has a voice now. Pandulph faces the Dauphin's threat to the authority of the Church, a threat that he himself raised by his immoral persuasions; and he faces an English ambassador, who tells him that John has used him "rather for sport than need" (5.2.175). We do not see Pandulph again. We hear that he negotiates the peace; the French, however, are mollified by the desertion of the English lords and the sinking of their supplies, not by Pandulph's persuasions. In addition, the English king whom Pandulph brought to yield the crown is dead.

In the last two acts of the play, the ideas about language emphasize rumor and war, the breakdown of national and international order. The voices of John, Philip, and Pandulph no longer dominate events. The great men are silenced; like their words, they are merely mortal. The fever after his poisoning leaves John "almost speechless" (5.6.24). "From the organ-pipe of frailty [he] sings / His soul and body to their lasting rest" (5.7.23–24). He is "a scribbled form, drawn with a pen / Upon a parchment," shrunk against the fires of his sickness (ll. 32–34) and, finally, "as dead an ear" as the deadly news the Bastard brings of English losses (l. 66). Narrowing the focus from the ever changing world of power politics to the brief life of an English king,[27] Shakespeare suggests an even larger question: is man no more than this? He who spoke with "the free breath of a sacred king" now speaks his last words from "the organ-pipe of frailty."

Shakespeare might have written a play like *The Troublesome Raigne,* on an English king's bold defiance of the Pope; instead, *King John* is a tragedy of many weak men in powerful offices, who, through corrupt language and self-serving words, turn social institutions to destructive ends and weaken the powers they sought to enlarge. Their world is mutable, fragmented, fallen, one where words lack stable significance. The transience and mutability of man, his falling off from former glories, are embodied in the ideas about speech in the play. This tragedy thus reaches its natural conclusion not in the Bastard's idealistic words, but in Prince Henry's elegy on human power:

> Even so must I run on, and even so stop.
> What surety of the world, what hope, what stay,
> When this was now a king, and now is clay?
>
> (5.7.67–69)

Notes

1. According to *The Riverside Shakespeare, Love's Labor's Lost* was composed about 1594–95, revised perhaps in 1597, and *King John* was composed about 1594–96.

2. The four plays with highest frequency of references to key terms concerning language are *R2*, one reference per sixteen lines; *Cor.*, one per seventeen lines; *LLL*, one per eighteen lines; and *Jn.*, one per nineteen lines.

3. Sigurd Burckhardt is the only critic I have read who has commented on the ideas about language in *King John*. In "*King John:* The Ordering of This Present Time," *ELH*, 33 (1966), 33–53, he argues that in the first three acts Shakespeare attempts "to expose an order and a language that has become false" (p. 147), while in the rest of the play he seeks but does

not find a stable language: "The play demonstrates the simultaneous disintegration of order and speech and truth" (p. 150).

4. The count for oral speech imagery is based on the terms tongue(s),
mouth(s), throat(s), ear(s), breath, air, and airy. *Jn.* is second of all the
plays with sixty-one such references; *LLL* is fifth with fifty. (*R2* is first with
sixty-five; *Wiv.* is last with eleven; the average for all plays is twenty-nine.)

5. The count for imagery of written speech is based on the terms pen,
ink, paper(s), and parchment. *LLL* is first with fifteen such references; *Jn.*
is twenty-second with two. (*AYL*, *Tmp.*, and *TNK* are last with zero; the
average for all plays is four.) *LLL* is first in reference to word(s) with forty-
eight; *Jn.* is nineteenth with twenty-two. (*Per.* is last with ten; the average
of all plays is twenty-four.)

6. See, for example, Willcock, "Language and Poetry in Shakespeare's
Early Plays" and "Shakespeare and Elizabethan English"; Walter Ong,
S.J., *Ramus, Method and the Decay of Dialogue* (Cambridge, Mass.: Har-
vard Univ. Press, 1948), esp. pp. 287-91, and "Oral Residue in Tudor
Prose Style," *PMLA*, 80 (1965), 145-54; and Marshall McLuhan, *The
Gutenberg Galaxy* (Toronto: Univ. of Toronto Press, 1962).

7. The problem of the relation between *The Troublesome Raigne* and
King John is vexing. I do not think that Shakespeare wrote *TR*, even at a
very early stage of his career: the play lacks the abundant imagery of
Shakespeare's early plays and includes many lines of Latin quotations in
the manner of Kyd, which Shakespeare uses nowhere else; and, while the
patriotism of *TR* is characteristic of Shakespeare in other plays, the pronounced anti-Catholic sentiments are not. That there is some relation between the two plays is obvious from the similar structures. If the playwright
of *TR* borrowed from *Jn.*, one would expect more verbal echoes, since the
poetry of *Jn.* is far superior to that of *TR*. On the other hand, revising the
language and conception of character while adhering to and condensing
the fable is characteristic of Shakespeare's method of using nondramatic
sources in his first ten years (as in *AYL*, for example). Yet *TR* remains a
better motivated and more unified play than *Jn.* My speculation is thus
that Shakespeare borrowed from *TR*, but reconceived the story of the anti-
Catholic tyrant as a story of many weak men and women who used their
positions to seek more power, and whose very efforts ironically lessened
what power they held. In the process of making character and story more
complex, Shakespeare sacrificed the clear motivation and simpler unity of
story in the source. For a review of the critical debate on the relation between *TR* and *Jn.*, see the introduction to *The Troublesome Raigne of
John, King of England*, ed. J. W. Sider (New York: Garland Publishing,
1979), pp. xxiii–xliii. For an argument that Shakespeare's play is not a
failure in structure but a deliberate attempt to provide a broader and more

ambiguous perspective for the events, see Larry S. Champion, " 'Confound Their Skill in Covetousness': The Ambivalent Perspective in Shakespeare's *King John,"* *TSL,* 24 (1979), 36–55.

8. On *King John* as a poor play, see, for example, Mark Van Doren, *Shakespeare* (New York: Henry Holt and Co., 1939), pp. 106–15; E. M. W. Tillyard, *Shakespeare's History Plays* (1944; rpt. London: Chatto & Windus, 1956), pp. 215–33; M. M. Reese, *The Cease of Majesty* (New York: St. Martin's Press, 1961), pp. 260–86; and Robert Ornstein, *A Kingdom for a Stage* (Cambridge, Mass.: Harvard Univ. Press, 1972), pp. 83–101.

9. *Jn.* and *R2* are first of all plays in references to speech as "breath" with eleven each; six plays have no such references, and the average is two. *TR* has five references to speech or speaking as "breath," but all at moments in the story different from those where the references appear in *Jn.*

10. On metonymy and synecdoche, see Sr. Miriam Joseph, *Shakespeare's Use of the Arts of Language,* pp. 315 and 336.

11. See Caroline Spurgeon, *Shakespeare's Imagery* (1935; rpt. Cambridge: Cambridge Univ. Press, 1971), pp. 245–53, on body images as the major ones of *King John.* She argues that they center on John, giving the "feeling of his being but a fragment — a mere counterfeit of humanity" (p. 249).

12. Cf. Hardin Craig, *An Interpretation of Shakespeare* (Columbia, Mo.: Lucas Brothers, 1948), p. 85: "No play illustrates better than *King John* that drama is debate."

13. Robinson, *Art of Pronuntiation,* sig. A3^V.

14. Castiglione, *The Courtier,* sig. F3^V.

15. See M. M. Reese's discussion of the political cynicism of *Jn.* in *The Cease of Majesty,* pp. 71–86; and Robert Ornstein's discussion, in *A Kingdom for a Stage,* of the play as "a uniquely crude representation of political casuistries and hypocrisies" (p. 93). Adrien Bonjour, in "The Road to Swinstead Abbey," *ELH,* 18 (1951), 253–74, sees the play as the fall of one hero (John) followed by the rise of another (the Bastard) — the latter possessing "absolute integrity" in contrast to John's "perfidy" (p. 268).

16. See Sr. Miriam Joseph, *Shakespeare's Use of the Arts of Language,* p. 328.

17. Ibid., pp. 318–19.

18. Van Doren, *Shakespeare,* pp. 109–10.

19. The extended conceits of *Jn.* are notably lacking in *TR,* except for occasional conceits, Marlovian in style, given to John when he is being particularly tyrannical. The style of *TR* is straightforward, clear language compared to that of *Jn.*

20. Ascham, *The Scholemaster,* sig. Oii^v.

21. Mulcaster, *Elementarie,* pp. 74 and 157-59.

22. Even though the Bastard is not alone on stage, this speech is yet a soliloquy because all the other characters are off to the side gathering up Arthur's body; the Bastard moves to join them only at the end of this speech.

23. See Agrippa, *Vanitie,* fols. 6^r-7^r; and Brinsley, *Ludus Literarius,* p. 247.

24. *Troublesome Raigne,* ed. Sider, Part I, sc. viii, ll. 263-64.

25. See Richard Knowles's discussion of "Rumor," in "Unquiet and the Double Plot of *2 Henry IV,*" *ShakS,* 2 (1966), 133-34.

26. See George Orwell, "Politics and the English Language," from *Shooting an Elephant* (New York: Harcourt, Brace, and Co., 1945), pp. 77-92.

27. Cf. Jonathan Price, "*King John* and Problematic Art," *SQ,* 21 (1970), who argues that in the second half of the play Shakespeare leaves the public issues to concentrate "on the personal collapse of John" (p. 27).

CHAPTER 6

The Merchant of Venice:
A Wealth of Meanings

No recurring ideas about language define the world of *The Mer-chant of Venice,* as they do the worlds of *Love's Labor's Lost* and *King John:* the play is average or below average in the relative fre-quency of all the key terms concerning language.[1] In this later play we see, instead, a new development in Shakespeare's dramatic prac-tice, one that becomes habitual in the middle plays: Shakespeare employs attitudes and ideas about language as a means of individu-alizing characters, rather than as a means of portraying the funda-mental tenets of their society. The play may be divided into three movements, each culminating in a task of imaginative interpreta-tion: the caskets, the trial, and the riddle of the rings.[2] In each case, accomplishing the task results in large degree from interpreting words: the mottoes, Shylock's bond and Venetian law, and the rid-dles. What we learn of the characters beforehand, from their styles of language and their attitudes toward words, prepares us for their success or failure in the tasks. Indeed, from the opening scenes, in which the Venetians try to interpret the riddle of Antonio's sadness and Portia judges her suitors, characterization depends on the atti-tudes toward language and the analogous methods of judging fig-ured forth in the variety of linguistic styles. In *The Merchant of Venice* Shakespeare fully embodies the Jonsonian principle that "No glasse renders a mans forme, or likenesse, so true as his speech."[3]

Antonio begins the play by asking for help:

> In sooth, I know not why I am so sad;
> It wearies me, you say it wearies you;
> But how I caught it, found it, or came by it,
> What stuff 'tis made of, whereof it is born,
> I am to learn;

189

> And such a want-wit sadness makes of me,
> That I have much ado to know myself.
>
> (1.1.1-7)

Everyone tries his hand at the riddle of Antonio's sadness, and everyone has a different answer. Salerio, his style as rich with images as his costume must be with patterned fabric and jewels, tells Antonio that it is his occupation to be sad: the merchant worries about the wealth invested in his argosies. Arriving at his conclusion allegorically, Salerio reads Antonio and his Venetian environment as a beginning student reads a poem, by finding in the images the preoccupations that he came to the poem with:

> Should I go to church
> And see the holy edifice of stone,
> And not bethink me straight of dangerous rocks,
> Which touching but my gentle vessel's side
> Would scatter all her spices on the stream,
> Enrobe the roaring waters with my silks,
> And in a word, but even now worth this,
> And now worth nothing?
>
> (1.1.29-36)

The church, towering in stone, reminds him not that a mighty fortress is our God; instead, he sees the treacherous rock that breaches ships and imagines the seawater that might stain the gorgeous silks he wears. Salerio does try to put himself in the place of Antonio, but all he manages is to discern his own meaning in the other's mind: "But tell not me; I know Antonio / Is sad to think upon his merchandise" (ll. 39-40). Epithets, imagery, piled-on clauses, taffeta phrases and silken terms precise—the very richness of Salerio's language prevents him from understanding a man who does not care much for the outward show of wealth. The other companion, Solanio, whose speech sparkles with alliteration and exotic oaths, wants Antonio to admit he is in love. Failing that, like the sun that shines on the just and the unjust, Solanio tolerantly accepts Antonio as he is: "Nature hath fram'd strange fellows in her time," some "like parrots," some like "vinegar" (ll. 51-54). Once he has uttered the abstract term "Nature" and placed Antonio in that category, he beams and shrugs and would be off on his own business. Even though their judgments do not seem to hit the mark, we cannot fault the two gentlemen: they demonstrate sympathy and generosity in their attempt to help a friend with a problem.

Indeed, Antonio does no better in his judgment of himself. His style reflects his age: plain words, short clauses, few tropes, and long, often balanced and periodic sentences. He is a plodder—he calls himself a "want-wit" from sadness. Paralleling this style of the traditional older man is Antonio's method of judging, the enthymeme, the form of syllogism with one premise suppressed so that the reasoning progresses from general truth to specific conclusion, from popular maxim to personal application:[4]

> I thank my fortune for it,
> My ventures are not in one bottom trusted,
> Nor to one place; nor is my whole estate
> Upon the fortune of this present year:
> Therefore my merchandise makes me not sad.
>
> (ll. 41-45)

Take a known principle: only a fortune that can be entirely lost (trusted to one ship, one place, or one year) makes a merchant sad. Fit the specific circumstance into the minor premise: my fortune of merchandise is not all trusted to one chance. And draw the conclusion: merchandise does not make me sad. Thus in his plain, systematic way, he judges himself:

> I hold the world but as the world, Gratiano,
> A stage, where every man must play a part,
> And mine a sad one.
>
> (ll. 77-79)

A man's life is merely a part that he plays; and so Antonio's is a sad part. In a sense, Antonio misuses the enthymeme because it brings him to no new knowledge; it allows him to do little more than rearrange what he already knows.

If men's lives are merely roles, counters Gratiano, "Let me play the fool" (l. 79). This young man's style is antithetical, amplified by schemes, similes, metaphors, personification, examples, and any other rhetorical device he can fit his quick wit and tongue to. His method is also antithetical; give him a general principle and he will stand it on its head:

> With mirth and laughter let old wrinkles come,

And let my liver rather heat with wine
Than my heart cool with mortifying groans.
Why should a man, whose blood is warm within,
Sit like his grandsire cut in alabaster?
Sleep when he wakes? and creep into the jaundies
By being peevish? I tell thee what, Antonio —
I love thee, and 'tis my love that speaks —
There are a sort of men whose visages
Do cream and mantle like a standing pond,
And do a willful stillness entertain,
With purpose to be dress'd in an opinion
Of wisdom, gravity, profound conceit.

(ll. 80–92)

And his "love" speaks on for many more lines until gravity becomes discourtesy, silence willfulness, and the sad and cautious Antonio a proud fool who wishes others to take his sadness for wisdom. By his sophistry, Gratiano is attempting to cheer Antonio out of his melancholy, but he is also commending himself: if the sad man is foolish, then Gratiano must be very wise. And for all his deft manipulation of the meanings of words, Gratiano convinces only himself. Thus Bassanio: "Gratiano speaks an infinite deal of nothing, more than any man in all Venice. His reasons are as two grains of wheat hid in two bushels of chaff; you shall seek all day ere you find them, and when you have them, they are not worth the search" (ll. 114–18).

By the end of the scene we are still at a loss to explain Antonio's sadness. Each of these men has offered a possible answer that does not exactly apply to Antonio. Values are shared: important in this society are wealth but not competitive gain, the community of good friends, tolerance of different personalities, wit and elegant speech, honor and generosity. The wealth of answers arises not from different values, but from different methods of judgment and from different attitudes toward language, these in turn generating the various styles of speech by which we interpret the characters. Perhaps we come to our own conclusion and judge Antonio melancholy because he is worried about his indebted friend. The scene itself provides no single answer, only a multitude to choose from; and, if we do not solve the riddle of Antonio, the variety of perspectives brought to bear on one problem makes us feel that this city is as rich in people as in gold.

Portia leads off the next scene by defining the difficulties of judgment and choice: "If to do were as easy as to know what were good to do, chapels had been churches, and poor men's cottages princes' palaces. It is a good divine that follows his own instructions; I can easier teach twenty what were good to be done, than to be one of the twenty to follow mine own teaching. The brain may devise laws for the blood, but a hot temper leaps o'er a cold decree. . . . But this reasoning is not in the fashion to choose me a husband" (1.2.12–22). Values and laws are not hard to come by; the difficulty is applying them. There are as many answers to Antonio's melancholy as there are suitors to Portia; the problem in either case is choosing one. Antonio cannot make a choice, and Portia may not: "O me, the word choose! I may neither choose who I would, nor refuse who I dislike; so is the will of a living daughter curb'd by the will of a dead father" (ll. 22–25). Free in her language, playing lightly on the two meanings of the word "will," Portia is yet bound by the words of her father. She does judge her possibilities, though, if only by way of a pastime. Her style, as well as Nerissa's, is a delicate euphuism. Colloquial proverbs, balanced antitheses (sharp and neat as boxed pins), wit and wordplay, even a light powdering of alliteration — all of Lyly's favorite prose patternings are here. Her method, freely ranging induction, is as flexible as her style is bright. She ticks off the faults of each suitor, adds them up, and hopes for a better bargain: not the Neapolitan who loves horses, or the German who loves wine; not the grave County Palatine, or the frivolous Monsieur Le Bon; not the English baron who lacks Italian, or the Scottish lord who lacks courage. Like Antonio, she says "no" to all the answers, but she seems a whole society in herself, with as many answers to her question as all of Venice had to Antonio's. And she does have a preference, when Nerissa reminds her of Bassanio: "I remember him well, and I remember him worthy of thy praise" (ll. 120–21).

Nerissa has already explained that the father's will may further Portia's choice, rather than frustrate it: "men at their death have good inspirations; therefore the lott'ry that he hath devis'd in these three chests of gold, silver, and lead, whereof who chooses his meaning chooses you, will no doubt never be chosen by any rightly but one who you shall rightly love" (1.2.28–33). Interpretation has thus appeared as a necessity of plot: the father will test Portia's prospective husbands by their skills in judgment. "Words are the Peoples," observed Ben Jonson, "yet there is a choice of them to be made."[5] As men and women reveal their strengths and weaknesses in their choice of words, the suitors will reveal their characters in their choice of the three caskets. Nerissa's faith in the test of the caskets rests on a belief that love and reason are not opposed, but apposite: out of the many possible meanings of the caskets and their mottoes, the suitor who picks the best ones will also best love Portia.

The same commonplace on the human condition that Portia uses to define her difficulties in choice, Sir Philip Sidney had used to define the end of poetry. Alerting us to the human condition—"our erected wit makes us know what perfection is and yet our infected will keeps us from reaching unto it"—Sidney had argued that good poetry addresses itself to this paradox: that men can conceive perfection, that they can easily know and hold appropriate moral values, but that they can only with difficulty enact those values in their daily lives. Thus poetry manifests general values in concrete particulars; it imitates "both to delight and teach, . . . to move men to take that goodness in hand which, without delight, they would fly as from a stranger, and . . . to make them know that goodness whereunto they are moved."[6] *The Merchant of Venice* does not teach social values; it assumes them. And, although they are mainly presented in Christian terms, they are less distinctively Christian values than the values that comedy always assumes: generosity, tolerance, and festivity.[7] Rather than teaching values, the play moves us, in the fashion described by Sidney, to exercise the values we already hold by making difficult judgments about the people and social problems that the characters are also making judgments about. In *The Merchant of Venice* language is an instrument of judgment, and the characters reveal their individual habits of mind by the way they use and interpret words.

In acts 2 and 3, when the three wooers make a choice of the caskets, each has an equal chance. Each understands that the riddling inscriptions are somehow symbolic and must be interpreted; and each receives the same clue from Portia: before each choice she uses the word "hazard," which is repeated in the inscription on the right chest. The first suitor is the Moor, Prince of Morocco:

> Therefore I pray you lead me to the caskets
> To try my fortune. By this scimitar
> That slew the Sophy and a Persian prince

That won three fields of Sultan Solyman,
I would o'erstare the sternest eyes that look,
Outbrave the heart most daring on the earth,
Pluck the young sucking cubs from the she-bear,
Yea, mock the lion when 'a roars for prey,
To win thee, lady. But alas the while!
If Hercules and Lichas play at dice
Which is the better man, the greater throw
May turn by fortune from the weaker hand:
So is Alcides beaten by his page,
And so may I, blind fortune leading me,
Miss that which one unworthier may attain,
And die with grieving.

(2.1.23-38)

The Moor's style is Tamburlaine's:[8] long sentences and verse paragraphs, frequent enjambment, exotic Asian names, classical allusions, and hyperbolic heroic boasts. Like Marlowe's hero, too, he thinks himself led by Fortune; from his style alone we might guess in what direction, since his ancestor sought obsessively "the sweet fruition" of a golden crown. Indeed, the Moor uses language less to signify than to adorn himself. He puts on his boasting words as the Renaissance knight put on his inlaid armor. He admits that he is at a loss to choose, for his method is the bold and violent one of simply taking what he wants. Trusting no words, only acts, he has no civil method to work within the bounds of law.

Thus, just as the Moor chooses words to adorn himself, so he chooses a casket and an inscription to augment his self-esteem. A lead chest and hazard are not appropriate to his golden mind; a silver chest and just desert are appropriate, but he aspires higher; only a golden chest decorously might adorn the fair Portia (who, as his wife, might be his decoration)—and off he flies in cosmic and angelic metaphors (2.7.14-60), led as the Marlovian hero was by "beauty's just applause":

One thought, one grace, one woonder at the least,
Which into words no vertue can digest.[9]

The dead father rejects the Moor's style, method, and character: "Had you been as wise as bold, / . . . Your answer had not been inscroll'd" (2.7.70-72). Just as for his literary ancestor, the reward for the Moor at the end of his golden quest is "A carrion Death" (2.7.63). It is by our evaluation of the Moor's language, however, that we understand the father's judgment of him: " 'All that glisters is not gold' " (l. 65). The Moor builds a colossus of words around himself while neglecting the man within. Romantic as he is, he could never rightly love Portia. He cannot even see the real woman whom he could love; he can only impose on her the fantasy of the perfect woman who would suit his heroic image of himself.

The second wooer of Portia is the Prince of Aragon, whose style is defined by schemes:

> I am enjoin'd by oath to observe three things:
> First, never to unfold to any one
> Which casket 'twas I chose; next, if I fail
> Of the right casket, never in my life
> To woo a maid in way of marriage;
> Lastly,
> If I do fail in fortune of my choice,
> Immediately to leave you, and be gone.
>
> (2.9.9–16)

Here are most of the figures of repetition: alliteration, especially on "w" and "f," anaphora in the repetition of "never" and "if" at the beginning of clauses, diacope by the repetition of "fail" twice in close proximity, and polyptoton in the variation on the forms of a word, "choose" and "choice." This is sound set before sense, a parody of the style of Sidney's Arcadian royalty. And, like the duke and princes in *The Arcadia,* after most careful reasoning on the nature of virtuous action, the Prince of Aragon solemnly chooses the wrong course of action for fear of doing wrong.[10] His method of choice, as well as his style of language, is simple pattern: he chooses by the Aristotelian moral pattern, the mean between extremes. Not for him the extremes of "base lead" (l. 20) or gold desired of "common spirits" and "barbarous multitudes" (ll. 32–33). His choice is the silver mean:

> Why then to thee, thou silver treasure house,
> Tell me once more what title thou dost bear:
> "Who chooseth me shall get as much as he deserves."
> And well said too; for who shall go about
> To cozen fortune, and be honorable

Without the stamp of merit? Let none presume
To wear an undeserved dignity.
O that estates, degrees, and offices
Were not deriv'd corruptly, and that clear honor
Were purchas'd by the merit of the wearer!

. . . .

Well, but to my choice:
"Who chooseth me shall get as much as he deserves."
I will assume desert.

(2.9.34-51)

Having chosen the silver chest by position in the pattern, Aragon
then finds a meaning in the inscription that will justify his choice.
Too proud to believe that words must be a social convention, based
on the consent of the many, Aragon interprets the motto as if his
own will might control significance. Scorning what might be understood by the common multitude, Aragon chooses not the father's
meaning, but rather his own.

Aragon would have only justice, reward based on merit alone,
works not faith. He is incensed at the arbitrary injustice of his reward, a fool's head:

"The fire seven times tried this:
Seven times tried that judgment is,
That did never choose amiss."

(2.9.63-65)

The Prince is rewarded with the opposite of what he "deserves" because he is not wise enough to know that fortune is blind: to each man
sometime comes mischance, not meritorious reward. In his choice,
Aragon carries the mean to extremes, and reveals that he could never
rightly love Portia: he who chooses "never . . . amiss" will never
choose well, since he will never choose merely for love, only for a
reason. Very different was Antonio, who swept aside all Bassanio's
reasons to lend him money merely for love. In Aragon's own schematic and patterned language the father judges him: " 'There be fools
alive, iwis, / Silver'd o'er, and so was this' " (ll. 69-70). Limited by
his trust in himself and his distrust of others' meanings—whether in
the father's casket or in the people's language—this wooer receives, if
not what he deserves, at least what he gives: cold-blooded wisdom.

Bassanio, who will not put off the choice at Portia's request, who is tortured by his love as if on a "rack" until he has her (3.2.25), possesses a temperament opposite to Aragon's. It does not follow, as some critics have maintained, that Bassanio chooses on impulse and wins by luck.[11] Did we not believe that Bassanio's choice results from his good judgment, we would feel cheated: the father's test would be a mere trick, and Portia would seem the prize of a gamble. In fact, Shakespeare has prepared us for Bassanio's success earlier, first by his way of speaking and judging in the first scene, then by Antonio's love for him and Portia's praise.

Let us look back at the first scene. We know from Bassanio's judgment of Gratiano that he distrusts mere words, that he knows one must seek meaning in words as one sorts through chaff for the grains of wheat. We have also seen him discard the superficial judgments of Antonio based on his melancholy outside for a deeper truth about the man in his inner love and generosity. Finally, we have seen him acknowledge his own limitations and find a means out of his straitened circumstances:

> In my school-days, when I had lost one shaft,
> I shot his fellow of the self-same flight
> The self-same way with more advised watch
> To find the other forth, and by adventuring both
> I oft found both. I urge this childhood proof,
> Because what follows is pure innocence.
> I owe you much, and like a willful youth,
> That which I owe is lost, but if you please
> To shoot another arrow that self way
> Which you did shoot the first, I do not doubt,
> As I will watch the aim, or to find both
> Or bring your latter hazard back again,
> And thankfully rest debtor for the first.
>
> (1.1.140–52)

Bassanio's style is based on similarity: the whole passage is a parable, comparing a former experience to a new one; his judgment of himself is in the form of a simile; and the passage moves naturally into an extended metaphor, based on likeness. The style mirrors the method: analogy. Like the boy who recovers his arrow by hazarding the second, Antonio will recover his money because Bassanio will not make the same mistake twice. The practical means Bassanio advances to get out of debt is marrying a rich wife. But his materialism is tempered by his intention:

> In Belmont is a lady richly left,
> And she is fair and, fairer than that word,
> Of wondrous virtues. Sometimes from her eyes
> I did receive fair speechless messages.
> Her name is Portia, nothing undervalu'd
> To Cato's daughter, Brutus' Portia.
>
> (1.1.161–66)

Again come the figures of comparison: this is an argument from the lesser to the greater degree (fair, but even better, virtuous), and amplified by metaphor and historical example. By this means Bassanio convinces Antonio that his pursuit of Portia is honorable, his intention, love: he chooses Portia not for her riches, but for her virtue and her promised love.

Thus Bassanio's method of judgment is grounded in experience and based on the likenesses of things—but not the mere surfaces of things. It takes intuition and imagination to see the crucial likeness between the arrow that the boy has lost and the money that Bassanio has lost, and to judge the relative similarity between the beauty of "fair" Portia and the even greater beauty of virtuous Portia. Bassanio's method gives him a way of living in both material and spiritual realms at once, and if his style leans often toward the metaphysical conceit, his method, too, seems metaphysical, a yoking of contraries by finding the deep-down similarities of things. We think of the metaphysical as a seventeenth-century style, but just at the time that Shakespeare was writing *The Merchant of Venice*, Donne was probably writing his elegies at Lincoln's Inn in London.

When Bassanio makes his choice of the caskets, we are already familiar with his analogical method of judgment. Having commented on the inscriptions while Portia, Nerissa, and Gratiano listen to the song on fancy, Bassanio comes forth with his interpretation: "So may the outward shows be least themselves" (3.2.73). Rather than immediately making his choice, however, he tests his interpretation against experience:

> The world is still deceiv'd with ornament.
> In law, what plea so tainted and corrupt

> But, being season'd with a gracious voice,
> Obscures the show of evil? In religion,
> What damned error but some sober brow
> Will bless it, and approve it with a text,
> Hiding the grossness with fair ornament?
> There is no vice so simple but assumes
> Some mark of virtue on his outward parts.
>
> (3.2.74-82)

Bassanio supports his conclusion with other examples, but these first two alert us to his attitude toward language. Like many Elizabethan logicians, Bassanio doubts that words mean what they seem to mean and accurately represent a truth until he has carefully tested and defined them. Having judged the mottoes by this principle, Bassanio turns to the caskets with the same distrust of appearances, and looks for their deeper significance:

> Therefore then, thou gaudy gold,
> Hard food for Midas, I will none of thee;
> Nor none of thee, thou pale and common drudge
> 'Tween man and man; but thou, thou meagre lead,
> Which rather threaten'st than dost promise aught,
> Thy paleness moves me more than eloquence,
> And here choose I. Joy be the consequence!
>
> (3.2.101-7)

The Moor had seen in the golden casket a likeness to Portia's outer beauty; Aragon had seen in the "silver treasure house" an analogy to his own value. Bassanio sees beyond these superficial likenesses to deeper truths: the "Hard food of Midas" that does not nurture, and the "common drudge" that is a slave to man's basest material desires. Promising wealth and beauty, the fair ornaments of gold and silver hide the gross use to which human greed may put them. Bassanio's final comparison is a most unlikely one: the lead casket, which seems to promise nothing, actually moves him more than eloquence, the proper business of which is to move. Just as Quintilian and the early humanists who followed him believed the power of eloquence to be derived from significance, not verbal ornament, so Bassanio judges the caskets by their meaning, not by their beauty. The lead casket may not look promising, but it speaks to Bassanio's imagination. By analogy to eloquence, through his loving knowledge of Portia, Bassanio has solved the father's riddle. How is a lead casket like loving Portia? In both cases, one finds that the inside is better than the outside.

In Bassanio's own comparative style the father judges him:

> "You that choose not by the view,
> Chance as fair, and choose as true:
> Since this fortune falls to you,
> Be content, and seek no new."
> (3.2.131–34)

As fair and true as Portia is Bassanio's choice. Unlike the other two suitors, who distrust words only to impose their own self-referent meanings on them, Bassanio distrusts words until he has carefully defined them by their best meaning—not necessarily his own. His method of interpretation allows him to choose the father's meaning and indeed also rightly love Portia. Bassanio, the only suitor open to the wealth of potential meanings in words, acknowledges the possibility of self-deception, and interprets all symbols in a way to learn from them. His open-minded judgment will further keep him from imposing his own meaning on Portia, and allow him to accept her for herself—as she means to be.

After Bassanio's choice, the scene exults in an abundance of similitude. Portia climbs by comparison from happy to happier to happiest and comes full circle from queen over herself to the unlessoned schoolgirl who commits herself to her lord to be directed (ll. 149–71). Bassanio is like the crowd after the oration of a beloved prince, "a wild of nothing, save of joy" (ll. 178–82). And Gratiano and Nerissa step forward to be like their lord and lady, having hazarded their love on the choice, and now to be married, too. Even when events turn somber, and we learn that Antonio has been arrested, Portia sends Bassanio to his "true friend" (3.2.308) on the basis of similarity. In scene 4, she explains her motive to Lorenzo:

> I never did repent for doing good,
> Nor shall not now: for in companions
> That do converse and waste the time together,
> Whose souls do bear an egall yoke of love,
> There must be needs a like proportion
> Of lineaments, of manners, and of spirit;
> Which makes me think that this Antonio,

> Being the bosom lover of my lord,
> Must needs be like my lord. If it be so,
> How little is the cost I have bestowed
> In purchasing the semblance of my soul,
> From out the state of hellish cruelty.
>
> (3.4.10-21)

Portia judges Antonio by the same analogical method that Bassanio used on the caskets. Since Antonio must be like Bassanio, she will naturally extend her love for Bassanio to his friend.

In the second movement of the play, that ending in the trial, linguistic styles and attitudes again prefigure success in judgment. Shylock, unique in alien garb and values, is without doubt the most powerful dramatic figure. His emotional intensity, too, lends tremendous weight to his speech. Yet power is not virtue. The story of the play requires Shylock's power, not because he is justified in his actions, but because of the dramatic reversal in the trial scene: the mighty are fallen and the low are raised high. Like the wicked in the Psalms, Shylock is condemned by his own counsel.

A great part of Shylock's power is owing to his style of language, but his style is not that of the usual Elizabethan villains: the rant of Herod or the cool equivocation of the Machiavel. Instead, Shylock's style is satiric, reminding us of the popularity of satire just at this time, in the 1590s. Like the diction of Lodge, Donne, and the author of the "Piers" satires, Shylock's is plain: words mainly of Anglo-Saxon origin, few Latin polysyllables, much tangy colloquialism and slang. Shylock speaks alternately prose and verse; satire of the period takes both forms. His prose is rough and simple: short sentences, or at least clauses, no balanced periods, no courtly schematic patternings. To my ear, moreover, his verse falls less often than that of the other characters into the standard iambic pentameter line. To illustrate, we may take his answer to Antonio's request for money, in the scene where we first meet Shylock:

> What should I say to you? Should I not say,
>
> "Hath a dog money? Is it possible,
>
> A cur can lend three thousand ducats?" Or

> x / x / x \ x / x /
> Shall I bend low and in a bondman's key,
>
> x / x / x / x / x \
> With bated breath and whisp'ring humbleness,
>
> x /
> Say this:
>
> / \ x / x / x / x /
> "Faith sir, you spet on me on Wednesday last,
>
> x / x \ x / x / x /
> You spurn'd me such a day, another time
>
> x / x / x \ x / x /
> You call'd me dog; and for these courtesies
>
> x / x / / / x
> I'll lend you thus much moneys"?

(1.3.120-29)

Like Donne's satiric verse, Shylock's depends on short clauses, few transitions, and many monosyllables—together creating an uneven rhythm that helps to sustain an appropriately indignant tone. Shylock's lines even pick up the couplets of the satiric verse of the period, although only with slant rhyme—in "humbleness," and "this," for instance, or in "courtesies" and "moneys" (ll. 124-29).

The satirist's tone and themes, as well as his form, may be discerned in Shylock's speeches. The merchant's tone results from verbal irony, usually the extreme form of sarcasm. In the passage just quoted, the sarcasm is clear, especially from "Shall I bend low" to the end. He means the opposite of what he asks: not should he be humble, but should he not taunt the Christians as they have previously taunted him. Throughout the speech his words seem to say that he would be friends, while his voice indicates his delight in provoking Bassanio and Antonio into losing their tempers. He uses his voice as a goad: he is indignant that Bassanio and Antonio take his thrift as mere usury, indignant that they ask him for money after they have railed at him, indignant that they become angry before he has made his "loving" offer of money without interest. Not just in this scene, but generally, Shylock's voice is that of the Elizabethan satirist as C. S. Lewis describes it, "a more or less continuous display of virtuous indignation."[12] The themes of Shylock's criticism of the Christians, moreover, are those economic and moral themes most common to the satire of the period: prodigality and hypocrisy.[13] Both these vices, for example, occur in Shylock's criticism of Bassanio:

> I am not bid for love, they flatter me,
> But yet I'll go in hate, to feed upon
> The prodigal Christian.
>
> (2.5.13-15)

Shylock even has affinities with a popular character type of the satiric "cony-catching" pamphlets: the cozener who mocks his gulls.

Satire depends on judging people according to general types, rather than according to their individual traits. When Greene, for instance, tells a tale about a collier beaten for cozening wives with short sacks of coal, he concludes with a warning to all colliers to become honest — assuming that all are indeed dishonest.[14] Shylock similarly places people in categories and criticizes Christians, rather than individuals. Thus he hates Antonio "for he is a Christian" (1.3.42); he argues that he will revenge because Christians take revenge on Jews in similar circumstances (3.1.65-73); and when Bassanio and Gratiano wish their wives dead sooner than Antonio, Shylock concludes, "These be the Christian husbands" (4.1.295). Shylock's criticism offers some wisdom: there is prodigality and hypocrisy enough in the Christians to warrant his satire. But it offers too little wisdom. Shylock's speech patterns show that he imposes the general type on the particular failing, with the result that his evaluation becomes to some degree untrue. Reducing a man with his unique strengths and weaknesses to a general category of his vices alone, Shylock operates on the hypothesis that the dram of eale calls all in doubt. Like Molière's misanthrope and Wycherly's plain-dealer, even like Hamlet in his bitter moments, Shylock demonstrates that the satirist's hypothesis, owing to the vices of men, is a workable one by which to live, but never a pleasant one.

If Shylock's style shows a man limited in judgment, his attitude toward language reveals the same limitation. Shylock, a man of the letter in both the religious and the rhetorical sense, treats words in as reductive a fashion as he does people. Shylock's literal interpretation of scripture — his using Jacob's deception of his father and of Laban to argue that God approves the man who helps himself to worldly gains (1.3.71-90) — has been discussed often enough to need no comment here.[15] What is more important to the general impression of Shylock's character is that his literalism extends beyond his religion to mold his distinctive attitude toward language. Under judicial rhetoric, classical and Renaissance rhetoricians defined the letter not only as opposed to any analogical extension of meaning, but also as opposed to the implied intention of a law.[16] Rigorously restricting meaning to its bare essentials, Shylock defines a "good man" as one who is "sufficient," possessing material wealth (1.3.12-17). To Shylock, "ships are but boards, sailors but men" (1.3.22), and his "daughter *is*" his "flesh and blood" (3.1.37-38, my italics). His argument that a Jew is also a man draws only upon those lesser properties that man shares with other animals: "hands, organs, dimensions, senses, affections, passions" (3.1.59-60). How different was the definition most Renaissance writers used! Thus Henry Peacham: "Herein it is that we do so far passe and excell all other creatures, in that we haue the gifte of speech and reason, and not they."[17] Shylock not only reduces words to the lowest material sense, he also opposes the letter to the intention, and values only the former. Thus he feels no qualms that he deceives Antonio about his intention in the bond, for he lives by the letter and counts that man a fool who does not. Furthermore, he preempts the words of others, to use them in a literal manner against their former intention. Reminding Antonio that his own words engendered the hatred now turned against him, Shylock accepts an insult in order to vindicate his revenge: "Thou call'dst me dog before thou hadst a cause, / But since I am a dog, beware my fangs" (3.3.6-7). Since Antonio has called him "dog," Shylock promises to live up to a strict definition of the word.

Unlike Shylock, Antonio defines words by the speaker's implied intention, not by the letter. In the scene where the two merchants draw up the bond, Antonio stops his railing when Shylock pleads, "I would be friends with you, and have your love, / . . . and you'll not hear me" (1.3.137-41). Calming himself, Antonio accepts the bond, despite its words, because Shylock indicates that his intention is friendship and a "merry sport" (1.3.145). Interpreting words in this manner requires trust in other people, a faith that they will not change their intention; and so Antonio's attitude toward language suggests the vulnerability that burdens the trusting man in the marketplace. Bassanio has no such faith—"I like not fair terms and a villain's mind" (1.3.179)—but Antonio overrules him, having already judged Shylock full of "much kindness" (1.3.153). As often in Shakespeare, a later parallel scene points up the extreme reversal of events. In act 3, scene 3, the roles of the merchants are reversed, and it is Antonio who pleads to be heard and treated kindly. But Shylock, unlike Antonio earlier, does not stop his railing to listen:

> I'll not be made a soft and dull-ey'd fool
> To shake the head, relent, and sigh, and yield
> To Christian intercessors. Follow not,
> I'll have no speaking, I will have my bond.
>
> (3.3.14–17)

Literal Shylock trusts his bond, as if words were as substantial as material things: reduce words to their basest meaning and stand firm. If Antonio is naive because he trusts words to mean always what the speaker implies as his intention, Shylock is equally naive because he trusts words to mean always the plain, stingy significance that he gives them. Both merchants are finally betrayed by their trust in words.

The first betrayed is, of course, Antonio. When he cannot repay the bond, he finds that Shylock's implied intention has nothing to do with its meaning according to the law. Even then, however, Antonio cannot see a way out of his situation because he holds to the same attitude toward language:

> The Duke cannot deny the course of law;
> For the commodity that strangers have
> With us in Venice, if it be denied,
> Will much impeach the justice of the state,
> Since that the trade and profit of the city
> Consisteth of all nations.
>
> (3.3.26–31)

Antonio assumes that the law requiring Venetians to honor their contracts with aliens can be interpreted only according to its original intention: to force the city's merchants to fulfill their bonds so that Venice will be an attractive mart for foreign trade. Even Antonio's outburst against Shylock at the trial suggests his faith in intention as the basis of language:

> You may as well do any thing most hard
> As seek to soften that—than which what's harder?—

His Jewish heart! Therefore I do beseech you
Make no moe offers, use no farther means,
But with all brief and plain conveniency
Let me have judgment and the Jew his will.

(4.1.78-83)

Now that Antonio knows that Shylock's purpose was what he signed
to in the bond, he assumes that the bond can mean only what Shylock wills it to. Surprisingly, Antonio's holding to the spirit or intention of words does not make him any more tolerant in judgment.
When Shylock pretended to mean well, he seemed to Antonio almost "Christian": "The Hebrew will turn Christian, he grows kind"
(1.3.178). Antonio assumes that "Christian" must be defined by the
spirit of the words, as "merciful," and that the word "Jewish" is its
opposite: it is not Shylock's unmerciful heart that incites him to vengeance, but "His Jewish heart." Despite their differences, Antonio
and Shylock are led to the same intolerance by their limited understanding of words.

But Shylock, as well as Antonio, is betrayed by his narrow trust in
his own way of meaning. Unmoved by the prayers, petitions, curses,
and persuasions advanced by the Duke, Gratiano, Bassanio, and
Portia, Shylock trusts that the words of the bond and the law mean
what he assumes they mean: "There is no power in the tongue of
man / To alter me: I stay here on my bond" (4.1.241-42). He holds
to the letter, and refuses to extend the interpretation of the bond
even as far as calling a surgeon for Antonio: "I cannot find it, 'tis not
in the bond" (4.1.262). What he learns, however, is that if only the
letter of the law guides interpretation, no man receives mercy. Portia restricts the meaning of the bond yet further, and tells Shylock
that he may take his "pound of flesh" but "no jot of blood" (ll.
306-7) without forfeiting his lands and goods to the state. Shylock,
for whom words are bondage, can only ask, "Is that the law?" (l.
315). Like Antonio, Shylock has been deceived by words because he
does not see that they may mean something other than what he
assumes.

In the trial scene, Portia does not stand for the spirit of the law
against the letter; rather, she mediates between these differing views
of Antonio and Shylock. At first, she attempts to do so by persuading Shylock to mercy:

> The quality of mercy is not strain'd,
> It droppeth as the gentle rain from heaven
> Upon the place beneath. It is twice blest:
> It blesseth him that gives and him that takes.
> 'Tis mightiest in the mightiest, it becomes
> The throned monarch better than his crown.
>
>   . . . .
>
> But mercy is above this sceptred sway,
> It is enthroned in the hearts of kings,
> It is an attribute to God himself;
> And earthly power doth then show likest God's
> When mercy seasons justice. Therefore, Jew,
> Though justice be thy plea, consider this,
> That in the course of justice, none of us
> Should see salvation. We do pray for mercy,
> And that same prayer doth teach us all to render
> The deeds of mercy.

                                        (4.1.184–202)

Here are all of Bassanio's figures of comparison: a simile, comparing mercy to rain; an argument from the lesser to the greater degree (like a king, even better, like God); and finally, the example of the Lord's Prayer. What Portia is offering Shylock at this point is another way to judge, one based on his likeness to other men. "The force of a similitude not being to prove anything to a contrary disputer but only to explain to a willing hearer"[18] — as Sir Philip Sidney observes — it is no wonder that Shylock is not persuaded. The only likeness between the Christians and himself that Shylock can see is hate.

With Shylock adamant, Bassanio pleads that the court "Wrest once the law to your authority" (l. 215); but Portia, as before when she might have helped Bassanio to leap "O'er a cold decree," will not allow it. The outcome of the first task of imaginative interpretation, however, has reassured us that language has many ways to mean, and men and women many ways to judge. And so, having failed to persuade Shylock to a just interpretation of his bond and the law, Portia provides one herself. In doing so, she not only unites the letter and the spirit of the law, but also employs the full range of methods of interpreting law that the classical and Renaissance rhetoricians discuss.[19] Thus she points out the *ambiguity* of the bond, and defines the "doubtful" words by the letter: Shylock may have only a pound of flesh, no more nor less, and no blood. If Shylock takes any more than his contract allows, he will fall under a *law contrary* to the one protecting aliens: one protecting Venetian citizens from violence by aliens. When Shylock consequently chooses not to take his pound of flesh, Portia has achieved the *end of the lawmakers:* to protect the inviolability of contracts and to insure a just relationship between citizens and aliens. But the law has another hold on Shylock: by *definition,* his is the crime of an alien's contriving against the life of a Venetian citizen. The bond, analogous to an attempt of murder, by *probation of things like* falls under the spirit of the law, and Shylock's life and goods are forfeit. To Portia, words are binding but not bondage: the wealth of meanings in words ensures that the general law may be adjusted to specific circumstances, and that the end of justice may be achieved.[20]

After Portia has presented her case, she turns to the judges: the Duke and, by virtue of the law against aliens, Antonio. The Duke is merciful. He grants Shylock his life before he asks it, and offers, in return for humbleness, a fine in lieu of the half of his wealth that might come to the state's coffers. Antonio, too, gives mercy, but not the open-handed generosity of the Duke. He requires the half of Shylock's wealth not for himself, but to support Shylock's daughter and new son-in-law, with the further stipulations that Shylock convert to Christianity and that he will the rest of his fortune to Jessica and Lorenzo. Thus Antonio's judgment imposes on Shylock the social bonds that he would not previously accept: turning Christian, he is forced to acknowledge his likeness to his fellow-citizens; supporting his daughter, he is forced to fulfill his paternal obligations. Nevertheless, I do not think that we violate the spirit of *The Merchant of Venice* when, in the modern theater, we feel pity for Shylock and troubled by Antonio's solution. Antonio's choices do not demonstrate the simple-minded vindictiveness of either Shylock toward him or of Gratiano toward Shylock. But Antonio's judgment is yet limited: if Christians are merciful and Jews are not, then Antonio will make Shylock "kind" (in both senses of the word) by naming him "Christian." That Shylock refuses to take joy in Antonio's mercy is a measure of the integrity as a dramatic character that Shakespeare has granted him.

The trial scene ends, however, not with the judgment of Shylock, but with Bassanio's giving up of Portia's ring, occasioned by the Duke's witty play on the word "bound": "Antonio, gratify this gentleman, / For in my mind you are much bound to him" (4.1.406–7). Antonio owes the lawyer not only gratitude and payment for his services, but also his very life; the word "bound" rings with new meaning since Antonio has been released from its old significance. Bassanio, following Antonio's example, steps in to take up his friend's bond and finds, as had Antonio, that he is committed to more than he intended. It is Bassanio now who will fall prey to the confusions of doubtful words. Those who judged before according to their own personal meanings—Morocco, Aragon, Shylock, even Antonio—found that words were barren, without power to help them gain their desires. In contrast, Bassanio and then Portia used the wealth of meanings in words to make them instruments of humane values and actions. The final test of interpretation, the riddle of the rings, will be a comic one: in wit and wordplay the characters will experience again the richness of language, and find this time that choosing the best of meanings may mean choosing them all.

But before turning to the festive wordplay that marks the final movement of the play, we may look to those characters whose use of language has prepared us for it. Launcelot is one such, although his love of the many meanings of words is more innocence than wisdom. His first speech parodies the dilemma of choice and interpretation that the characters in the main action continually confront. Just as Portia loves Bassanio but is bound by her father's will, just as the state desires to preserve Antonio's life but is bound by the law, so Launcelot wants to give his service elsewhere but is bound to Shylock:

> "Bouge," says the fiend. "Bouge not," says my conscience. "Conscience," say I, "you counsel well." "Fiend," say I, "you counsel well." To be rul'd by my conscience, I should stay with the Jew my master, who (God bless the mark) is a kind of devil; and to run away from the Jew, I should be rul'd by the fiend, who, saving your reverence, is the devil himself. . . . The fiend gives the more friendly counsel: I will run, fiend; my heels are at your commandement, I will run.
>
> (2.2.19–32)

Launcelot is caught between the letter and the spirit of the law, the one saying that he must stay with his master, the other saying that staying with this master is unjust. He chooses to run, but not before providing himself a witty reason: the devil tells him to run, but the

Jew, too, is a "devil," and so he may run from him. Like Antonio, Launcelot escapes by means of the doubtful word.

Not Portia but Launcelot is the first character to see the advantage in turning Shylock's letter against him. When Shylock calls Jessica before going to Bassanio's, Launcelot calls, too, and at Shylock's objection, echoes his own words taken too literally: "Your worship was wont to tell me I could do nothing without bidding" (2.5.8-9). The clown is not beyond the one-sided interpretations of others, but he uses them for frolic. At Belmont he imitates Shylock's literal interpretation of scripture, as well as, in blockheaded fashion, the Christians' prejudices: "for look you, the sins of the father are to be laid upon the children; therefore, I promise you, I fear you. I was always plain with you, and so now I speak my agitation of the matter; therefore be a' good cheer, for truly I think you are damn'd. There is but one hope in it that can do you any good, and that is but a kind of bastard hope neither. . . . Marry, you may partly hope that your father got you not, that you are not the Jew's daughter" (3.5.1-12). His argument is a curious compound of mockery and ignorance. One doubts that Launcelot could contrive a more reasoned one, but he at least knows that such limited methods of judging are best employed only in games.

The verbal games that Launcelot plays with Jessica and Lorenzo at Belmont anticipate the serious struggles with interpretation that directly follow at the trial in Venice. Lorenzo tries to persuade Launcelot to serve in dinner as the Christians in the next scene try to persuade Shylock to give up the bond. Launcelot, like Shylock after him, turns each persuasion away by resort to the letter. Launcelot will not bid the servants "prepare for dinner" because it is already done — "they have all stomachs" (3.5.46-48). When Lorenzo asks him to "cover" — lay the table — Launcelot will not because he knows his "duty" — he may not put on his hat before his betters (ll. 51-54). And, as Portia will finally resort to the letter in the trial scene, Lorenzo resorts to the plainest of meanings in order to beat Launcelot at his own game: "I pray thee understand a plain man in his plain meaning: go to thy fellows, bid them cover the table, serve in the meat, and we will come in to dinner" (3.5.57-60). Lorenzo's comment on Launcelot's sophistry thus serves as much as an introduction to the trial scene as an evaluation of the clown and his attitude toward language:

> O dear discretion, how his words are suited!
> The fool hath planted in his memory
> An army of good words, and I do know
> A many fools, that stand in better place,
> Garnish'd like him, that for a tricksy word
> Defy the matter.
>
> (3.5.65-70)

Lorenzo, assuming the position of the humanist, draws the moral: although the fool with his misplaced love of words causes only laughter, other, greater fools, who love words more than what they signify of truth and value, cause great harm. Shylock, too, has tricksy words — "law," "bond," "justice," "A Daniel come to judgment" — which seem to help him defy the humane values that should be their intention. Nor are the Christians exempt from this attitude toward language. Sophistical Gratiano picks up all of Shylock's phrases and begs the court to drop them on the Jew's own head. So Launcelot had picked up the proverbs of scripture and dropped them — however facetiously and unfairly — on Jessica. In both scenes, however, language is rescued from the limits of the letter by a speaker who perceives that even the letter may be given a meaning that does not contradict the spirit of the words. Lorenzo saves Jessica and his dinner from Launcelot's sophisms in a comic anticipation of Portia's rescue of Antonio and justice from Shylock's bond.

Jessica and Lorenzo also play with words, although they take from them more gentle recreation than does Launcelot. Their interchange on "such a night" (5.1.1-22) is a case in point. While Launcelot uses a meaning contrary to his companion's in order to score against him, Jessica and Lorenzo share the abundance of meaning in words. Each of their comparisons between this night and another celebrates an example of loyal romantic love, but implies destructive results: on such a night Troilus's sighs followed Cressida, but to the Grecian tents, and Thisbe sought Pyramus, but found a lion; on such a night Dido longed for Aeneas, but must also have planned her suicide, and Medea gathered the herbs for her gift to Jason, the last and greatest gift before she monstrously punished his unfaithfulness. The lovers end their comparisons by describing their own romantic night: on such a night Jessica loves Lorenzo even though his vows are untrue, and Lorenzo loves Jessica despite her shrewishness. The lyric words of the passage tell us about their love;

the ironic delivery must tell us about the knowledge of human faults and weaknesses that will keep their love generous and forgiving. That they treat with irony these historic examples indicates their own realistic expectations from love; that they do not allow the irony to overwhelm romance suggests that they will trust, no matter what defective human love will be the return of their faith. Their ironies do not deny one meaning for its opposite but, instead, incorporate two disparate meanings into a whole. Their teasing acceptance of two meanings at once allows them full expression of the mixed nature of human love. If ideal love is denied merely human lovers, then they will love in what fashion they can. Just so, they gladly listen in the moonlight to the music that is only an imperfect realization of the heavenly music, which earthly lovers cannot hear.

In their use of language, Jessica and Lorenzo are an appropriate prelude to the teasing riddles when the other wives and husbands return. Love finds expression at the end of this play in wit and wordplay. From her arrival at Belmont, Portia plays her double role as wife and lawyer to generate double meanings in her words: "We have been praying for our husbands' welfare, / Which speed we hope the better for our words" (5.1.114-15). "Praying" is not what Lorenzo assumes, but the persuading of the court to justice for Antonio; the ladies' "words" in interest of their husbands' welfare were more legal than religious. Similarly, when Bassanio and Gratiano admit their gift of the rings, Portia and Nerissa reply with ambiguous accusations and threats: the husbands, they are certain, gave the rings not to men but to women (ll. 158-60); the wives will never come to their husbands' beds until they see the rings (ll. 190-92); the wives will take the doctor and the clerk as their bedfellows should they ever meet them, since the rings now bind them to these persons (ll. 223-35); and, finally, the wives did lie with the doctor and his clerk in return for their rings (ll. 258-62). All these riddles depend on the double meanings of words: that "doctor" and "clerk" mean Portia and Nerissa, not men, and that those words with sexual connotations, "bedfellow" and "lie," have a literal rather than extended meaning. While Portia and Nerissa are teasing their husbands with these double meanings, they are pretending that they only adhere to their bonds: Bassanio and Gratiano had promised to keep the rings forever, and, since they broke their promises, the ladies may take revenge. They have adopted Shylock's literalness, but to play with, as if by putting on the role of the villain they might exorcize its power. Although to Bassanio and Gratiano the riddles are real threats to happiness, to us they are further proof that words offer many interpretations to be used in shaping a happy society.

With the return of the rings and the final riddle, Bassanio and Gratiano, like many before them in this play, find themselves handicapped by the assumption that words have only one meaning. But just as they have begun to think that they are cuckolds before they have fully become husbands, Portia reveals the double identity of the doctor and his clerk, and so the double meaning of her words. As Thomas Wilson had suggested, on the subject of conflict arising from verbal confusion, "the double meanyng being ones knowen . . . endes the whole matter."[21] Bassanio, however, takes the teases in the vein in which they were given. He does not deny the former for the new meaning; he takes up both: "Sweet doctor, you shall be my bedfellow — / When I am absent, then lie with my wife" (ll. 284–85). Thus Bassanio's payment to the "doctor" comes home to him again, with interest: he has found that Portia's ring binds him to one wise and witty, as well as one fair and virtuous.

One who welcomes the lustier joys of love, one might add. The extra meanings abounding at the end of the play include the double entendres that young lovers always see as proof that all men and women share their desires. It is Portia who calls these new meanings into the language of the play, from which they are absent in the earlier scenes. Thus she replies to her husband's romantic greeting, comparing her to the sun, with a series of puns:

> Let me give light, but let me not be light,
> For a light wife doth make a heavy husband,
> And never be Bassanio so for me.
>
> (5.1.129–31)

Playing on the meanings of *light* ("brightness," "sexually loose," and "weighing little") and *heavy* ("weighing much" and "sad") Portia prepares her last line to be an ambiguous double vow of fidelity: may she never make Bassanio sad by being unfaithful, and may she never think Bassanio too much weight for her to hold. Portia does not deny Bassanio's former meaning, but adds something less idealistic: her wordplay admits that sensuality and jealousy, as well as romance, may enter into love without endangering its central faith.

Like Jessica and Lorenzo, who in their ironies acknowledge the imperfections of love in order to strengthen it, these other lovers, with their bawdy puns, incorporate an earthier reality into their lyricism. Most telling is Gratiano's closing pun: "Well, while I live I'll fear no other thing / So sore, as keeping safe Nerissa's ring" (ll. 306–7). Body and soul come together in Gratiano's pledge: vowing to keep safe the token of their spiritual union, he is also vowing to keep a jealous eye on their physical union. In the last scene, equivocation becomes the poetic kind, an economic means of saying more than one true thing at once. The lovers take an attitude toward language directly opposite to Shylock's: rather than paring meaning down to its bare essentials, they welcome the many meanings in any single word.

In *The Merchant of Venice,* those who make themselves open to the generous supply of meaning in words live happier lives and succeed better in solving problems of judgment. Language, signifying what the many, not the individual, will, offers its bounty to those who listen carefully to the words they speak and hear. In contrast, those who shut themselves up in their own meanings find that what little significance they have dwindles to less. Even Antonio's melancholy may be on its way to a cure at the end of the play: he who formerly rejected all the meanings of his sadness that his society offered now welcomes in new meanings. His last speech includes a play on words: "Sweet lady, you have given me life and living" (l. 286). Portia has not only rescued him from Shylock's knife; she has also handed him a letter recounting the return of his ships and prosperity. "Life" and "living": the meanings of these two words that sound almost alike are quite different, and yet in concord. Thus Antonio joins the other characters who, having paid dearly to buy themselves free from life's problems, turn at last to life's unbought joys: the beauty of moonlight, stars, and a fresh morning, the harmony of music, the company of good friends, and the wealth of meanings that language offers every speaker.

Notes

1. In oral speech imagery (based on the count of the terms tongue(s), mouth(s), throat(s), ear(s), breath, air, and airy) *MV* has nineteen. (*R2* is first with sixty-five; *Wiv.* is last with eleven; the average is twenty-nine.) In

writing imagery (based on the count of the terms pen, ink, paper(s), and parchment) *MV* has six. (*LLL* is first with fifteen; *AYL, Tmp.,* and *TNK* are last with zero; the average is four.) Of references to word(s), *MV* has twenty-two. (*LLL* is first with forty-eight; *Per.* is last with ten; the average is twenty-four.)

2. *The Merchant of Venice* has been called "a fairy tale" by Harley Granville-Barker, in *Prefaces to Shakespeare* (Princeton: Princeton Univ. Press, 1946), I, 335. Although because of the realistic characters it does not seem so, it has affinities with fairy tales, especially with those in which the hero's growing up is symbolized by his or her answering riddles and achieving impossible tasks. See, for example, Bruno Bettelheim's analysis of "The Queen Bee," "The Three Languages," and "The Three Feathers," in *The Uses of Enchantment* (New York: Random House, 1977), pp. 76-78 and 97-111.

3. *Timber,* in *Ben Jonson,* VIII, 625.

4. On the enthymeme, see Sr. Miriam Joseph, *Shakespeare's Use of the Arts of Language,* pp. 358-61. The enthymeme may be based on fallible signs and probabilities.

5. *Timber,* in *Ben Jonson,* VIII, 621.

6. Sidney, *Defense,* pp. 10-12. Later Sidney speaks of the "imaginative and judging power" as one faculty, a faculty which poetry speaks to better than philosophy does (p. 17).

7. Norman Rabkin, in "Meaning and Shakespeare," in *Shakespeare 1971,* ed. Clifford Leech and J. M. R. Margeson (Toronto: Univ. of Toronto Press, 1972), p. 103, makes a telling objection to much of the criticism on *MV:* "In terms of moral content that we can extract [from the play], we come away with precious little: by the end we know as we knew before that cruelty is bad and love better." Rabkin's thesis, that those critical attempts to find a unifying central theme in *MV* deny the variety of responses we have to the characters, is borne out by much of the criticism. The stumbling block is usually Shylock, for whose feelings we have sympathy at the same time that thematic interpretations require us to see him as a value or idea that we must only condemn: see, for example, M. C. Bradbrook, *Shakespeare and Elizabethan Poetry* (London: Chatto and Windus, 1951), pp. 170-79; Barbara K. Lewalski, "Biblical Allusion and Allegory in *The Merchant of Venice,*" *Twentieth Century Interpretations of The Merchant of Venice,* ed. Sylvan Barnet (Englewood Cliffs, N.J.: Prentice-Hall, 1970), pp. 33-54; *The Merchant of Venice,* ed. John R. Brown (1955; rpt. London: Methuen & Co., 1964), esp. pp. lvii-lviii; Sylvan Barnet, "Prodigality and Time in *The Merchant of Venice,*" *PMLA,* 87 (1972), 26-30; Neil Carson, "Hazarding and Cozening in *The Merchant of Venice,*" *ELN,* 9 (1972), 168-77; and John S. Coolidge, "Law and Love in

The Merchant of Venice," SQ, 27 (1976), 243-63. In contrast, Barber, in *Shakespeare's Festive Comedy*, pp. 163-91, describes the comic values assumed by the play, and at the same time the means by which Shakespeare makes Shylock a sympathetic character who yet must not be allowed to disrupt society and pervert its values.

8. Bradbrook, in *Shakespeare and Elizabethan Poetry*, pp. 175-76, mentions the likeness of the Moor's "accents" to those of Tamburlaine, but does not elaborate. In "Shakespeare's Recollections of Marlowe," in *Shakespeare's Styles*, ed. Edwards et al., pp. 191-204, Bradbrook further suggests that *MV* 2.7.37-47 is modeled on Tamburlaine's speech at the death of Zenocrate, and that the Father's judgment is appropriate to Morocco's character: "like Tamburlaine's the conclusion of his quest is a death's head" (p. 191).

9. Marlowe, *Tamburlaine, Part I*, 5.1.172-73, in *Works*, I, 137.

10. Thus, after reasoning against the wise advice of Philanax, Duke Basilius retires into the country to try to prevent the wrongs prophesied by the oracle, and so brings them on himself; and Pyrocles and Musidorus, after considering the viciousness of passion and the virtue of love, follow passion into sins while they think they are pursuing love into glory. See Sir Philip Sidney, *The Countess of Pembroke's Arcadia*, ed. Albert Feuillerat (1912; rpt. Cambridge: Cambridge Univ. Press, 1970), pp. 2-6, 8-23, and 36-39.

11. Both Barber, in *Shakespeare's Festive Comedy*, p. 174, and also Barnet, in "Prodigality and Time," p. 28, argue that Bassanio relies not on reason but on impulse and guess to choose the correct casket. Yet the stage direction tells us that while the song plays, *"Bassanio comments on the caskets to himself"* (3.2.63), and he follows the song with a long, reasoned speech on his choice (ll. 73-106).

12. Lewis, *English Literature in the Sixteenth Century*, p. 470.

13. See Hallett Smith, *Elizabethan Poetry* (Cambridge, Mass.: Harvard Univ. Press, 1952), pp. 194-205.

14. For the tale of the collier, see Robert Greene, "A Notable Discovery of Cozenage (1591)," in *Elizabethan Prose Fiction*, ed. Merritt Lawlis (New York: Odyssey Press, 1967), pp. 432-34.

15. See, for example, Lewalski, "Biblical Allusion," pp. 39-40; and Coolidge, "Law and Love," pp. 246-47. On Shylock's use of language, also see Barber, *Shakespeare's Festive Comedy*, p. 181; and Lawrence Danson, *The Harmonies of the Merchant of Venice* (New Haven: Yale Univ. Press, 1978), p. 139.

16. See, for example, Quintilian, *Institutio Oratoria*, VII.xi.1-4; and Wilson, *Arte of Rhetorique*, sigs. Niiii[v]-Oi[r].

17. Peacham, *Garden* (1577), sig. Aii[r].

18. Sidney, *Defense,* p. 53.

19. See Cicero, *De Inventione,* I.xiii.17; Quintilian, *Institutio Oratoria,* VII.iii–x; and Wilson, *Arte of Rhetorique,* sigs. Niiii^r-Oi^r. The five methods of interpreting a law from which the lawyer may draw his arguments are, in Wilson's words, "i. Definition. ii. Contrarye Lawes. iii. Lawes made, & thende of the law maker. iiii. Ambiguitye, or doubtfulnes. v. Probation of thinges like." In *definition,* the lawyer decides what the crime should be called — whether murder or manslaughter, for example. Facing *contrary laws,* he attempts to resolve the contradiction or give one precedence over the other by interpreting each. With regard to the *end of the lawmaker,* he argues for either the letter or the spirit of the law. He must also clarify any *ambiguity* in the law caused by words meaning more than one thing, and, if no law applies to his case, he must argue, by *probation of things like,* that his client's situation, analogous to that under the law, falls under the spirit of its jurisdiction.

20. For readings based on sixteeth-century English legal practices that support this one based on judicial rhetoric, see E. F. J. Tucker, "The Letter of the Law in 'The Merchant of Venice,' " *ShS,* 29 (1976), 93–101; and Alice N. Benston, "Portia, the Law, and the Tripartite Structure of *The Merchant of Venice,*" *SQ,* 30 (1979), 367–85. But see also William Chester Jordan, "Approaches to the Court Scene in the Bond Story: Equity and Mercy, or Reason and Nature," *SQ,* 33 (1982), 49–59, who argues from an examination of many versions that the bond story presents a fictive world where ordinary law does not apply, but where men yet manage to overcome the unreasonable and unnatural desires of the lender by an even more strict reading of the law than he proposes.

21. Wilson, *Rule of Reason,* sig. Sii^r.

CHAPTER 7

All's Well That Ends Well: Words and Things

No book on Shakespeare and ideas about language would be complete without a look at the play containing Parolles. Unexpectedly, even *All's Well That Ends Well* illustrates Shakespeare's subordination of ideas about language to larger dramatic interests. Although named after "words," Parolles is no less an individualized character than Lafew, named after "fire"; and, for all Parolles's importance to the story, language is not a major theme of the play. Instead, as in *The Merchant of Venice*, linguistic ideas and attitudes serve the purpose of characterization; not Parolles alone, but all the major characters acquire particularity by the way that they use and value words. Moreover, in *All's Well That Ends Well* the ideas about language contribute as well to our sense of a distinctive fictional world. From the conflicting ideas and attitudes of the characters emerges a social world with the human potential for growth and decay. Words in the society of *All's Well That Ends Well* are what the Renaissance humanists imagined them to be: agents of confusion when loved for themselves, and guides to wisdom and virtuous action when loved for what they speak of truth. We shall see this same double purpose of ideas about language in *Hamlet;* at the turn of the century, Shakespeare is developing a new way of putting together a play. At this point, however, it is more useful to look at the later play because it is simpler. In *All's Well That Ends Well* the seams show, while in *Hamlet* they do not.

Even though a thorough defense of the play is not within the scope of this chapter, I must admit at the outset that I like *All's Well That Ends Well,* and that I do not hold with much of the criticism on it: that Shakespeare fails to bring off the mingling of romantic story and realistic characterization; that the character of Helena is inconsistent, both humble wife and also shrewd trickster; that she wins

Bertram by mere deceit; that Bertram is a brute and Helena's love for him implausible; that the elders are tyrants whom the youth must rebel against if society is to be renewed; that the wit of the clown is so crude as to be humorless; and that the language is completely without poetry.[1] Others have defended *All's Well That Ends Well*,[2] and I shall only add that it plays very well with good actors — a spirited Helena, a handsome Bertram, kindly elders each with integrity, and a Parolles not overtheatrical.[3] The play, I think, is a modest success, the prosy kind of romantic comedy that Thomas Heywood was master of in Shakespeare's day: the story of a nobody, like you or me, who suddenly finds herself in the middle of romantic adventures on account of love, and who succeeds not by heroism or grandeur of mind, but by the simple virtues that a nobody has — common sense, loyalty, perseverance, cunning, pluck, and a sense of worth that she will not disown in the company of her "betters."[4]

Another of these ordinary virtues, which Helena possesses and which anyone may claim some share in, is language. Helena's influence results not from birth or station, but from words: her "words all ears took captive," Lafew asserts, and her "dear perfection hearts that scorn'd to serve / Humbly call'd mistress" (5.3.17–19). Lafew's estimation, of course, is not quite accurate. Helena's words take the King captive and he assents to try her cure; but Bertram scorns her, despite her perfection, when she chooses him for her husband. Consequently, the play may be divided into two movements, marked by the scene of Helena's choice: in the first, Helena wins her husband in the eyes of family and society and gains the *name* of wife; in the second, she wins Bertram by putting meaning into his riddle, and so becomes a wife in *deed*. As M. C. Bradbrook long ago pointed out, Shakespeare has interpreted the reuniting of husband and wife not only as the heroine's earning of her title, but also as the hero's education up to his.[5] The scene of Helena's choice further reveals what Bertram has to learn in order to be worthy of her: the distinction between words and things that will enable him to see clearly his society's values, and so to achieve them. As far as the story goes, as soon as Bertram has his values straight, he naturally accepts the wife who embodies them.

Part of the focus that Shakespeare has given Boccaccio's story of the wife who wins a husband by her wit[6] is the humanists' distinction between *res et verba*, words and things. Let us begin, then, with the scene that holds the play together, and in which this focus becomes clear. In act 2, scene 3, having cured the King, Helena takes her reward and moves down the line of young lords to choose a husband. She expects rejection for her lack of rank and titled family, yet each courtier surprisingly seeks to be her husband, and it is she who refuses them. Lafew, supposing that the young men have denied Helena, grumbles a chorus of disapproval: they deserve to be sent "to th' Turk to make eunuchs of" (2.3.87-88); they are "boys of ice" and "bastards to the English" (ll. 93-94). These are Lafew's salty ways of saying that Helena is the test, not the one tested, that he who refuses her is a boy, lacking both the blood and wisdom of manhood. Bertram, unlike the other wards of the King, proves such a boy: "A poor physician's daughter my wife! Disdain / Rather corrupt me ever!" (ll. 115-16). Lafew has already shaped our response to Bertram's refusal: "I am sure thy father drunk wine — but if thou be'st not an ass, I am a youth of fourteen" (ll. 99-101). Along with Lafew, we think Bertram not so much evil as not yet the man his father was, still young and very foolish.

The King thinks so, too, and tries to enlighten Bertram:

> 'Tis only title thou disdain'st in her, the which
> I can build up. Strange is it that our bloods,
> Of color, weight, and heat, pour'd all together,
> Would quite confound distinction, yet stands off
> In differences so mighty. If she be
> All that is virtuous — save what thou dislik'st,
> A poor physician's daughter — thou dislik'st
> Of virtue for the name. But do not so.
> From lowest place when virtuous things proceed,
> The place is dignified by th' doer's deed.
> Where great additions swell's, and virtue none,
> It is a dropsied honor. Good alone
> Is good, without a name; vileness is so:
> The property by what it is should go,
> Not by the title. She is young, wise, fair,
> In these to nature she's immediate heir;
> And these breed honor. That is honor's scorn,
> Which challenges itself as honor's born,
> And is not like the sire. Honors thrive,
> When rather from our acts we them derive
> Than our foregoers. The mere word's a slave

> Debosh'd on every tomb, on every grave
> A lying trophy, and as oft is dumb
> Where dust and damn'd oblivion is the tomb
> Of honor'd bones indeed. What should be said?
> If thou canst like this creature as a maid,
> I can create the rest. Virtue and she
> Is her own dower; honor and wealth from me.
>
> (ll. 117-44)

Shakespeare has conceived the King as a humanist, and his speech is a humanist's sermon, both in style and in argument. The style is rhetorical: abstract diction, metaphors only for clarity, balanced antitheses, with many of the ideas presented in the terse form of moral maxims. The matter is also humanistic: the King explains to Bertram that he dislikes Helena not for want of virtue, which she has, but only because of her name, derived from a poor physician. The King's arguments thus address Bertram's confusion of names with things: a title without virtue is not honorable, while virtue without a title is; good and evil must be seen for what they are, not by what they are called; honor derives from acts, not from ancestors; and words are untrustworthy guides to honor, gracing the tombs of the worthless and leaving unmarked the graves of the truly honorable. In this speech the King repeats the arguments of his ancestors in the humanistic dialogues and interludes we have looked at already, in the third chapter: Medwall's Flaminius, Heywood's Plowman, Erasmus's boys, and Vives's Flexibulus.[7] The King concludes that Bertram's assumption of Helena's unworthiness is false: Helena possesses the essentials of honor—the gifts of nature and the achievements of virtue—and the King will provide the circumstances—recognition of her honor and wealth. If Bertram can see beyond the mere word he will accept her gladly as his wife.

In this scene, Bertram speaks from an ignorance similar to that of Grympherantes, the arrogant young nobleman in Vives's dialogue, and the King's admonition is similar to that of Flexibulus, the wise old teacher. Bertram thinks that words are things, that Helena's lack of title is lack of nobility. In the earlier dramatic debates on nobility, as well as in the school-boy dialogues, this ignorance does not last; the side of merit wins acceptance through persuasive education. By the general principle that good is good no matter what it is called, that one must judge not by the "lying trophy" but by the thing itself, the King attempts to clear out a way for Bertram to see essential values. The King's speech is not about language; it is about virtue and honor. Yet the King must teach Bertram the distinction between names and things, title and virtue, before he can teach him the thing itself.[8] The confrontation ends as if Bertram had been led to the truth; he corrects himself before the King and marries Helena. But we soon learn Betram's plans: "Although before the solemn priest I have sworn, / I will not bed her" (2.3.269-70). Unlike the teachers in the dialogues and interludes, the King is unsuccessful. Bertram clings to the old habit: he allows even his marriage vow to be a "lying trophy." Rather than Helena's essential virtue he chooses the mere word — Parolles — as his companion and leaves for the wars.

Between Bertram's apparent education and his reversion to boy's foolishness, however, comes an episode serving as a comic variation of his confrontation with the King. As Bertram had bridled at the offense to his honor by offering him Helena, so Parolles bridles at Lafew's insult to his honor by naming Bertram his "master":

Laf. Your lord and master did well to make his recantation.
Par. Recantation? My lord? My master?
Laf. Ay; is it not a language I speak?
Par. A most harsh one, and not to be understood without bloody suc-
   ceeding. My master?
Laf. Are you companion to the Count Rossillion?
Par. To any count, to all counts: to what is man.
Laf. To what is count's man. Count's master is of another style.
Par. You are too old, sir; let it satisfy you, you are too old.
Laf. I must tell thee, sirrah, I write man; to which title age cannot
   bring thee.

(2.3.186-99)

Having offended Parolles, Lafew resorts to a more polite phrase: Parolles, perhaps, is a "companion." When Parolles haughtily re-fuses even this title, Lafew lets his anger speak the truth: Parolles is a worthy companion only to a "count's man," or servant. In the face of Lafew's anger, Parolles retreats from his threats of a challenge; and, in a full rage now, Lafew judges Parolles not even worth the ti-tle "man."

As soon as he whom Parolles called "too old" to challenge passes

safely out of earshot, the braggart soldier works himself into a perfect dither of vengeful vows—all immediately undercut by Lafew's
reentry and Parolles's servility:

> *Laf.* Sirrah, your lord and master's married, there's news for you.
>   You have a new mistress.
> *Par.* I most unfeignedly beseech your lordship to make some reserva-
>   tion of your wrongs. He is my good lord; whom I serve above is my
>   master.
> *Laf.* Who? God?
> *Par.* Ay, sir.
> *Laf.* The devil it is that's thy master.
>
> (ll. 242-49)

Parolles, in a much more obvious fashion than Bertram, lives by the
mere word: in his empty threats, in his claim to a higher title than
he deserves, and in his extended plea that Lafew apologize for
speaking the truth. He belongs with those characters whom Erasmus
advances as men pursuing "names" not "things": "Aren't men fools
who rush off and enlist in the army in hope of booty—not very much
booty at that—at risk to body and soul? Who toil to amass wealth
when they have a soul in need of every good? Who wear fancy
clothes and live in fine houses when their souls lie sloven and neglected? . . . And though you see these fools everywhere, you'd find
scarcely any who would put up with the *name* of fool, yet they don't
object to *being* fools."[9]
   Like Erasmus's fools, Parolles objects to being called so: "This is
hard and undeserv'd measure, my lord" (l. 257). But he does not object to being one: gartering his sleeves and disguising his body with
scarves; stuffing his speech with repetition and overblown courtesy;
hoping to gain the title of captain by mere squatter's rights—by tales
of war and by propinquity to the titled Bertram. A humanist of the
same school as the King, Lafew thinks that vileness, like goodness,
should go by its true name: "You are a vagabond and no true
traveller. You are more saucy with lords and honorable personages
than the commission of your birth and virtue gives you heraldry.
You are not worth another word, else I'd call you knave" (ll.
259-63). Lafew takes the measure of Parolles's virtue and names
him "knave."
   Thus, in the climactic scene[10] in *All's Well That Ends Well*, Ber-

tram and Parolles come into conflict with the King and Lafew on just those issues debated in the humanist dialogues and interludes. It is in this scene that we may see most clearly Shakespeare's techniques for handling ideas about language in this play. Each of these men is distinguished by his ideas: the King thinks that virtue is more important than family name as an indication of honor; Bertram thinks that Helena's lack of title makes her unworthy; Parolles presumes to titles he has not earned; Lafew thinks that even the title "man" should be earned by deeds. Yet the values of the society are apparent: the characters with authority and experience see that names are not things, that people are not what they are called, and that one must value the essentials beneath the titles; Bertram and Parolles are making mistakes. Linguistic ideas and attitudes provide individuality, and yet also contribute to the making of a coherent world. Ideas about language are not themselves the theme of this scene: the nature of honor, whether inherited or achieved, is. But the ideas about language are a means of translating the theme of education in honor into the experience of young and old in conflict. The sins and follies that threaten society result not from senility, but from juvenility; the suspense of the play derives from this threat. Will the young increase in wit and wisdom to the degree that they may preserve the values of society? Throughout the play attitude toward language is a measure of maturity.

If we trace the ways that characters use the words "nature" and "virtue" or their synonyms in the first half of the play, we can see at work this translation of the theme of honor into characterization by attitude toward language. The elders share sensitivity to the various meanings of the words, precise distinctions, and conclusions: virtue is achieved not inherited. The young people vary widely in their interpretations of these words, depending on their degree of wisdom. The individuality of the characters is further heightened by contrast. It is not until the middle of the play that we see the young together in conversation (with the exception of Helena and Parolles). Most of the opening two acts is taken up with wise elders attempting to pass on their wisdom to the young.[11] Furthermore, the focus of episodes alternates, from definitions based on essentials, to definitions based on verbal confusions, and back again.

The first scene, Bertram's leave-taking, brings naturally to the fore the values that his mother wishes him to carry with him. The

Countess assures Lafew that Helena "derives her honesty, and achieves her goodness" (1.1.45), that she both inherits her disposition toward virtue and also lives up to her inheritance. Less certain of Bertram's untested virtue, the Countess reminds him of the difference between nature and achievement in her blessing: "Thy blood and virtue / Contend for empire in thee, and thy goodness / Share with thy birthright" (1.1.62–64). To the Countess, the importance of "blood" or "birthright" is the potential for goodness, and goodness, while an inheritance, is one that must be earned. When Bertram arrives at court, the King continues his mother's instruction, but makes a slightly different distinction:

> Youth, thou bear'st thy father's face;
> Frank Nature, rather curious than in haste,
> Hath well compos'd thee. Thy father's moral parts
> Mayst thou inherit too!
>
> (1.2.19–22)

To the King, blood is only blood: the father's nature has been recapitulated in Bertram's handsome features. Morality, while an inheritance, is not a natural one, and the King is still in doubt whether Bertram will achieve it. We have already heard Lafew trying to teach Parolles that neither his "birth" nor his "virtue" has entitled him to the names by which he would be known. Lafew's lecture to Parolles suggests yet another understanding of nature: one may claim even nature's gifts only as he realizes their potential. Although the elders differ in their definitions of "nature," they share the precise use of words and the definition of "virtue" by deeds, not blood.

With the elders speaking more or less in concert, the young provide the variation. The method of characterizing by contrasts begins immediately: in the first scene Parolles's folly follows hard upon the heels of the Countess's wisdom. When Helena inquires how a maid may defend her virginity, Parolles answers — with intimations of his soldierly capabilities — that she may as well surrender it. "It is not politic in the commonwealth of nature to preserve virginity," advises Parolles, for "Loss of virginity is rational increase, and there was never virgin got till virginity was first lost" (l.1.126–29). Virginity, in fact, is a sin: "'tis against the rule of nature," and taking its part is disobedience to one's mother; "virginity murthers itself," and so is "a desperate offendress against nature" (ll. 135–41). Parolles's arguments are, of course, sophistical: he arrives at his conclusion by juggling the various senses of his words. One can call virginity self-murder only by taking the property for the person: a virgin begets no virgins, and so virginity murders itself by taking itself to the grave. And one can argue that virginity is a sin only by confusing physical with moral nature. Like the fools that the Tudor humanists warned against, Parolles takes words for realities and, so, confusion for truth.

Helena will not accept Parolles's arguments, and he leaves promising to "return perfect courtier," and "to naturalize" her to the role (1.1.207–8). But in her soliloquy following Parolles's exit, Helena rejects "nature" in the sense that Parolles has used the word, distinguishes between "nature" and "merit," and chooses the latter:

> The mightiest space in fortune nature brings
> To join like likes, and kiss like native things.
> Impossible be strange attempts to those
> That weigh their pains in sense, and do suppose
> What hath been cannot be. Who ever strove
> To show her merit, that did miss her love?
>
> (1.1.222–27)

In an elliptical argument, moving from one thing to its opposite, Helena assesses her chance of success, according to her motive, in her love for Bertram. She decides that "nature" cannot be her motive, at least in the sense of the procreator that Parolles extolls. Such a motive can only bring Countess to Count, as it brings body to body. Helena's love is "impossible," that which is beyond nature and sense. And so her goal, in one way Bertram, is in another way "merit": she who achieves goodness will surely achieve her love as well—and thus follows her plan to cure the King and earn her right to Bertram's love. Earnest and good, Helena is also very young. She sees through to the heart of the matter and distinguishes between "nature" and "merit"; but she assumes that life is as easy as a fairy tale, where the heroine is loved on account of her goodness. There is none of the melancholic assessment of human nature and the doubt about achieving virtue that experience has led the wiser elders to.

In the third scene Lavache picks up Parolles's arguments for procreative nature in his request to marry: he wishes to have "the blessing of God" in the "issue a' [his] body" (1.3.24–25), and his "poor body . . . requires it" (l. 28). Lavache's wit, far from humorless, is a mischievous expounding of the scriptures: "I have been, madam, a wicked creature, as you and all flesh and blood are, and indeed I do marry that I may repent" (1.3.35-37). Lavache's "blood" is the frailty of human nature, which St. Paul bemoans and forgives, but which Lavache simply and slyly accepts. Lavache is a cynic, wiser than Parolles, sufficiently witty to use his play with words to point up human failures, but not enough to use it to work men toward virtue. When Lavache tells the Countess that he has been wicked, we expect him to tell her that he marries in order to reform; instead, he says that he marries to repent. His comment demands the reply of the Countess: "Thy marriage, sooner than thy wickedness" (1.3.38).

As Helena when alone corrects the view of Parolles on nature, the Countess, in her soliloquy on Helena's love for her son, corrects the view of Lavache:

> Even so it was with me when I was young.
> If ever we are nature's, these are ours. This thorn
> Doth to our rose of youth rightly belong;
> Our blood to us, this to our blood is born.
> It is the show and seal of nature's truth,
> Where love's strong passion is impress'd in youth.
> By our remembrances of days foregone,
> Such were our faults, or then we thought them none.
> Her eye is sick on't; I observe her now.
>
> (1.3.128-36)

The Countess knows herself. Out of this wisdom she recognizes yet forgives faults in others. She views human nature ("blood"), not as Parolles, who sees it as virtue, not as Lavache, who sees it as a necessary evil, not even as Helena, who seeks to rise above it. Instead, with sympathy she recognizes that one's strength and failing are often the same thing: love is both a passion in the blood that leads to faults and, also, nature's truth that leads to virtue. Her sensitivity to the underlying meanings of words allows her to see and express what experience has led her to know. Shakespeare grants her poetry for her wisdom, as if the beauty of seeing clearly were worth the sadness one pays for it — a double sadness in the case of the Countess, who understands Helena's love because of her own former joys, now lost, and who shares the pain that Helena will inevitably feel before she gains the Countess's perspective.

We have considered the King's speech to Bertram, in which he
carefully distinguishes the gifts of nature—blood, youth, beauty,
even wit—from the goodness by which Helena achieves her honor.
But we have not considered Bertram's response, which betrays the
confusion of merit with nature that leads him to fly the marriage he
seems to accept:

> When I consider
> What great creation and what dole of honor
> Flies where you bid it, I find that she, which late
> Was in my nobler thoughts most base, is now
> The praised of the King, who so ennobled,
> Is as 'twere born so.
>
> (2.3.168-73)

To Bertram, merit is only blood; since Helena was not "born so," she
cannot be noble—and what resentment shows in Bertram's contrast
of her baseness with his "nobler thoughts"! He appears to accept the
King's opinion, but he advances his own argument for doing so: the
King's word possesses the power of "creation," and so Helena may be
as noble now as if she were by nature. The argument reveals that Bertram yet cannot see beyond words and title to the merit necessary to
support them.

The wise understand that words are not things and distinguish between the underlying meanings of words; the foolish do not. Hence
the importance of Parolles: if one sees through "Words," he has a
degree of wisdom—the process would be allegorical were not Parolles himself an individualized character. To Lafew, Parolles is "my
good window of lettice . . . for I look through thee" (2.3.213-15);
and the Countess complains that her "son corrupts a well-derived
nature / With his [Parolles's] inducement" (3.2.88-89). The King,
although he does not know Parolles, knows his kind, and repeats the
words of Bertram's father on them:

> —"Let me not live," quoth he,
> "After my flame lacks oil, to be the snuff
> Of younger spirits, whose apprehensive senses
> All but new things disdain; whose judgments are
> Mere fathers of their garments; whose constancies
> Expire before their fashions."
>
> (1.2.58-63)

It is no accident that Parolles combines flashy dress with glib chatter. From Socrates, who advised that rhetoric compares with politics as the cosmetic with the gymnastic art,[12] to the Elizabethans, who called inflated speech "bombastic," decking oneself out with words or with clothes has seemed the same failing. All the elders — even the spirit of Bertram's father — see through the like of Parolles, and warn against him.

Most of the young do, too. Lavache, pretending to praise Parolles for discretion, judges that "To say nothing, to do nothing, to know nothing, and to have nothing, is to be a great part of your title, which is within a very little of nothing" (2.4.24-27). And Helena judges Parolles acutely:

> I know him a notorious liar,
> Think him a great way fool, soly a coward;
> Yet these fix'd evils sit so fit in him,
> That they take place when virtue's steely bones
> Looks bleak i' th' cold wind. Withal, full oft we see
> Cold wisdom waiting on superfluous folly.
>
> (1.1.100-105)

Parolles combines not the great vices of the world, but its small vanities: his speech is empty verbosity, his apparel fantastical, his reasoning sophistical; he is full of words, empty of wisdom, wanting in deeds. He would be harmless, were he not so attractive. In the responses to Parolles, Shakespeare joins together the functions of the ideas about language in the early and middle plays: each character in his individual way confronts and recognizes the danger of mere words; the sum of their responses establishes as a basic value of this humanistic society the importance of truth and deeds over mere words. Until the end of the play, Bertram — all promise and little achievement — is separated from his society by his inability to see through Parolles.

What is set in contrast to mere words in this play is not simply deeds, but also loyalty, or holding to one's word; graciousness and restraint in speech; and eloquence, or making one's words into acts of virtuous persuasion. If there is an opposite to Parolles in the play, it is Bertram's father as the King remembers him. In his youth the Count showed himself a brave soldier, a wit without the levity of the

younger generation, and a man whose honor spoke as often in restraint as in challenge:

> his honor,
> Clock to itself, knew the true minute when
> Exception bid him speak, and at this time
> His tongue obey'd his hand.
>
> (1.2.38-41)

He had no contempt in his pride, but treated others, of whatever
class, with gracious respect: "Such a man / Might be a copy to these
younger times" (ll. 45-46). His youthful prowess withered — "on us
both did haggish age steal on, / And wore us out of act" (ll. 29-
30) — but his maturity provided strength of a different kind, the
wisdom of a "good melancholy" (l. 56), and the power of a fruitful
eloquence:

> his plausive words
> He scatter'd not in ears, but grafted them,
> To grow there and to bear.
>
> (ll. 53-55)

In the years after those of brave deeds, the father's words became his
acts. If in his youth the Count achieved the ideal of a noble man, living in such a way that his example might influence others to grow in
goodness, in his age he continued the process of generation, with
words that nurtured the good in others. Generally the play assures us
that the young inherit only nature, not virtue; this scene dramatizes
the fact that virtue has its own lineage. Bertram has not received his
father's wisdom in his blood, but it has been planted in the King's
mind by the Count's eloquence; in the King's words the promised
seed lies ready for Bertram's reaping.

The ideal of education inspires the elders of the play, as it did
Bertram's father when he was past action.[13] The King, the Countess,
and Lafew share the inability to act: the King, physically disabled,
cannot go to war; the Countess does not accompany Helena to
court; Lafew does not give Parolles the beating he deserves. Although no longer in deeds, they yet enact their values in words. The
King welcomes Bertram to court not with ceremony or social niceties, but with a generous praise of Bertram's father turned to the end

of moral instruction. The King eloquently conveys the weight of Bertram's obligation to his inheritance, and warns him against men of false values among his peers. Not narrowly parental, the elders show concern for the growth of all the young. The Countess, in whose love for Helena "Adoption strives with nature, and choice breeds / A native slip . . . from foreign seeds" (1.3.145–46), sympathetically plays on the meanings of the words "mother" and "daughter" until Helena reveals her love for the Countess's son (1.3.139–70). When Helena, embarrassed, tries to blur the truth with equivocation, the Countess corrects her confusion of words with things:

> *Count.* Love you my son?
> *Hel.*   Do not you love him, madam?
> *Count.* Go not about; my love hath in't a bond
>   Whereof the world takes note. Come, come, disclose
>   The state of your affection.
>
> (ll. 187–90)

When the Countess hears Helena's plan to cure the King in hopes of deserving Bertram's love, she neither prevents Helena, nor acts in her stead; she merely lends support to Helena's attempt. The Countess's purpose is education in the largest sense: making it easier for the young to achieve their own goodness. Lafew's style is neither as high as the King's, nor as imperturbable as the Countess's; his words are full of fire, as his name indicates, and testy wit. But equally generous with his words, he smooths the way for Helena's audience with the King, tries to teach Parolles the truth about himself, and, failing that, attempts to show Bertram his error in choosing such a companion as Parolles.

The elders use their words to encourage virtue in others. The result is a society, shaped by them, intent on continually educating itself: wise words come home. The Count's words to the King are spoken years later to the Count's own son. By her eloquence Helena leads the King to trust in God's ability to work impossible cures:

> Methinks in thee some blessed spirit doth speak
> His powerful sound within an organ weak;
> And what impossibility would slay
> In common sense, sense saves another way.
>
> (2.1.175–78)

When the King promises Helena, "If thou proceed / As high as word, my deed shall match thy deed" (2.1.209-10), his "deed" turns out to be his words persuading Bertram to take her to wife. The "impossibility" that Helena convinces the King to attempt results in her own achieving of the "impossible": marriage to Bertram.

Mere words do not possess the generative powers of the society's ideal of eloquence and education, but they are more dangerous than this negative appraisal suggests. When Lavache is called to visit the court, he prepares a fashionable phrase to answer all questions: "O Lord, sir!" (2.2.13-51).[14] He tries it out on the Countess, parodying the courtly vice of polite verbosity, until the threat of whipping teaches him that "things may serve long, but not serve ever" (ll. 58-59). We delight in the Clown's ingenuity, his fitting this response to each of the Countess's questions, but laughter comes with the realization that the phrase suits all occasions only because it means very little. The Clown's satire of courtiers thus sets up the humor of the following scene: as Parolles and Lafew discuss the miracle of the King's cure, after every item in Lafew's account, Parolles intrudes with "So I say" (2.3.1-40). Parolles fulfills the Clown's prediction of courtly verbosity — long in wind and short in invention — and it is this aspect of his character that makes him a dangerous companion for Bertram. Bertram is young, and his inexperience will inevitably lead him into trouble; he is his own tempter. Parolles is not a tempter, but a flatterer:[15] he confirms men in their virtues and vices indiscriminately by seconding their views with his words. Parolles's words reflect the status quo and work no change for the good. They work no change at all: neither good nor evil, they obscure such differences. Parolles, like his words, serves all occasions, and so serves none of them well.

The events of the second half of the play grow naturally out of the world created in the first half. In the confusion of youthful ignorance, Bertram chooses words, not things, leaving his wife his name but no deeds of love, not even a kiss to seal the marriage vows (2.5.77-87). Even his riddling letter to Helena indicates his reliance on mere words: "When thou canst get the ring upon my finger, which never shall come off, and show me a child begotten of thy body that I am father to, then call me husband; but in such a 'then' I write a 'never'" (3.2.57-60). Unless Helena can lend these words significance through her deeds, she cannot gain the reality behind her new title. But Bertram's point is that the tasks are impossible: Helena cannot make these words true. In fact, she alone does not. It takes the entire society—the widow and Diana, the lords who expose Parolles for their friend's education, even Parolles himself—to fill Bertram's words with the weight of truth. In this society no divinity calls meaning into words, as happens with the oracles of the late romances. This society keeps words true and creates significance through sheer human industry.[16]

We are reassured by the first scene in Florence that the values of Bertram's society have little to do with geography. As the young of France had the guidance of their elders, so Diana has the guidance of hers—her widowed mother and Mariana. Mariana's advice to Diana reiterates the lessons we have heard before, in Rosillion and in Paris: "Well, Diana, take heed of this French earl. The honor of a maid is her name, and no legacy is so rich as honesty" (3.5.11-13). One's "honor" depends not on birth or blood, but on virtue; better than wealth is the legacy of honesty, achieved not inherited. Words are not deeds, continues Mariana, and one must judge by merit, not promises: "I know that knave, hang him! one Parolles, a filthy officer he is in those suggestions for the young earl. Beware of them, Diana; their promises, enticements, oaths, tokens, and all these engines of lust, are not the things they go under" (3.5.16-20). Mariana sees through Parolles, and recognizes his influence on Bertram: neither young man is above using words and gifts to signify what he has no intention of fulfilling.

Diana has learned her lesson well. When she meets with Bertram in order to further Helena's cause, she delivers to him Mariana's lecture:

> Ber.   How have I sworn!
> Dia. 'Tis not the many oaths that makes the truth,
>   But the plain single vow that is vow'd true.
>   What is not holy, that we swear not by,
>   But take the High'st to witness. Then pray you tell me,
>   If I should swear by Jove's great attributes
>   I lov'd you dearly, would you believe my oaths
>   When I did love you ill? This has no holding,
>   To swear by Him whom I protest to love
>   That I will work against Him; therefore your oaths

Are words and poor conditions, but unseal'd—
At least in my opinion.

(4.2.20-31)

Diana is reminding Bertram that his oaths to her can only be empty words, unsealed, because he has already given his plain single vow to his wife. In a line of argument reminiscent of the King's—"The property by what it is should go, / Not by the title" (2.3.130-31)— Diana asserts that calling on God's name to affirm evil does not make evil good. More important, Diana is urging on Bertram the requirement of honor to hold steady in a course that will make and keep words true. To others in the play, as well as Diana, the value of words rests precisely in the effort speakers put into making them good. When Helena offered her "life" as pledge of her promise, the King weighed the meaning underlying the word:

Thy life is dear, for all that life can rate
Worth name of life in thee hath estimate:
Youth, beauty, wisdom, courage, all
That happiness and prime can happy call.

(2.1.179-82)

As Helena has made her life worth the name, the King trusts her promise. Bertram has nothing to offer to support his vows of love, Diana points out to him; he has already called God and himself to witness as he offered his life to his wife. In the world created in this play, Bertram's resentment and reluctance in the marriage have no importance; once he has given his word in the marriage ceremony, he must be brought to keep it. According to Diana, Bertram's obstinacy justifies the bed-trick:

My mother told me just how he would woo,
As if she sate in 's heart. She says all men
Have the like oaths.

. . . .

I think't no sin
To cozen him that would unjustly win.

(4.2.69-76)

Especially so, one might add, because Diana is merely helping Bertram to keep his word.

While Diana goes busily about Bertram's education in the town, the lords are similarly engaged at the camp. They wish to convince Bertram that Parolles is "a most notable coward, an infinite and endless liar, an hourly promise-breaker" (3.6.9-10). They concoct a plan to catch Parolles in the net of his own words. He has been talking up his courage, offering to fetch the drum lost to the enemy and, under Bertram's inducement, he promises to makes his boasts good. The encounter fulfills not the braggart's promises, however, but the lords'. Parolles is overheard admitting the distance between his promises and deeds: "I find my tongue is too foolhardy, but my heart hath the fear of Mars before it, and of his creatures, not daring the reports of my tongue" (4.1.28-31). And when the "manifold linguist" (4.3.236), who "hath a smack of all neighboring languages" (4.1.15-16), faces the lords, disguised in their nonsensical words as Parolles has been in his, he attempts no action, fearing only that he will die "for want of language" to betray the Florentines (4.1.70-73). Parolles, too, learns that words may serve long, but not serve ever.

When Bertram enters and the lords question their captive, Parolles reveals himself a coward despite his boasts, betraying military secrets in order to save his life, and slandering his fellow-soldiers in order to ingratiate himself with his captors. Shakespeare denies Parolles even the dignity of pathos. When he is sentenced, he begs, "O Lord, sir, let me live, or let me see my death" (4.3.309-10). If the actors set up their lines properly, the humor associated with Lavache's empty phrase — "O Lord, sir!" — will carry over to Parolles's use of it in this context. Then, instead of feeling Parolles's dismay, we shall laugh at his self-serving words and savor the appropriateness of the final punishment: "Fare ye well, sir, I am for France too. We shall speak of you there" (4.3.328-29). The lords keep their promise. When Parolles meets Lafew at court, the old lord's first question is "How does your drum?" (5.2.41). For this fool whose only realities are words, the tales told by the lords are punishment enough.

The lords do not intend the exposure of Parolles to be an education for the braggart himself, whom they think beyond the benefit of instruction; they intend it for Bertram. In their discussion of Bertram's seduction of Diana, and his boasts of it afterwards (4.3.14-34), they hope that he will take the example of Parolles to heart: "I would gladly have him see his company anatomiz'd, that he might take a measure of his own judgments, wherein so curiously he had set this counterfeit" (4.3.31–34). They desire Bertram to recognize not only Parolles's vices, but also his own. Bertram begins to learn. He points out Parolles's equivocation, the use of the contradictory meanings of words to mislead hearers: "Come, bring forth this counterfeit module, h'as deceiv'd me like a double-meaning prophesier" (4.3.98–100). But the education fails in its chief point, for Bertram does not accept it with the patience he is admonished to use (ll. 108–17). While Captain Dumain takes with good humor Parolles's revelation of his faults, including an escapade similar to Bertram's with Diana, Bertram does not (ll. 210–38). Bertram, who was willing to act the fool with Diana, is not yet willing to be called a fool. Thus, ironically, it is Parolles who learns most from the episode:

> Captain I'll be no more,
> But I will eat and drink, and sleep as soft
> As captain shall. Simply the thing I am
> Shall make me live. Who knows himself a braggart,
> Let him fear this; for it will come to pass
> That every braggart shall be found an ass.
>
> (4.3.331–36)

Parolles has given up presumptuous titles; he is now the thing itself. He is still a character whose speech is foolish verbosity (as in 5.2.1–14), but he is now willing to accept the titles which before gave him offense. Subsequently, he finds that the world has room for a fool that goes by his true name. When Parolles returns to Paris, Lafew takes him under protection: "though you are a fool and a knave, you shall eat" (5.2.53–54).

Bertram may have learned something about Parolles in the unmasking, but he does not apply the lesson to himself. The Count returns to court, dressed cap a pie with two-pile-and-a-half velvet covering a scar on his left cheek (4.5.94–98). Just as Parolles's scarves are all one with his bombastic speech, so Bertram's clothing signifies that he has yet to learn his lesson in full. Bertram's velvet, however, covers a real scar; and, because of this proof of honor, we shall more readily forgive him when he does learn. Lafew is the first to see that Bertram's experience has made him less of a fool, just as he was the first to see him for what he was: "A scar nobly got, or a noble scar, is a good liv'ry of honor" (4.5.99-100). And if neither the wise words of the elders nor the concerted efforts of his peers have taught Bertram anything, then time and loss have: Helena, says Bertram, "she whom all men prais'd . . . / Since I have lost, have lov'd" (5.3.53-54).

Even wise words were not enough. As is always the way, these young people have had to learn from experience what the elders would gladly have spared them by their words. Helena, too, has learned from time and loss: "But O, strange men, / That can such sweet use make of what they hate" (4.4.21-22). In bed with Bertram, who thinks that she is Diana, Helena discovers that the pains of love achieved may be as great as love denied—even while keeping Bertram's word, as well as her own. The best poetry in this play, as we have seen in the case of the Countess, comes not with passion, but with the steady wisdom that looks on the faults of passion and is not dismayed. Thus Helena, steadying herself, asks Diana to continue with her to the end:

> *Hel.*   You, Diana,
>   Under my poor instructions yet must suffer
>   Something in my behalf.
>   . . . .
> *Dia.*   I am yours
>   Upon your will to suffer.
> *Hel.*   Yet, I pray you:
>   But with the word the time will bring on summer,
>   When briers shall have leaves as well as thorns,
>   And be as sweet as sharp.
>
>   (4.4.26-33)

"Yet" is the word that, like time, will bring on fruition: the word signifies the perseverance that makes words true and brings sweetness into imperfect human love.

During the series of unfolding surprises that make up the denouement—the betrothal of Bertram to Lafew's daughter, the appearance of Diana, the exposure of Bertram, and the "resurrection" of Helena—Bertram learns that his name depends not upon his birth and blood, but upon his actions, whether worthy or not. Put in the same position as Helena earlier, he finds that his society ignores his title and judges him ignoble and disgraced by his deeds. Lafew retracts the offer of his daughter after Diana's intelligence: "Your reputation comes too short for my daughter, you are no husband for her" (5.3.176–77). And the King warns Bertram that he has yet to earn his title by achieving merit:

> Sir, for my thoughts, you have them ill to friend
> Till your deeds gain them; fairer prove your honor
> Than in my thought it lies.
>
> (5.3.182–84)

Unlike Helena, who proved her deeds equal to her words, Bertram faces witness after witness who demonstrate his words to be false. Bertram gradually loses credibility until even Parolles's word is accepted before his by the King:

> *Par.* He did love her, sir, as a gentleman loves a woman.
> *King.* How is that?
> *Par.* He lov'd her, sir, and lov'd her not.
> *King.* As thou art a knave, and no knave. What an equivocal companion is this!
>
> (ll. 245–50)

For once Parolles inadvertently uses his equivocation in the service of truth. He explains that Bertram loved Diana to bed her, not to marry her, expecting his apologetic joke about the illicit amours of gentlemen to amuse his courtly audience. The court is not amused, and Bertram's shame is doubled: not only has he acted dishonorably with Diana; he has also shared his confidences with a knave.

Diana equivocates as well, suddenly explaining that she did and did not give Bertram the ring, that she did and did not sleep with him, and that he is and is not guilty. Her riddles do not emphasize her likeness to Parolles and Bertram, but her difference: words with double meanings may be used to circumvent truth and to obscure evil actions; Diana's words, however, like the wives' riddles at the end of *The Merchant of Venice*, express more than one truth at once. It is at this point that Helena is brought in to put meaning into Bertram's riddle and his former vows, and also to make sense of Diana's riddles:

> Dead though she be, she feels her young one kick.

So there's my riddle: one that's dead is quick—
And now behold the meaning.

(ll. 302-4)

If Helena must represent something in the play opposite to what Parolles stands for, it is "meaning": that which gives words life and
power. "The sense," Ben Jonson reminded his contemporaries, "is as
the life and soule of Language, without which all words are dead."[17]
Helena literally puts life into Bertram's and Diana's words: despite
the report of her death she is alive, and she carries new life within
her. The King speaks for all in his astonishment, and Bertram finally achieves the knowledge that his society has been trying to teach
him all along:

> *King.*   Is there no exorcist
> Beguiles the truer office of mine eyes?
> Is't real that I see?
> *Hel.*   No, my good lord,
> 'Tis but the shadow of a wife you see,
> The name, and not the thing.
> *Ber.*   Both, both. O, pardon!

(ll. 305-8)

Bertram at last grasps the relation between honor and deed, title
and person, name and thing. Since verbosity has been associated
throughout the play with folly, Bertram's brevity simply emphasizes
his conviction. He speaks the right words at the right time, and we
are only too happy—finally—to take a noble young soldier at his
word. Helena achieves her title in the end, not by the bed-trick, but
by Bertram's sincere acknowledgment of the significance of his marriage vows.

Learning the difference between words and things, persons and
titles, promises and deeds, is the first step toward wisdom in this humanistic society. Wisdom itself, nevertheless, lies not in words; Ben
Jonson follows his statement on "sense" as the "life of Language" with
the observation that "Sense is wrought out of experience, the knowledge of humane life, and actions."[18] Wisdom lies in knowing the values that enable men to judge well, to act virtuously, and to help
others to a similar wisdom; and words are only a means to this end.
At the beginning of *All's Well That Ends Well*, the old are wise. By

the end of the play, the young seem to have acquired the values and
the wisdom of their elders. As the King supposes, "All yet seems
well" (l. 333). We leave the play hoping that Helena and Bertram
will live to be like the Countess and the King, "a copy to these
younger times." That they achieve and hold to such merit is imperative: the next copier is on the way.

Notes

1. See, for example, Frederick S. Boas, *Shakspere and his Predecessors*
(New York: Charles Scribner's Sons, 1904), p. 352, on Helena's faults;
W. W. Lawrence, *Shakespeare's Problem Comedies* (New York: Macmillan Co., 1931), p. 36, on the lack of "sunshine" in the comic relief; J. Dover
Wilson, *The Essential Shakespeare* (Cambridge: Cambridge Univ. Press,
1932), p. 116, on the "mirthless" wit, the "detestable" bad characters and
the "unattractive" good ones; Hazelton Spencer, *The Art and Life of
William Shakespeare* (New York: Harcourt, Brace and Co., 1940), p. 297,
on the lack of poetry in the play; E. M. W. Tillyard, *Shakespeare's Problem Plays* (London: Chatto & Windus, 1950), pp. 89–112, on the "defective poetical style," the unfortunate linking of fairy-tale plot and realistic
characters, and the incredibility of Helena's loving such a "stupid . . .
youth"; Albert H. Carter, "In Defense of Bertram," *SQ,* 7 (1956), 21–31,
on Helena's faults and the necessity that the youth rebel against the older
generation; A. P. Rossiter, *Angel with Horns,* ed. Graham Storey (London: Longmans, 1961), pp. 89–105, on the defects of Bertram and the unsuccessful mingling of romantic and realistic elements; Jay L. Halio, *"All's
Well That Ends Well,"SQ,* 15 (1964), 33–35, on the lack of unity and the
elders as symbols of death and decay; J. M. Silverman, "Two Types of
Comedy," *SQ,* 24 (1973), 33, on Helena's deceit and guile; and Nicholas
Brooke, " 'All's Well That Ends Well,' " *ShS,* 30 (1977), 83, on the curious
mingling of realistic language with romantic story.
2. For defenses of the play, see E. E. Stoll, *From Shakespeare to Joyce*
(New York: Doubleday, Doran and Co., 1944), pp. 237–68; Harold S. Wilson, "Dramatic Emphasis in *All's Well That Ends Well,"HLQ,* 13 (1950),
217–40; John F. Adams, *"All's Well That Ends Well," SQ,* 12 (1961),
261–70; and Joseph G. Price, *The Unfortunate Comedy* (Toronto: Univ. of
Toronto Press, 1968), esp. pp. 133–72.
3. The production of *All's Well That Ends Well* on which I base this
opinion was that of the Folger Shakespeare Theater, directed by Jonathan
Alper, in the spring of 1976.
4. See, for example, Thomas Heywood, *A Fair Maid of the West* (Parts

I and II) and *A Challenge for Beautie,* in *Dramatic Works* (London: John Pearson, 1874), vols. II and V.

5. See Bradbrook, *Shakespeare and Elizabethan Poetry,* pp. 162–68.

6. See Geoffrey Bullough, *Narrative and Dramatic Sources of Shakespeare* (London: Routledge and Kegan Paul, 1958), II, 389–96.

7. By "ancestors" I mean not sources but previous characters like the King, conceived along humanist lines. For the argument that title without virtue is not honor, see Medwall, *Fulgens & Lucres,* Part II, ll. 620–44; and Vives, *"Educatio,"* in *Tudor School-Boy Life,* pp. 229–30. For the argument that good and evil should be seen for what they are, not as they are called, see Erasmus, "Things and Names," in *The Colloquies,* pp. 383–85; and Vives, *"Educatio,"* pp. 227–28. For the argument that honor derives from acts, not from ancestors, see Medwall, *Fulgens & Lucres,* Part II, ll. 620–26; John Heywood, *Gentleness and Nobility,* Part I, ll. 222–26, and Part II, ll. 501–20; and Vives, *"Educatio,"* p. 231. For the argument that praising words are not truths, see John Heywood, *Gentleness and Nobility,* Part II, ll. 551–76; and Vives, *"Educatio,"* pp. 228 and 230.

8. Cf. Flexibulus to Grympherantes, in Vives's *"Educatio,"* p. 227: "The circumstance that you do not understand the significance of words leads you far from the knowledge of truth."

9. Erasmus, "Things and Names," p. 385.

10. I use the term "climax" in the traditional sense of the turning point in the middle of the play from which the subsequent action follows, not in the loose sense of a scene of heightened emotional pitch.

11. Until act 2, scene 4, the young have no scene completely to themselves, and, with the exception of Parolles and Helena, hardly speak to each other; from act 2, scene 5, until the last scene, the elders appear infrequently, and only Diana's elders act as advisors; in the final scene old and young solve problems together and seem at last a unified society.

12. See Plato, *Gorgias,* 465.

13. Cf. the suggestion that the rhetorician and statesman, once past the age when he can act and speak vigorously, should become a teacher of eloquence and moral values to the young, in Quintilian, *Institutio Oratoria,* XII.xi.4–6.

14. Lavache's phrase, "O Lord, sir!" may be a borrowed joke. When Clove invites Orange to "talk fustian a little," all that Clove can manage is "O lord, sir," in Jonson's *Euery Man out of his Humour,* 3.4, in *Ben Jonson,* III, 502–3.

15. This point has been made before, most notably by Robert G. Hunter, *Shakespeare and the Comedy of Forgiveness* (New York: Columbia Univ. Press, 1965), pp. 120–21.

16. Cf. Anthony Brennan, "Helena versus Time's Winged Chariot in

All's Well That Ends Well," MQ, 21 (1979-80), 391-411, who argues that "Our hope in Shakespeare's comedies usually resides in the ability of the younger generation to grasp and reaffirm enduring values" (p. 394), and that at the end of *AWW* we have neither "the old world of the King's youth," nor "the shallow world of the feckless young courtiers," but rather "a new world achieved by a pragmatic determination to salvage some of the older values that men had once so easily taken for granted" (p. 410).

17. *Timber,* in *Ben Jonson,* VIII, 621.

18. Ibid.

CHAPTER 8

·᛭·

Hamlet:
Voice, Gesture, and Passion

In *All's Well That Ends Well* Shakespeare succeeds in using ideas about language to shape a coherent world and yet also to distinguish particular characters. The ideas even influence the story: the society's education of Bertram consists largely of a feeling demonstration of the difference between words and things, titles and merit. In this play, however, there is neither the range of individual attitudes toward language belonging to the characters in *The Merchant of Venice,* nor the rich detail of the linguistic worlds created in *Love's Labor's Lost* and *King John.* With regard to ideas about language, *All's Well That Ends Well* is a simple play: the ideas derive mainly from a single source, the humanists' distinction between words and things; and, while the ideas affect all the dramatic elements of the play, coherence is achieved mainly through the agency of a single character—the society defines its values by opposition to the mere word, and the characters define their values by their responses to Parolles. In *Hamlet,* where Shakespeare also uses ideas about language to particularize characters, to define an imagined world, and to structure the story, the effect is rich and complex. The ideas are drawn from a variety of sources—medical theory, rhetoric, and the arts of poetry and acting—and their abundance reminds us that Shakespeare followed his age in its taste for amplitude in expression. In a textbook Shakespeare might have studied in school, Erasmus advises that an abundance of ideas as well as words, *copia rerum et verborum,* should go into a speech. One should judge what to employ by the standard of appropriateness: different ages, different types of people, even individuals of the same type, favor different words and ideas.[1] In his mature plays, Shakespeare's choice of ideas from the sixteenth-century study of language reflects these Renaissance guides to composition: copiousness and decorum. Just as he varies styles of speech from one play to another, and from one character to another, so he varies ideas about language. The variation in both cases helps to make characters distinctive and to give the societies dramatic form. In *Hamlet* Shakespeare demonstrates his mastery over this aspect of his medium: men and women define themselves by their attitudes toward language; if not in words, then in the alternative language of voice and gesture, they reveal their inner, emotional life; and from the conflicting ideas and attitudes of the characters emerges a tragically mutable world.[2] Ideas about language further mark the stages by which Hamlet comes to terms with his world and, so, the nature of the task events thrust upon him. Speaking and listening, the characters of *Hamlet* create and transform themselves and their world.

Speech is not a social bond in the world described in the first two acts of *Hamlet:* Shakespeare's Denmark is a world of frustrated attempts at communication and casual distrust of words.[3] Horatio's "ears . . . are . . . fortified against" the guards' "story" of the ghost (1.1.31-32). Only the "whisper" (1.1.80) goes about to tell the rumors of Fortinbras's attempted invasion. According to Claudius, Fortinbras is allowed to raise his army because "Norway . . . impotent and bedred, scarcely hears / Of this his nephew's purpose" (1.2.28-30). Politely denying his friend's joke about truancy from Wittenberg, Hamlet tells Horatio, you shall not "do my ear that violence / To make it truster of your own report / Against yourself" (1.2.171-73). Hamlet commands the guards that the subject of the ghost "be tenable in your silence still, / . . . Give it an understanding but no tongue" (1.2.247-49); and Polonius warns Ophelia not to "slander any moment leisure / As to give words or talk with the Lord Hamlet" (1.3.133-34). Despite the simple, natural style of the guards' talk, Horatio's easy, vivid recount of the state of affairs in Denmark, Claudius's compressed, dramatic explanations to his court, Laertes' moving remonstrance to Ophelia about Hamlet's love, and the ghost's majestic words — all products of Shakespeare's eloquence in this play — the characters of the play continually remind us of their failures to communicate.

Meaning in this world is not straightforward, but hidden in the biases and indirections of thought. Polonius sends Reynaldo to slander his son, directing him to "breathe his faults . . . quaintly" (2.1.31) — to insinuate, rather than to accuse. The ghost tells

Hamlet that "the whole ear of Denmark / Is by a forged process of my death / Rankly abus'd" (1.5.36-38). It is no accident in this world that Polonius begins his advice to his son with the maxim, "Give thy thoughts no tongue" (1.3.59), and reinforces it with another proverb: "Give every man thy ear, but few thy voice" (l. 68).

The characters of *Hamlet* reveal an automatic distrust of the meaning of others that is nothing like the healthy distrust of words shown by those of mature judgment in *The Merchant of Venice*, or in *All's Well That Ends Well*. In the society of Denmark, it is assumed that even honest men have motives in opposition to their words. Laertes warns Ophelia that she has no choice but to discount Hamlet's offers of love:

> Then if he says he loves you,
> It fits your wisdom so far to believe it
> As he in his particular act and place
> May give his saying deed, which is no further
> Than the main voice of Denmark goes withal.
>
> (1.3.24-28)

Without considering that men could be otherwise, Laertes coolly instructs his sister in deceit: that the Prince must be lying in this matter, even if he does not mean to, is to be expected. Yet more distrustful is Polonius, recalling his own experience: "I do know, / When the blood burns, how prodigal the soul / Lends the tongue vows" (1.3.115-17). And so, Hamlet's words must also not be trusted: "Do not believe his vows, for they are brokers, / . . . Breathing like sanctified and pious bonds, / The better to beguile" (1.3.127-31). Were language no more than a system of untrustworthy signs, in the Denmark of *Hamlet* communication would seem scarcely possible.

From the Renaissance viewpoint, however, language includes not only rational symbols, but also voice, expression, and gesture, conveying and purging the passions. It is this side of language, what Thomas Wilson called "the speache of [man's] bodie," and Montaigne "the proper and peculier speech of humane nature," that receives special emphasis in the first two acts of *Hamlet*.[4] The ghost, silent at first, yet speaks through expression and gesture, his "countenance more / In sorrow than in anger" (1.2.231-32), and his "courteous action" (1.4.60) waving Hamlet to follow him. Horatio compares this ghost to the "sheeted dead" who, as omens of Julius Caesar's death, "Did squeak and gibber in the Roman streets" (1.1.115-16). Because they prefigure some monstrous disorder in the world, ghosts do not address men in ordinary, rational discourse.

Even when the ghost does talk to Hamlet, he begins by listing the sorts of things he may not tell, the horrors of purgatory, not meant for "ears of flesh and blood" (1.5.21-22). And we are held in suspense while the ghost describes the passionate gestures that would express Hamlet's involuntary terror were his father to tell him these forbidden truths. The language of voice and action thus speaks fear in response to the disordered world of Denmark. Barnardo cannot resist an "I told you so" to Horatio, bold only until the ghost enters: "How now, Horatio? you tremble and look pale. / Is not this something more than fantasy?" (1.1.53-54). Horatio similarly describes the guards and their "fear-surprised eyes" to Hamlet: "they, distill'd / Almost to jelly with the act of fear, / Stand dumb and speak not to him" (1.2.203-6). In these descriptions of fear Shakespeare captures the paradox of art championed by Renaissance painters: the language of gesture, though dumb, speaks the passions most eloquently.

In *Hamlet*, moreover, the gestures are heightened and given significance by description; Peacham's comment that good poetry, like good painting, represents "by outward countenance of the inward spirite and affection"[5] fully applies. Shakespeare does not show us Hamlet's visit to Ophelia; he has her describe it:

> Lord Hamlet, with his doublet all unbrac'd,
> No hat upon his head, his stockins fouled,
> Ungart'red, and down-gyved to his ankle,
> Pale as his shirt, his knees knocking each other,
> And with a look so piteous in purport
> As if he had been loosed out of hell
> To speak of horrors—he comes before me.
>
> (2.1.75-81)

Ophelia comes so close to guessing the cause of Hamlet's perturbation that we trust her reading of his silent language, with grief and horror dominating his complex emotional response to events. Even Hamlet's attire speaks his emotions; the whole vocabulary of "action," as presented by rhetoricians under *"pronuntiatio,"* is called upon to render Hamlet's condition. When Polonius asks Ophelia what Hamlet said, she replies with a description of his expression and gestures: his hand over his forehead, his shaking and sighing, his eyes fixed on her as he leaves. What is gained by substituting this description of Hamlet's action for speech between the lovers is doubt as to the cause of his distress; what is retained is the force of a direct emotional encounter. Captured vividly is the impression of fear and the insubstantiality of its causes, fear being a response to what is unknown. And fear is more accurately conveyed through bodily reactions than through the inevitably more secure language of rational symbols.

At the court, one way we perceive very early the conflict between Hamlet and Claudius is their reliance on different aspects of language. Claudius, feeling no sorrow, desires others, too, to control the natural side of speech and the passions spoken by it:

> Though yet of Hamlet our dear brother's death
> The memory be green, and that it us befitted
> To bear our hearts in grief, and our whole kingdom
> To be contracted in one brow of woe,
> Yet so far hath discretion fought with nature
> That we with wisest sorrow think on him
> Together with remembrance of ourselves.
>
> (1.2.1-7)

No "brow of woe" for Claudius, because his "discretion" denies his emotions before they are born; and grief for the former king he can only see as dangerous to his own rule. As surely as his balanced antitheses make the improbable link between marriage and funeral seem necessary, Claudius makes his coldness seem reasonable.[6] Gertrude joins him in wishing that Hamlet would recover from grief:

> And let thine eye look like a friend on Denmark.
> Do not for ever with thy vailed lids
> Seek for thy noble father in the dust.
>
> (1.2.69-71)

The King and Queen object to Hamlet's embarrassing expression of his grief; it speaks in his face, in his lowered eyes. Although for different reasons, they both ask Hamlet to turn even this naturally straightforward side of language to deceptive ends: they do not ask that he *be* a friend to the new king, but that he *look like* a friend.

Even in a first acquaintance with the play, before one knows the story, I do not think that the King's reasons can excite so much sympathy as Hamlet's emotions. By explaining the language of grief he speaks, Hamlet tells us that his response is the sincere one:

> 'Tis not alone my inky cloak, good mother,
> Nor customary suits of solemn black,
> Nor windy suspiration of forc'd breath,
> No, nor the fruitful river in the eye,
> Nor the dejected havior of the visage,
> Together with all forms, moods, shapes of grief,
> That can denote me truly. These indeed seem,
> For they are actions that a man might play,
> But I have that within which passes show,
> These but the trappings and the suits of woe.
>
> (1.2.77-86)

Hamlet admits that even voice and gesture may be counterfeited. But he defends his way of expressing himself with his sincerity: his sighs, tears, and dejected expression are not seeming; they are outward signs of his true inner grief. What the King and Queen ask of Hamlet—to disguise his feelings with false expressions and gestures in the interest of political order—his stubborn sincerity will not allow him to do.

The unhealthiness of the King and Queen's request to Hamlet is suggested when Hamlet ends his grieving first soliloquy, "But break my heart, for I must hold my tongue" (1.2.159). According to Elizabethan medical theory, Hamlet's assertion must be taken literally: unless he spills his grief at his father's death and his mother's hasty marriage, his heart will burn itself up with the confined passions, or break with the pressure. Indeed, Hamlet cannot confine his feelings. When both Claudius and Gertrude ask him to stay at court, he replies, "I shall in all my best obey you, madam" (1.2.120). Hamlet's feelings break out in his sarcasm, where he sets the grief and anger in his voice against what the rational symbols say.

In the emotive language of voice and gesture, there is thus a force to oppose the deceptiveness of words. Rosencrantz and Guildenstern may hide their motives in silence or uneasy lies, but the truth proclaims itself in their expressions. "Were you not sent for?" asks Hamlet: "Come, come, deal justly with me. Come, come—nay speak.

. . . You were sent for, and there is a kind of confession in your looks, which your modesties have not craft enough to color" (2.2.274–80). That they continue to speak their lies against the truth in their faces appalls Hamlet and turns him with deep rancor against his old friends.

Combining distrust of words with frequent mention of the body's language—and with eloquent verse—Shakespeare achieves what would seem to be mutually exclusive effects. We understand that the social bond of language is broken, and yet we explore the consequences of this rupture in passionate words. Shakespeare solves in *Hamlet* one problem that he failed to solve in *King John:* how to represent the corruption of language in a play that remains eloquent and clear. The burden that was carried in *King John* by the shrill insults and hyperbolic conceits is carried in *Hamlet* by the description of the outward countenance speaking inner turmoil. But the success is more than this summary suggests. The effect for us of combining distrust of words with vividly described expression and gesture is disorientation: we find ourselves in a nightmare world, irrational and emotional. In form we experience something like that which Hamlet experiences, although from a safe distance.

This nightmarish quality is nowhere more obvious than in Hamlet's language after his meeting with the ghost:

> O all you host of heaven! O earth! What else?
> And shall I couple hell? O fie, hold, hold, my heart,
> And you, my sinows, grow not instant old,
> But bear me stiffly up. Remember thee!
>
> (1.5.92–95)

Hamlet's passions at first leap out in interjections and in sentences so compressed that they seem more exclamations than thoughts. Indeed, Renaissance grammarians defined interjections not as rational symbols, but as sounds conveying attitudes and emotions.[7] Addressing his heart and sinews, Hamlet attempts control. But these words also alert us to Hamlet's fear of losing himself to his emotions: feeling the rising passions, he begs that his heart hold them in and not break, and that his muscles continue to hold him up. Unlike Claudius, whose sophisticated reason denies his feelings, Hamlet touches his emotions so close that he might be overwhelmed by them. When Horatio and the guards enter, the fear that Hamlet bears with his

new knowledge remains, obvious even though he tries to hide it from
his companions:

> And so, without more circumstance at all,
> I hold it fit that we shake hands and part,
> You, as your business and desire shall point you,
> For every man hath business and desire,
> Such as it is, and for my own poor part,
> I will go pray.
>
> (1.5.126-32)

In the polite acknowledgment and dismissal of Horatio and the
guards, inappropriate to the circumstances, in the repetitions and
meaningless elaborations, Horatio senses Hamlet's perturbation:
"These are but wild and whirling words, my lord" (l. 133). Inde-
cipherable to Horatio, Hamlet's response speaks clearly to us his
closeness to hysteria: his passions pour out in the multitude of words,
if not in their meaning. Shakespeare seems to realize, as do the Renaissance grammarians and rhetoricians, that language has re-
sources for communicating not only to the intellect, but also directly
to the emotions.

In the middle of the play, Hamlet reaches inside himself to make
something out of nothing, courage out of his own weakness. Shakespeare employs ideas about language to help define the special nature of Hamlet's courage in the sense that Hamlet transforms his
expression of passion in voice and action into the controlled and artful
moving of others to emotional response.[8] To begin with, Hamlet's
"wild and whirling words" *become* the style of his "antic disposition."
The Prince had suggested to himself this transformation, when to
Gertrude and the court he admitted that voice, expression, and
gesture, the "forms, moods, shapes of grief" are "actions that a man
might play."

We might see in Hamlet's change from contempt at seeming to
the role of madman another instance of the quick alternation of sys-
tems of value, which gives to the audience of the play, Stephen
Booth argues, a direct experience of "the agonies of decision, knowing, and valuing."[9] Certainly we are uneasy with Hamlet's feigned
madness, as the countless explanations of it attest. But we may also
see a development of Hamlet's character that begins to allow him to
face and master his fears. Hamlet's disdain of deception and his role

of madman are not necessarily opposites. On the basis of such an assumption, Renaissance poets defended their art: fables are not merely lies, but rather truths presented in heightened and artful form.

What Hamlet makes of his mad language is a political weapon. Many critics have written on the equivocations of Hamlet's antic disposition—the puns by which he vents his hate for Claudius and his disgust at his mother, the ambiguous phrases which he lays out as bait for Polonius's and Rosencrantz and Guildenstern's politic ingenuity—all the while seeming the mad, grieving son and brokenhearted lover.[10] But sufficient emphasis has not been given to the combination of truth and fiction in Hamlet's role. Combining the sarcasm he had used with Claudius, his excited language in response to the ghost, and the grotesque action of his visit to Ophelia to make up the role of madman, Hamlet is like the rhetorician who, according to Quintilian, gives his speech power by conveying *true* but *fictional* emotions in delivery.[11] Hamlet's emotions—fear, anger, grief—are true, but he uses them to shape the fiction of the mad Hamlet. Thomas Wilson, whose English rhetoric Shakespeare may have read, follows Quintilian: the orator must "from his harte fetche his complaintes, in suche sort, that the matter maie appere . . . more greeuous to the eare, and . . . so heinous, that it requires . . . a spedy reformacion."[12] In his role of madman, Hamlet may thus speak the truths of his fears: that Polonius, like Jephthah, sacrifices his daughter; that Claudius has turned Denmark into a prison; that his mother and Ophelia use beauty against honesty. Yet Hamlet may also use his passion to sane ends. By playing mad, Hamlet neither gains time, as Amlethus did in the source (Hamlet, unlike Amlethus, does not need to grow up physically). Nor does he gain knowledge, which comes later, from Claudius's response to the play-within-the-play. Rather, Hamlet gains power over Claudius, and thus confidence in his own powers. The King could coolly respond to Hamlet's sarcasm because he knew the cause: nothing other than the main, his father's death and Gertrude's marriage. But confronted with Hamlet's "transformation"—as Claudius calls it (2.2.5)—not knowing the cause, the King is himself afraid.

Hamlet faces a world which has changed irrevocably at the death of his father, and which is changed even further by the message from the ghost. He sees his mother turn from funeral to marriage;

he sees Claudius turn from uncle to king, adulterer, finally murderer; he sees Ophelia change from beloved to stranger, his kingdom from a golden one to a congregation of vapors, man from angel to dust. Hamlet must learn not only to understand and, to some degree, to accept the passionately varying nature of humankind, but also to admit with honesty and yet control his own varying, even conflicting, emotions. In this sense, Hamlet's task is not that of the Senecan revenger—the task that Pyrrhus accomplishes in the Player's speech on Hecuba, the task that Laertes sets himself later in the play, the task that Seneca assigns his tragic heroes. Hamlet's task, instead, is that which Seneca assigns himself, in his *Epistulae Morales:* "There is this difference between ourselves [the Stoics] and the other [Epicurean] school: our ideal wise man feels his troubles, but overcomes them; their wise man does not even feel them."[13] The first step in Hamlet's mastery of himself is transformation of his own fear into a means to speak the truth and to make Claudius afraid of a man who is himself fearful. In the true fiction of Hamlet's madness, Claudius encounters a potent mysteriousness, something for which his reason can find no cause. Thus the King comes to fear the unknown inside Hamlet, as Hamlet already fears the unknown in the unrecognizable world his has become.

Hamlet's antic disposition consequently gives him an advantage, but only until the King observes Hamlet in the "nunnery" scene. Then the King, "seeing unseen" (3.1.32), perceives that the "something-settled matter in [Hamlet's] heart" which "puts him thus / From fashion of himself" (3.2.173-75) is not madness, but something far more dangerous. Claudius's resolve, however, comes only after Hamlet's next move ahead: the plan of the play.

As Hamlet had done in his "antic disposition," the players transform the expression of emotion into the actors' language, an artful means to move an audience. Hamlet calls for a "passionate speech" (2.2.432), and the Player's speech is indeed full of passion: Pyrrhus's anger, Priam's courageous but pitiable fight, Hecuba's grief—so moving that the actor himself weeps over Hecuba. Alone after the exit of the actors, Hamlet speaks a soliloquy which is a passionate contemplation of the effects of acting:

> O, what a rogue and peasant slave am I!
> Is it not monstrous that this player here,

> But in a fiction, in a dream of passion,
> Could force his soul so to his own conceit
> That from her working all the visage wann'd,
> Tears in his eyes, distraction in his aspect,
> A broken voice, an' his whole function suiting
> With forms to his conceit? And all for nothing,
> For Hecuba!
> What's Hecuba to him, or he to Hecuba,
> That he should weep for her? What would he do
> Had he the motive and the cue for passion
> That I have? He would drown the stage with tears,
> And cleave the general ear with horrid speech,
> Make mad the guilty, and appall the free,
> Confound the ignorant, and amaze indeed
> The very faculties of eyes and ears.
>
> (2.2.550–66)

Hamlet responds primarily to the actor's delivery: the contorted features, the tears, the broken voice. What Hamlet ponders is the combination of truth and fiction in the actor's special language. Like Dekker's ideal actor, who is inspired by the poet's fiction to feel and deliver true emotion,[14] this one is moved to weep over the fiction of Hecuba. Such an action seems "monstrous" to Hamlet, not because the Player can imagine a passion well enough to communicate it with his entire form, but because Hamlet cannot render his own passion, motivated by a real death, in as forceful a manner. Were his motive true rather than fictional, the Player might "make mad the guilty" by arousing emotions to a level beyond control. Hamlet does not yet pick up his own clue to a method of trapping Claudius, because he is himself moved by the Player's speech to a desperate grief and guilt.

Swayed by the actor's grief to feel his own, Hamlet involuntarily purges his own passion:

> Why, what an ass am I! This is most brave,
> That I, the son of a dear father murthered,
> Prompted to my revenge by heaven and hell,
> Must like a whore unpack my heart with words,
> And fall a-cursing like a very drab,
> A stallion. Fie upon't, foh!
>
> (2.2.582–87)

The tenuous mastery of his emotions that Hamlet achieved through his antic disposition is undone by the Player's speech, and the Prince is repelled by the lack of restraint shown in his own exclamatory and passionate words—a use of language appropriate to the vulgar, or even to beasts.[15]

Thinking of the actor's ability to move passions through voice, expression, and gesture, however, Hamlet turns his passions once more to active use:

> I have heard
> That guilty creatures sitting at a play
> Have by the very cunning of the scene
> Been strook so to the soul, that presently
> They have proclaim'd their malefactions:
> For murther, though it have no tongue, will speak
> With most miraculous organ.
>
> (2.2.588-94)

If the players moved Hamlet, they might also move Claudius. In this way Hamlet's discovery of a method to expose Claudius anticipates Heywood's later defense of the aesthetic means of acting to reach a moral end. Hamlet has been moved to respond to events in his own life by watching the Player's acting of the story of Pyrrhus, Priam, and Hecuba, much in the same way that, Heywood argues, Hercules was moved to action by the "liuely and well-spirited action" of the "personated" life of his father, Jupiter.[16] Heywood furthermore offers a parallel to what Hamlet expects of Claudius: he cites two instances where spectators at a play were moved, by the actor's personation of a murderer, to confess their own guilt.[17] Hamlet's first act of revenge is thus acting: he hopes that by the players' art he will move Claudius to become again accessible to human emotions and to feel his own guilt. If he cannot make him speak, he may at least make him confess his guilt in his looks (ll. 596-98)—"the miraculous organ" through which murder may speak without a tongue.

Hamlet's remarks to the players (3.2.1-45) are necessary because his plan absolutely depends on the actors' presenting fictional passions so convincing that they arouse in Claudius a real feeling of guilt. The Prince emphasizes communication of emotion by voice, expression, and gesture: no bellowing to split the ears of the groundlings, no mouthing of the lines, no overdone sawing of the air—but not the reverse, either. The reason for his concern may be inferred from his general advice: "Suit the action to the word, the word to the action, with this special observance, that you o'erstep not the modesty of nature: for any thing so o'erdone is from the purpose of playing, whose end, both at the first and now, was and is, to hold as 'twere the mirror up to nature: to show virtue her own feature, scorn her own image, and the very age and body of the time his form and pressure" (3.2.17–24). If the passion presented is too extreme, the audience will not apply the actions of the play to themselves; if the passion is underplayed, the audience will not be moved. Hamlet hopes that with a natural balance between the two, Claudius will see his own vices in the "mirror" of the players and be moved to reveal his guilt. From the actors, Hamlet turns to Horatio, directing him to give Claudius "heedful note" (3.2.84). If Claudius will not be moved to speech, he may yet reveal his guilt in the alternative language of expression and gesture.

We have some reason to hope that Hamlet's plan will succeed because Claudius has responded even to the inadvertent remarks of Polonius. When the old counselor makes polite talk while waiting for Hamlet to meet Ophelia, he involuntarily triggers an emotional response in the King: "We are oft to blame in this," Polonius observes, "that with devotion's visage / And pious action we do sugar o'er / The devil himself" (3.1.45–48). Claudius starts, and in an aside admits his guilt:

> O, 'tis too true!
> How smart a lash that speech doth give my conscience!
> The harlot's cheek, beautied with plast'ring art,
> Is not more ugly to the thing that helps it
> Than is my deed to my most painted word.
>
> (3.1.48–52)

This is the first time we have seen any indication of guilt in Claudius himself; up to this point he has successfully presented his "most painted word" for the thing itself. That even Polonius's moldy proverbs might move him, though, encourages us to give credit to Hamlet's plan.

Hamlet's plan does work.[18] With Hamlet as chorus, Claudius breaks off the play the second time he sees the murder performed, and we learn that the look of guilt was there. "Didst perceive?"

Hamlet asks Horatio; "Upon the talk of pois'ning?" And Horatio affirms that Claudius spoke his guilt in his expression: "I did very well note him" (3.2.287-90). The plan does not miss, but it succeeds not quite fully. The court do not interpret Claudius's reactions as do Horatio and Hamlet, and Claudius does not confess to anyone but God and us.[19] Or perhaps only to us, for Claudius betrays the disjunction of words from meaning that presupposes, in Shakespeare's plays, the man alienated from his society and even from God: in his confession, his "words fly up," his "thoughts remain below" (3.3.97).

After the play, the exclamations and short clauses of Hamlet's hysterical voice reappear. When Rosencrantz and Guildenstern bring the Queen's message, they can find no sense in Hamlet's words: "Good my lord, put your discourse into some frame, and start not so wildly from my affair" (3.2.308-9). What we hear in Hamlet's voice, though, is not incoherence, but rather tense exultation: Hamlet is drawn as taut as a string tuned to concert pitch on an old piano, and he is in as much danger of breaking. His restraint with his mother is thus an act of strength, and ideas about language are again used to point up this courage. The Prince will put his passions to use:

> Let me be cruel, not unnatural;
> I will speak daggers to her, but use none.
> My tongue and soul in this be hypocrites—
> How in my words somever she be shent,
> To give them seals never my soul consent!
>
> (3.2.395-9)

Here is just the opposite of the problem confronted by speakers in *All's Well That Ends Well,* that of giving their sayings deeds. Hamlet feels compelled by his anger to seal these words with acts, but he resists the compulsion. He plans to ease his own passion and punish his mother at once—but in words, not in violent acts.

When Hamlet meets with his mother, his force with her frightens her, and her cry frightens Polonius: the scene is a chain reaction of fear. Hamlet, too, is caught up in the panic. He stabs through the arras, breaking through his thin cloak of restraint to the fear beneath it. It is not surprising that Hamlet kills Polonius; it is surprising that he does not harm his mother as well.

Instead, he turns his anger and disgust into a sermon to "wring"

Gertrude's "heart" (3.4.35) and to force on her a feeling horror at her wrongs. His speech, like the play that was a "mirror" for Claudius's crime, is a "glass" wherein she will see the "inmost part" of herself (ll. 19–20). It is an impassioned reflection of Gertrude's fault in marrying Claudius: how could she not see the difference between the two brothers—the one all that is a man, the other a "mildewed ear" (ll. 60–64). Hamlet chastises Gertrude for her hypocrisy, which makes her "marriage vows / As false as dicers' oaths," and her "religion . . . / A rhapsody of words" (ll. 44–48); her example as mother calls all sons and daughters to succumb to shameless lust (ll. 81–88). And Gertrude responds: "These words like daggers enter in my ears. / No more, sweet Hamlet!" (3.4.95–96). The image suggests the ability of words to pierce the ear and pain the heart of the listener: Gertrude has been moved to see her faults and feel guilt for them.

When the ghost enters, he speaks only once, calling up Hamlet's purposed revenge on Claudius, and expressing concern for Gertrude. But he speaks again in action before he leaves:

> look you how pale he glares!
> His form and cause conjoin'd, preaching to stones,
> Would make them capable. —Do not look upon me,
> Lest with this piteous action you convert
> My stern effects, then what I have to do
> Will want true color—tears perchance for blood.
>
> (ll. 125–30)

At this crucial moment the ghost's look does convert Hamlet's anger into pity, enabling him to restrain his rage at his mother within the bonds of words.[20] Thus Hamlet urgently asks Gertrude to put her new knowledge into practice, to leave Claudius and "Assume a virtue" even if she does not have it (l. 160). What Hamlet asks of the Queen is the courage he himself shows, that of imposing restraint on a heart without it.

In this respect, as in many others, Ophelia and Laertes serve as foils to Hamlet in the final acts of the play: in speech, as well as in action, they betray a lack of the restraint that becomes Hamlet's courage. A gentleman reports Ophelia's madness, mirrored in her speech:

> She speaks much of her father, says she hears
> There's tricks i' th' world, and hems, and beats her heart,

Spurns enviously at straws, speaks things in doubt
That carry but half sense. Her speech is nothing,
Yet the unshaped use of it doth move
The hearers to collection; they yawn at it,
And botch the words up fit to their own thoughts,
Which as her winks and nods and gestures yield them,
Indeed would make one think there might be thought,
Though nothing sure, yet much unhappily.

(4.5.4-13)

Having no logical movement in thought or syntax, Ophelia's speech is merely voice, gesture, and passion: what men share with animals, according to classical and Renaissance grammarians. Pointing out that one cannot understand her speech, however, makes the audience pay more attention to it, and we pick out the themes of the betraying lover and the dead father, just as we grasped the significance of Hamlet's hysterical and antic voices. As in the first two acts, this language of passion speaks more truth than the rational discourse of the court. Indeed, Horatio and Gertrude recognize that hearers may make a sense not Ophelia's, one dangerous to the ruling family (4.5.4-16); and when Laertes sees and hears Ophelia, he interprets her speech exactly as they feared someone might: "Hadst thou thy wits and didst persuade revenge, / It could not move thus" (4.5.169-70). Ophelia gives way to the emotions that Hamlet had restrained and directed to political use; her irrational speech, directed to no end, yet moves Laertes to give way to his passions.

Laertes' words and actions, on the other hand, are directed to the wrong end. Out of control, he rushes to Claudius to demand revenge, and quickly falls under the King's control. When Laertes promises to avenge his father's death on Hamlet, Claudius warns him not to waste his anger in words:

That we would do,

We should do when we would; for this "would" changes,
And hath abatements and delays as many
As there are tongues, are hands, are accidents,
And then this "should" is like a spendthrift's sigh,
That hurts by easing.

(4.7.118-23)

Like the prodigal's sigh that frees him from the burden of guilt, Laertes' hot promises may purge the passion that should be saved, according to Claudius, to incite him to kill Hamlet. Ironically, Laertes is exactly this sort of man; he curses Claudius, cools off, and becomes his ally.

In the graveyard scene, Hamlet, incensed by Laertes' rash words, mocks them bitterly:[21]

> And if thou prate of mountains, let them throw
> Millions of acres on us, till our ground,
> Singeing his pate against the burning zone,
> Make Ossa like a wart! Nay, and thou'lt mouth,
> I'll rant as well as thou.
>
> (5.1.280-84)

If love is only words, Hamlet avers, then he has more love for Ophelia than Laertes has. To Hamlet, Laertes is the rash young man whom the Prince has accused himself of being—one who curses and, dissipating his passion in words, takes no risk in direct action. Although choleric, Laertes is no Hotspur, for his spirit does not equal his hot words. It is not courage that leads Laertes to face Hamlet in a match where only he holds an unguarded, poisoned foil.

Hamlet itself, like the Player's speech on Priam and Hecuba, is a story of human passions: the guards' fear of the ghost, Laertes' anger, Ophelia's grief, the King's and Gertrude's remorse, and Hamlet's conflicting fear, grief, and anger. Yet how different is Hamlet, unpacking his heart with words, from Rosencrantz and Guildenstern, who confess their hearts in their looks. Ophelia, like "pictures, or mere beasts" (4.5.86), speaks her grief in her winks and nods and songs, while her brother has "a speech a' fire" (4.7.190), hot words always ready. Ideas about language thus help to differentiate the characters in this play by pointing up their individual ways of handling emotions. In acts 2 through 4, the distrust of symbolic speech continues or even grows. In imitation of Gertrude, the Player Queen speaks her vows of love and breaks them. Ophelia sings of the broken promises of young lovers. "The rabble" follow Laertes in his anger,

> And as the world were now but to begin,
> Antiquity forgot, custom not known,
> The ratifiers and props of every word,
> They cry, "Choose we, Laertes shall be king!"
>
> (4.5.103-7)

Society seems not only to return to the primitive state before the rule of kings, but also to the chaos of ignorance before words held significance by certainty of ancient use and custom. Still, all the characters do speak their perturbations, in one form of language or another. The general impression of their speech is one of mutability owing to the passionately varying nature of mankind.

Human mutability is not something that Hamlet easily accepts, in himself or in others. How can his mother be first "Niobe, all tears" at his father's death (1.2.48-49) and then wife to Claudius? How is it that Hamlet, "Prompted to . . . revenge by heaven and hell" (2.2.584), yet waits to do something, four months later?

The graveyard scene is a turning point in Hamlet's response to changing human passions. As he reflects upon the insignificance of human action that the skulls represent, Hamlet extends his observation to speech: "That skull had a tongue in it, and could sing once" (5.1.75-76). The courtier no longer greets his lord and praises his horse to beg it (ll. 82-86). The lawyer no longer tells of actions of battery (ll. 102-3). In the mirror of human speech, Hamlet, like many other Renaissance men, sees not so much human reason as the transience of all human powers. Thus the Count in Castiglione's *The Courtier* contemplated the continuing change in language and concluded, "at the last both wee and whatsoeuer is ours, are mortall."²² In the graveyard Hamlet finds that only the jester continues to repeat the same message: "Now get you to my lady's chamber, and tell her, let her paint an inch thick, to this favor she must come" (ll. 192-94). What the jester said in satire and bitter song, his skull, a *memento mori*, may still speak, though dumb. The message is mortality. The whirlwind of passions, whether turned to words or actions, will end. The play gives to all characters the epitaph that Hamlet speaks over the body of Polonius:

> This counsellor
> Is now most still, most secret, and most grave,
> Who was in life a foolish prating knave.
>
> (3.4.213-15)

The graveyard scene universalizes the epitaph and prepares Hamlet for his own, "the rest is silence."

Hamlet is a story not only of passion, but also of restraint of passion—in Fortinbras's men, who for honor "Go to their graves like beds" (4.4.62); in Hamlet, who overcomes his premonitory fear before the fencing match. More important, it is a story of getting from one to the other, from passion to restraint; courage, in fact, is not possible without this initial human weakness.[23] We see such courage in Horatio's speaking to the ghost despite his fear, in Hamlet's growth in the soliloquies, from the bitterly passionate first one to the final praise of reason and honorable sacrifice, even in Claudius's confession, when he almost takes the courage to bend his heartstrings to remorse, but lets all slip for his crown, his own ambition, and his queen. The language of the play appropriately changes to make a special place for this kind of courage in the last scene: it is language no longer filled with perturbation, speech no longer distorted by madness, feigned and real, or by hypocrisy and politic indirection. Hamlet has thrown off his antic disposition, and clearly, calmly speaks simple and informative sentences. Osric, spending his "golden words" (5.2.131-32) with no thought to their significance, obscuring ideas rather than clarifying them,[24] simply underscores the difference. Claudius and Laertes, intent upon their purpose, speak little.

At the end of the play, ideas about language reinforce our final sense of courage in the characters of *Hamlet*. Elizabethan medical writers warned that speech, generally beneficial as a purge of the passions, at death might hasten the loss of life, by what Stephen Batman called "too great exhalation and wasting of the kinde heate."[25] The men and women of *Hamlet* die by their sacrificial words, as well as by poison and swords, Gertrude spending her last breath to warn Hamlet of the drink (5.2.309-10), Laertes exchanging forgiveness with Hamlet in his final words (ll. 329-31). Only Claudius refuses to face death with restraint, his last words a futile plea for life: "O, yet defend me, friends, I am but hurt" (l. 324).

Hamlet begins his dying speech without such restraint, but takes courage and stops himself:

> You that look pale, and tremble at this chance,
> That are but mutes or audience to this act,
> Had I but time — as this fell sergeant, Death,
> Is strict in his arrest — O, I could tell you —
> But let it be. Horatio, I am dead,

Thou livest. Report me and my cause aright
To the unsatisfied.

(5.2.334-40)

When Hamlet approaches his final speech, he has the benefit of his
experience in the graveyard: life, in any case, is as brief as a song or a
jibe, as transient as speech. The final scene is thus Senecan not
merely in the sense of revenge completed and the stage heaped with
bodies, but in the more important sense of Hamlet's understanding
of his final role in the scene: "It is with life as it is with a play," Seneca writes in his *Epistulae*, "it matters not how long the action is spun
out, but how good the acting is. . . . Stop whenever you choose;
only see to it that the closing period is well turned."[26] For Hamlet,
there is no time for melodrama and passionate self-justification; he
has other business for his last words: "Fortinbras," he tells us, "has
my dying voice" (l. 356). Horatio's line, "Now cracks a noble heart"
(l. 359), emphasizes that Hamlet's words are tragic ones, spending
breath and the heat of the heart to hasten death.

Before his last speech, however, Hamlet passes his office of speaker
to Horatio, concerned that the truth about him be known. Horatio,
vowing himself more Roman than Dane, reaches for the poisoned
cup, but Hamlet requires of him a different kind of courage:

> O God, Horatio, what a wounded name,
> Things standing thus unknown, shall I leave behind me!
> If thou didst ever hold me in thy heart,
> Absent thee from felicity a while,
> And in this harsh world draw thy breath in pain
> To tell my story.

(ll. 344-49)

Hamlet asks his friend to live and heal his name; Horatio must suffer
to do it, not only from the knowledge of this harsh world, but also
from the passions he feels at the death of his friend, passions that
will be raised again when he tells Hamlet's story. Until this moment
in the play, Horatio's stoicism may seem too easily won. Here in Horatio's one rash act, then Hamlet's requirement of greater restraint
from the man already under great strain, we see again the depth
and humanity of the courage celebrated in the play.

With Hamlet's "the rest is silence" (l. 358), we have come full circle. The uneasy silence of the midnight guard has given way to the voices of passion, and those in turn to the mysterious silence of death. While we shall take with us the echo of the passionate players who out-Herod Herod, we shall also retain some of the sympathetic understanding of silence that Hamlet has learned from the dead.

Hamlet's final limit of silence, though, is transcended. In the feeling restraint and formal parallelism of his account, Horatio lives up to Hamlet's requirement of courage:

> And let me speak to th' yet unknowing world
> How these things came about. So shall you hear
> Of carnal, bloody, and unnatural acts,
> Of accidental judgments, casual slaughters,
> Of deaths put on by cunning and forc'd cause,
> And in this upshot, purposes mistook
> Fall'n on th' inventors' heads: all this can I
> Truly deliver.
>
> (5.2.379–86)

The final transformation is not after all from speech to silence, but from the destructiveness of human passions to the truth in the story of them. Fortinbras listens and commands that, for Hamlet, "The soldiers' music and the rite of war / Speak loudly" (ll. 399–400). Music, the sublimation of the voice of passion into something transcendent, is Hamlet's final voice.

In *Hamlet* Shakespeare reaches a consummate ability to make his characters and their world come alive in our imaginations through their ideas about language. The men and women create a tragic world, distrusting words, speaking their varying passions in the universal but primal language of voice and gesture, and changing themselves and each other through words. Through Hamlet's experience we may come to understand that speech is a human instrument reflecting the limitations as well as the transcendence of the human spirit. *Hamlet,* however, is not Shakespeare's final word on language. In the most important sense, there is no final word, for in each of the later comedies, tragedies, and romances, Shakespeare creates a fictional world where characters not only speak and listen, but also share their ideas on why and how they do so. In *Measure for*

Measure, for example, characters reveal their strengths and failings by their responses to the disjunction of heart and tongue, of motive and meaning. The Duke warns Angelo of his dual responsibility: "Mortality and mercy in Vienna / Live in thy tongue and heart" (1.1.44–45). Isabella pleads with Angelo that he acknowledge the guilt like Claudio's in his own heart, and speak accordingly: "Let it [your heart] not sound a thought upon your tongue / Against my brother's life" (2.2.140–41). Angelo, however, finds his tongue and heart at odds: "Heaven hath my empty words, / Whilst my invention, hearing not my tongue, / Anchors on Isabel" (2.4.2–4). In his judgment Escalus looks into the meaning behind names and finds the motives of Froth and Pompey; while in his slander Lucio allows his mischievous motive to corrupt his tongue, later pleading, "I spoke it but according to the trick" (5.1.504–5). Drawing on the grammarians' separation of voice from symbol, the etymologists' searches into the significance of names, the rhetoricians' methods of interpreting law, and the humanists' ideal of the man united in himself, speaking wise eloquence, Shakespeare creates in this play a world that moves from disorder to order — from a society where citizens "To have what we would have, / . . . speak not what we mean" (2.4.118), to one where all recognize their weaknesses and speak from their best selves: "They say best men are molded out of faults" (5.1.439). Similarly, in *Coriolanus* and *The Tempest,* ideas about language help to define the natures of the characters, the values of their societies, and the progress of the story, from problems to resolution. Informing *Coriolanus* are ideas drawn from medical theory and rhetoric — ideas on speech as a purge of passion, on irony as voice speaking a message opposed to words, and on the powerful effect of the body's language to persuade uncivil hearts. In *The Tempest* Shakespeare draws on ideas from the arts of poetry and acting, as well as magic, to distinguish the wise and the foolish and to suggest in the denouement that man's power to remake himself is of greater worth than his power to control the natural world. In his career after *Hamlet,* although Shakespeare borrows ideas about language from many sources, the plays reveal worlds, people, and languages not as we know them, not even as people in the Renaissance generally thought of them, but as Shakespeare created them: mirrors in which to see what might be, rather than simply what is.

Notes

1. See Erasmus, *On Copia of Words and Ideas,* tr. Donald B. King and H. David Rix (Milwaukee: Marquette Univ. Press, 1963), esp. pp. 15-16 and 52.

2. *Hamlet* especially shows Shakespeare's interest in language. In references to key terms concerning language, it is sixth of all the plays, with one reference per twenty lines. (*R2* is first with one reference per sixteen lines; *TNK* is last with one reference per forty-five lines; the average for all plays is one reference per twenty-six lines.)

3. This point has been made before. See, for example, H. Granville-Barker, *Prefaces to Shakespeare* (London: B. T. Botsford, 1930), I, 221; H. B. Charlton, *Shakespearian Tragedy* (Cambridge: Cambridge Univ. Press, 1949), p. 111; Maynard Mack, "The World of Hamlet," *YR*, 41 (1952), 505-7; Robert Hapgood, "*Hamlet* Nearly Absurd," *TDR*, 9 (Summer, 1965), 139; and George T. Wright, "Hendiadys and *Hamlet,*" *PMLA*, 96 (1981), 179-80.

4. Wilson, *Arte of Rhetorique,* sig. Ggii^v; and Montaigne, "Apologie," *Essayes,* p. 261.

5. Peacham, *Garden* (1593), sig. Tiii^v.

6. On Claudius's style in this speech, see Doran, *Shakespeare's Dramatic Language,* p. 40; to this essay on "Language in *Hamlet,*" I owe more than my notes can show.

7. See *Ars Minor of Donatus,* p. 55; and Richard Carew, "Epistle," p. 5.

8. My interpretation thus opposes that of Kirby Farrell, in *Shakespeare's Creation: The Language of Magic and Play* (Amherst: Univ. of Massachusetts Press, 1975), p. 5, who argues that Hamlet's "tragedy is his failure to achieve an adequate 'art.'" On the other hand, I think that Lionel Abel, in *Metatheatre* (New York: Hill and Wang, 1963), extends the metaphor of the playwright too far when he argues that "Almost every important character acts at some moment like a playwright, employing a playwright's consciousness of drama to impose a certain posture or attitude on another" (p. 46).

9. Stephen Booth, "On the Value of *Hamlet,*" in *Reinterpretations of Elizabethan Drama,* ed. Norman Rabkin (New York: Columbia Univ. Press, 1969), p. 152.

10. See, for example, J. Dover Wilson, *What Happens in Hamlet* (Cambridge: Cambridge Univ. Press, 1936), pp. 93-95; and Doran, *Shakespeare's Dramatic Language,* pp. 52-57.

11. See Quintilian, *Institutio Oratoria,* XI.iii.61-62.

12. Wilson, *Arte of Rhetorique,* sig. ti^v.

13. Seneca, *Epistulae Morales,* IX.3.

14. See "Prologue" to *If This Be Not a Good Play,* in *Dramatic Works of Thomas Dekker,* III, 22.

15. On voice and gesture as the universal language, especially appealing to the ignorant and even beasts, see Cicero, *De Oratore,* III.lix.223; and Fraunce, *Arcadian Rhetorike,* sig. I7^v.

16. Thomas Heywood, *Apology,* sig. B3^r.

17. Ibid., sigs. G1^v-G2^v.

18. Cf. Nigel Alexander, *Poison, Play, and Duel* (Lincoln: Univ. of Nebraska Press, 1971), p. 28: "The words [of the play-within-the-play] are not a substitute for an attack upon the King. They are an attack. Hamlet's choice of weapons is correct. Words are a weapon against which the policy and poison of Claudius is ineffective. Sitting at a play the King is poisoned by a mortal self-knowledge."

19. See Bertram Joseph, *Conscience and the King* (London: Chatto and Windus, 1953), pp. 55-63, on Elizabethan theories of physiognomy, gesture, and action, and on Claudius's expression and gesture at the play, correctly interpreted only by Horatio, Hamlet, and the audience of *Hamlet.*

20. In *The Character of Hamlet* (Chapel Hill: Univ. of North Carolina Press, 1941), pp. 51-52, John Erskine Hankins argues that seeing the ghost a second time marks an emotional catharsis for Hamlet in which his anger is converted into pity and his planned revenge into justice.

21. See Doran, *Shakespeare's Dramatic Language,* pp. 43-45, on Hamlet's impatience with Laertes' kind of speech. She sees Hamlet's ability to see through false words as a general principle in the play: "His sensitivity to the affected or false or strained note is our touchstone of honesty" (p. 45).

22. Castiglione, *The Courtier,* sig. F3^v.

23. Cf. Seneca, *Epistulae Morales,* LIII.11-12: "There is one point in which the sage has an advantage over the god; for a god is freed from terrors by the bounty of nature, the wise man by his own bounty. What a wonderful privilege, to have the weaknesses of a man and the serenity of a god!"

24. Cf. Mack, *Killing the King,* p. 106: "Osric is merely an extreme case of a contagious disease in which words become treacherous, either as masks to hide false meanings, or as levers that enable meanings to be shoved around at will."

25. *Batman vppon Bartholome,* fol. 17^r.

26. Seneca, *Epistulae Morales,* LXXVIII.20.

Index

Abel, Lionel: on Hamlet, 266*n*8
Acting, Elizabethan: theory of influenced by 16thc study of language, 7, 83-98, 244, 265; style of, 81, 102-3*n*49; compared to oratory, 102*n*48
Adam of Balsham: on logic as an art of language, 137*n*11
Aesthetic, Renaissance: drama as mirror in, 13-14, 15; painting-poetry debate in, 79-83, 92; of painting, 102*n*38, 247; of poetry, 252. *See also* Acting, Elizabethan; Diction; Language
Agricola, Rudolph: his theory of discourse, 106-8
Agrippa, Cornelius: his Neoplatonic view of words, 26; on grammar, 32-33; on change in language, 34, 180
Alexander, Nigel: on *Hamlet*, 267*n*18
Alper, Jonathan: directed *All's Well That Ends Well*, 241*n*3
Ambiguity. *See* Fallacies; Wordplay
Anglo-Saxon: 16thc view of, 30-31, 34, 52*n*62
Aquinas, Thomas: on language, 6, 50*n*44
Aristotle: influenced 16thc view of language, 4, 9-10*n*10, 29, 51*n*56, 109, 139-40*n*44; influenced Priscian, 48*n*22; on relation of words to things, 50*n*39; his distrust of words, 110-11; on metaphor, 117; influenced 12thc renaissance, 137*n*11; on fallacies, 137-38*n*14; mentioned, 66, 196
Ascham, Roger: on love of words, 128, 177; mentioned, 52*n*60

Augustine, Saint: on language as divine, 5-6, 10*nn*13-14, 50*n*39

Bacon, Francis: his distrust of words, 6, 111, 113, 125-26, 129; on relation of words to things, 27; on etymology, 29; on death, 68; on gesture, 75, 100*n*28; mentioned, 47*n*16, 53*n*73, 115
Barber, C. L.: on wordplay in *Love's Labor's Lost*, 162*n*8; on Shylock, 217*n*7; on Bassanio, 217*n*11
Barnet, Sylvan: on Bassanio, 217*n*11
Bartas, Guillaume de Saluste du. *See* Du Bartas, Guillaume de Saluste
Bartholomeus Anglicus. *See* Batman, Stephen
Batman, Stephen: on speech organs, 51*n*52; on death by exhalation, 68, 262
Beckerman, Bernard: on 16thc acting, 102*n*45
Bible: influence on 16thc view of language, 4, 5, 31, 50*n*51; alluded to in Shakespeare, 154-55, 163*n*14, 175, 204, 208, 228; mentioned, 38, 39. *See also* Language, biblical history of
Blundeville, Thomas: on categories of terms, 111, 137*n*12; on fallacies, 111, 138*n*14
Boccaccio, Giovanni: as peak of language to the Renaissance, 34, 35, 52*n*62; *Decameron* as source of *All's Well That Ends Well*, 220
Bonjour, Adrien: on *King John*, 187*n*15
Booth, Stephen: on *Hamlet*, 251

269

A Note on the Author

Jane Donawerth received her Ph.D. in English from the University of Wisconsin (Madison) and is now on the English faculty at the University of Maryland. She assisted S. Schoenbaum in editing *Shakespeare in Context*, a book-length microfilm project, and has published several articles on Shakespeare.